DEVIANCE AND MORAL BOUNDARIES

NACHMAN BEN-YEHUDA

DEVIANCE AND MORAL BOUNDARIES

Witchcraft
the Occult
Science Fiction
Deviant Sciences
and Scientists

The University of Chicago Press
Chicago and London

NACHMAN BEN-YEHUDA is a lecturer in sociology at
Hebrew University in Jerusalem.

The University of Chicago Press, Chicago 60637
The University of Chicago Press, Ltd., London
© 1985 by The University of Chicago
All rights reserved. Published 1985
Printed in the United States of America

94 93 92 91 90 89 88 87 86 85   54321

LIBRARY OF CONGRESS CATALOGING IN PUBLICATION DATA

Ben-Yehuda, Nachman.
   Deviance and moral boundaries.

   Bibliography: p.
   Includes index.
   1. Deviant behavior—Case studies. 2. Social
change. 3. Witchcraft—Case studies. 4. Science
and civilization—Case studies. I. Title.
HM291.B386   1985   30 2.5'42   85–1167
ISBN 0–226–04335–5

To Morris Janowitz and Barry Schwartz
—true mentors

CONTENTS

ACKNOWLEDGMENTS

Researching and writing this manuscript was a very long process. Many friends and colleagues helped along the way with information, advice, jokes, and above all with patience, listening to more than a few bizarre tales, helping to cope with tough ethical problems. Etti, Tzach, and Guy were the most patient of all—and I love them for it. The help and support of Dina, Hanna, and Yehuda, our parents, were indispensable. We are grateful to Bessie and to Bernard Schindell, who were ideal relatives.

Menachem Amir, Ruth Alroy, Steve Dubin, Jim Rule, S. N. Eisenstadt, Menachem Horowitz, Rachel Rosen, Mike Inbar, Gerald Krumer, Lester Kurtz, Stephen Cole, Ivan Chase, Lyle Hallowell, Norman Goodman, Judith Tanur, Kai Erikson, Andrea Tyree, Mark Granovetter, Hannan Selvin, Joe De Bolt, Yaron Ezrahi, Baruch Kimmerling, Rafael Mechoulam, Amos Yahill, Stanley Einstein, Don Handelman, Ken Feldman, and Said Arjomand all contributed good advice, information, and lengthy discussions of various ideas. Joseph Ben-David's comments on the ideology of the European witchcraze and on the early work in radio astronomy were most helpful. Woodruff T. Sullivan and Grote Reber provided indispensable advice on radio astronomy. Erik Cohen helped me develop and apply his concept of recentralization to the occult and science fiction. Barry Schwartz, Victor Azaria, and Stanley Cohen read the entire first draft of the manuscript thoroughly. Their comments were invaluable. The time they put in reading and commenting on a long manuscript renewed my faith in my colleagues. My debt to them is simply beyond anything that can be said. Morris Janowitz's constructive help and guidance were most useful. My discussions with Erich Goode, his detailed comments, and warm generous help and support, are gratefully acknowledged.

I could not have managed without the competent technical assistance of Sabina Honigwacks, Anna Ketof, Moshe Lissak, Glenn Yago, Barbie Zelizer, Veronica Abjornsen, Lora Ben-Shmuel, Nili Sobol, and the editing staff of Moshav Shorashim. Marilyn Muroff's endless patience and superb typing are greatly appreciated. I am most grateful to the Department of Sociology, University of Chicago, whose grants helped research the section on witchcraft, and to the faculty of Social Sciences, Hebrew University, who provided all the necessary funds for researching and writing the manuscript. I would also like to thank the Department of Sociology at the State University of New York, Stony Brook, who enabled me to rewrite this manuscript during one fruitful sabbatical.

Last, but not least, I would like to express my deepest gratitude to Al and Goggie Blitstein, whose generosity and warmth helped make all this possible.

THEORETICAL BACKGROUND
An Enigma and Its Solution

Introduction

Since its inception, the sociology of deviance seems to have suffered from at least two major problems. The first is a theoretical chaos. Describing the field of social pathology (which preceded the field of the sociology of deviance), in 1943, C. Wright Mills stated that "The level of abstractions . . . is so low that often they seem to be empirically confused for lack of abstraction to knit them together. . . . The 'informational' character . . . is linked with a failure to consider total social structures. Collecting and dealing in a fragmentary way with scattered problems and facts [results in a] lack of systematization [and] perspectives [that] are usually not explicit" (1943, pp. 166, 167, 168). Many of the same criticisms have been lodged against the field of the sociology of deviance, which did not exist at the time of Mills's devastating critique. Nonetheless, in the ensuing years we have witnessed substantial progress in the sociology of deviance, rendering much of Mills's original criticism invalid; some of his criticism, however, remains as relevant today as it was in the 1940s.

Since 1943, an enourmous quantity of literature, research, and theoretical formulations in the sociology of deviance has been generated. Specific subareas—sex, juvenile delinquency, mental illness, drug abuse, and political deviance—have been thoroughly researched, both theoretically and empirically. Despite this treasure of knowledge, the field still lacks an eclectic theory, a conceptual framework, that can encompass all the manifestations of deviance (e.g., Thio 1983; Rubington and Weinberg 1971). Scull's (1984) recent criticism maintains that the sociological study of deviance is still characterized by theoretical and epistemological confusion. Thus even today, the sociology of deviance can be character-

ized as fragmented and chaotic. In the next few pages, I shall substantiate
this claim and suggest that what I call the "Durkheimian double bind" is
the major cause for this state of affairs. Later I shall suggest a theoretical
solution for this problem.

The second major problem was also mentioned by Mills in 1943, and
echoed by Scull in 1984, and that is that the sociology of deviance
generally failed to consider total social structures and fell into a deep
(however interesting) trap of small-scale studies about various esoteric,
sensational types of deviance. Thus Rock (1974) claims that the emphasis
on studying the phenomenon of deviance has given rise to a radical type
of phenomenalism that defines society as a collection of small units
lacking an overall structure. In a 1973a essay, he claims that the sociology
of deviance has created an artificial contradiction between *phenomenalism* (emphasizing the need for an accurate and reliable reconstruction of
the social world as seen by those living in it) and *essentialism* (searching
for the underlying properties of the social order). Supporting Rock's
criticism, Gouldner (1968) and Liazos (1972) accuse sociologists of ne-
glecting major problems in favor of small-scale, meaningless studies. The
lack of comprehensive conceptual formulations, coupled with rivalry
among different sociologies of deviance, have caused much discontent
and have probably hindered the development of coherent frameworks.
Both the labeling approach and the more recent phenomenological
theories indicate that sociologists have become increasingly aware of the
absence of such frameworks. Thus, we witness their attempts to create
formulations that are anchored in larger sociological-philosophical
theories. While back-ups are certainly feasible, they nevertheless create
further problems regarding the quantity and quality of involvement between the larger theoretical framework (e.g., symbolic interaction, phenomenology) and its derivative in the sociology of deviance (Goode 1978,
Douglas and Waksler 1982).

The problem is further aggravated by substantive issues. While the
labeling theory can be best applied to explain so-called soft deviance (sex,
drug abuse, and mental illness), it is not as efficient as, for example, the
deviant-behavior approach (Clinard 1974; Wolfgang, Savitz, and Johnson 1970; Rubington and Weinberg 1971) to explain "hard" deviance
(murder, organized crime, burglary, rape, and other violent crimes).
Another development is the attempt of recent textbooks in the field to
discuss deviance in relation to "how society works" (Goode 1978; Suchar
1978).

In view of all this, this study has two goals. First, I shall examine the
theoretical problems of the sociology of deviance. I shall analyze why

sociologists have been attracted to "small-scale" deviant acts and have refrained from developing integrative conceptual frameworks or theories. The analysis will focus on the nature of deviance itself and on the early contributions to the field of Emile Durkheim. Second, I shall suggest an integrated conceptual approach to the study of deviance. This will focus on the redefinition of moral and social boundaries, on change and stability. I will show that deviance is, not a marginal phenomenon in society, but rather a central one. In this regard, "deviance" will be used to explain the nature of change and stability. Thus, this work does not aim to explain deviance per se but rather to use the phenomenon to explain much wider societal processes. This approach certainly considers total social structures by examining deviance as part of larger social processes of change and stability in the moral boundaries of societies. In this sense, it presents a very different interpretation of deviance than is usual.

The Durkheimian Double Bind

Defining deviance has always been problematic.[1] With the exception of the general statement that deviance involves violation of norms, a satisfactory solution to the problem has apparently not yet been found. Such a broad definition, however, only begs the question. In addition, the subject is approached by some as one facade of a defined social reality and by others as an analytical concept.

The literature in the field reflects this confusion. On the one hand, we have the so-called Eastern school (perhaps best exemplified by textbooks and readers such as Wolfgang, Savitz, and Johnson 1970) focusing primarily on hard deviance and very close to positivistic criminology. On the other hand, we have the "Western school" (perhaps best exemplified by textbooks and readers such as Rubington and Weinberg 1978), which concentrates for the most part on soft deviance. Even a superficial perusal reveals how truly different these two classes of books are.[2] The differences are not in subject matter only but in methodology as well. The first school concentrates on so-called official statistics, cohort studies and

---

1. I use the term "double bind" in the same sense that Bateson et al (1956) use it. The Durkheimian message regarding the functionality of deviance certainly contains a double, contradictory meaning.

2. The first is apparently more positivistic and influenced by the perspectives of "deviant behavior," "culture conflict," and perhaps, the "Chicago school," while the second is based more on humanistic orientations such as labeling (symbolic interaction) and, to some extent, phenomenology. The difference is striking (Rubington and Weinberg 1971; Davis 1975).

the like. The second school points to the unreliability of official statistics and emphasizes participant observations and interviewing. Studies in the first school somehow convey that "deviance" is a real construct, well-defined and embedded in statistics and descriptions. In the second, the differences between deviance and nondeviance are not as patent, and the demarcation is not always well defined.

How is it possible then, if at all, to resolve the theoretical and empirical problem of the enigma that is "deviance"? Even phrasing the question accurately is a problem. In order to understand the question and the solution better, we shall go back to the sources of the problem and answer the question of why the study of deviance has developed as it has. Understanding the fundamental issues will better enable us to comprehend the problems of the field and to suggest a solution.

It is my contention that the basic problem of the sociology of deviance lies with one of its founding fathers (perhaps its "totemic father"), Emile Durkheim. When René Descartes made his famous distinction between mind and body, he helped separate the study of the one from that of the other and created a dilemma for psychological and psychiatric theory and practice that has yet to be satisfactorily resolved.[3] Durkheim, in my opinion, initiated a similar problem for the sociology of deviance, although not quite as explicit as Descartes's. First, he set out to establish that deviance is an inevitable aspect of any society: "To classify crime among the phenomena of normal sociology is not to say merely that it is an inevitable, although regrettable phenomenon, due to the incorrigible wickedness of men; it is to affirm that it is a factor in public health, an integral part of all healthy societies. . . . Crime is, then, necessary; it is bound up with the fundamental conditions of all social life, and by that very fact it is useful" (1938, pp. 67, 70). Furthermore, in a famous and frequently quoted passage, he states, "Imagine a society of saints, a perfect cloister of exemplary individuals. Crimes, properly so called, will be there unknown; but faults which appear venial to the layman will create there the same scandal that the ordinary offense does in ordinary consciousness. If, then, this society has the power to judge and punish, it will define these acts as criminal and will treat them as such" (ibid., p. 69). Having established that deviance is an inevitable part of any society, Durkheim then attempted to specify exactly why this is so. In answering this question, he created a paradox and a contradiction.

In *The Rules of Sociological Method* (1938), Durkheim argues that

3. Only later did Freud suggest a limited solution to this dilemma. Modern theories of "psychosomatic medicine" are also struggling to overcome this distinction.

"what is normal, simply, is the existence of criminality. . . . Crime is normal because a society exempt from it is utterly impossible. . . . Crime implies not only that the way remains open to necessary changes, but that in certain cases it directly prepares these changes. Where crime exists, collective sentiments are sufficiently flexible to take on a new form, and crime sometimes helps to determine the form they will take" (pp. 65–73). The conclusion, simply put, is that crime is a necessary and vital part of any social system. Its main function is to create and sustain the flexibility necessary for the social system to adapt itself to varying conditions. Crime or, in this framework, deviance is functional and good because it is one (if not the only) mechanism for social change. Durkheim offers as evidence an example of a renowned criminal: Socrates. "According to Athenian law Socrates was a criminal, and his condemnation was no more than just. However, his crime, namely the independence of his thought, rendered a service not only to humanity but to his country. It served to prepare a new morality and faith" (ibid., p. 73). Defined as such, deviance serves an important function in the social system.

Although these passages from *The Rules of Sociological Method* are reprinted in many textbooks on deviance, Durkheim's statement there is not his only one on crime and deviance. In *The Division of Labour in Society,* he has quite different things to say about the subject.

> The only common characteristic of all crimes is that they consist . . . in acts universally disapproved of by members of each society. . . . Crime shocks sentiments which . . . are found in all healthy consciences. . . . An act is criminal when it offends strong and defined states of the collective conscience. . . . Crime is everywhere essentially the same, since it everywhere calls forth the same effect. . . . Its primary and principal function is to create respect for . . . beliefs, traditions, and collective practices. . . . What characterizes crime is that it determines punishment. . . . Crime damages . . . unanimity [and] since it is the common conscience which is attacked, it must be that which resists, and accordingly the resistance must be collective. [Punishment's] true function is to maintain social cohesion intact. (1933, pp. 70–110)

Even more specifically, Durkheim notes that

> Crime brings together upright consciences and concentrates them. We have only to notice what happens, particularly in a small town, when some moral scandal has just been committed. They stop each other on the street, they visit each other, they seek to come together to talk of the event and wax indignant in common. From all the similar impressions which are exchanged, for all the temper that

gets itself expressed, there emerges a unique temper—which is everybody's without being anybody's in particular. That is the public temper. (Ibid., 102)

What Durkheim implies in this passage is that crime threatens the collective conscience (specifically, so-called mechanical solidarity), eliciting a collective action called "punishment." Crime's main function, then, is positive, since it causes punishment, which in turn facilitates cohesion and maintains societal boundaries. K. T. Erikson, continuing Durkheim's theoretical direction, stated that "Deviance makes people more alert to the interests they share in common and draws attention to those values which constitute the *collective conscience* of the community. . . . Boundary-maintaining devices . . . demonstrate to whatever audience is concerned where the line is drawn between behavior that belongs in the special universe of the group and behavior that does not. . . . For these reasons, deviant behavior is not a simple kind of leakage which occurs when the machinery of society is in poor working order, but may be, in controlled quantities, an important condition for preserving the stability of social life" (1966, pp. 4, 11, 13). George Herbert Mead also supported this thesis:

While the most admirable of humanitarian efforts are sure to run counter to the individual interests of very many in the community, or fail to touch the interest and imagination of the multitude and to leave the community divided or indifferent, the cry of thief or murder is attuned to profound complexes, lying below the surface of competing individual effort, and citizens . . . separated by divergent interests stand together against the common enemy. . . . The criminal does not seriously endanger the structure of society by his destructive activities, and on the other hand he is responsible for a sense of solidarity, aroused among those whose attention would otherwise be centered upon interests divergent from those of each other. (1918, p. 590)

In modern societies, the widespread reporting of deviance in the mass media indirectly fulfills the integrative function of deviance, replacing more direct "degradation ceremonies" (Garfinkel 1950). Erikson also pointed this out.

Today we no longer parade deviants in the town square or expose them to the carnival atmosphere. . . . It is interesting to note that the "reform" which brought about this change in penal policy coincided almost precisely with the development of newspapers as media of public information. . . . Newspapers (and now radio and television) offer their readers the same kind of entertainment once supplied by public hanging or the use of stocks and pillaries. (1964, p. 29)

Since Durkheim's original essays on the functionality of deviance, there have been numerous scholars who have utilized this idea to illustrate that in many cases, a way of coping with pressures exerted by the social order is to commence or maintain a deviant career. Thus, Cohen suggested several positive functions for deviance, such as creating cohesion, facilitating flexibility, serving as a safety valve for unhappy members of society and as a warning signal that something is wrong in society (1966, pp. 6–11). Farrell and Swigert's review (1982, chap. 2), documents how deviance maintains behavioral boundaries. Harris (1977) implied that deviance designations may help draw lines between the powerful and the powerless. Berger and Luckmann (1966) point out that societies react very intensely to any deviant interpretation of their symbolic universe. Lauderdale (1978) suggested that society's moral boundaries fluctuate, exposing different people, depending on time and place, to the label "deviant."

While many scholars accepted the idea that deviance enhances stability, fewer pursued the idea that it produces change. Douglas's 1977 analysis is certainly an exception. In it, he suggests the term "creative deviance" and argues that "deviance is the mutation that is generally destructive of society, but it is also the only major source of creative adaptations of rules to new life situations" (p. 60). Thus, he suggests that whole societies can change through deviance.

It is clear that the two Durkheimian ideas are contradictory, both in their content and in their implications. On the one hand, one learns that deviance is functional because it creates and maintains flexibility, thus enhancing the survival value of the social system. Deviance here is a potential mechanism for social change. On the other hand, one learns that deviance is functional because it elicits punishment, which causes cohesion, promoting rigidity and inflexibility. But before we continue our analysis, it is important to clarify an important linguistic issue. The passages quoted from Durkheim clearly indicate that there is a problem in the way we conceptualize the "functionality" of deviance.[4] Is it de-

---

4. Roshier claims that "there are some important and dangerous implications of the function of crime myth which require the effort of disposing of it" (1977, p. 310). Roshier tries to show that the idea that crime is necessary is either fallacious or devoid of meaning. He argues that some activities are, in fact, functional and beneficial to society (e.g., prostitution, pornography, and gambling). However, their definition as "deviance" is not what makes them functional. It is my hope that the arguments in this book will persuade the reader that Roshier's arguments are wrong.

viance per se itself or is it the reaction to deviance that is functional? It seems that Durkheim envisioned an "interaction model." Deviance for him was, not only the breaking of norms or rules, but also the reaction to the real or assumed violation. For both of his claims, it is essential that either the rule-breaking be visible or that the assumption of a transgression becomes public knowledge. Invisible breaches of conduct cannot provoke a societal reaction and are, therefore, not functional in the Durkheimian sense. Thus the "function of deviance" refers to societal reactions to it. These responses (for or against the deviant) are the crucial mechanism through which deviance becomes functional.

We must also note that only recently has Durkheim been recognized as a key figure in the theoretical, historical, and substantive evolution of the sociology of deviance (see, e.g., Tiryakian 1981; Lidz and Walker 1980). Jones (1981) realized that Durkheim's ideas on crime and punishment were not fully developed and that they had thus led to many problems within the field. He tried to resolve the double bind by positing that Durkheim's ideas on crime and punishment had undergone a transition. At first, he had perceived deviance as contributing to rigidity, but later in his career he saw it as facilitating social change. Jones's historical explanation, however, does not really solve the Durkheimian contradiction. First, it does not answer any of the aforementioned questions. Second, Jones infers that Durkheim in the end was concerned only with social change, whereas he in fact maintained a concern with social stability as well. Third, it is doubtful that Durkheim himself saw his work as evolutionary. Last, while Jones's interpretation is illuminating, it is based totally on Durkheim's treatment of legal evolution, ignoring his broader social thought.

If we accept the idea that reactions to deviance create much-needed flexibility, then deviance is good. If, however, we argue that reactions to deviance create inflexibility and ossification of the system, the implications are quite different. Either stand affects theoretical developments, research priorities, and strategies and points to the different moral and value commitments of the researchers. The dilemma directly concerns the important issue of the true nature of deviance, both as a real phenomenon and as a sociological abstraction.[5]

5. It is noteworthy that Marx had an approach to deviance similar to Durkheim's (see Taylor, Walton, and Young 1973, pp. 209–36). Although Marx wrote little on either crime or deviance directly, one infers from his writings virtually the same contradictory conclusion one draws from Durkheim. On the one hand, Marx hints that deviance is functional for the capitalistic social order because it sustains existing social arrangements and protects the bourgeoisie. On the other hand, he clearly implies that deviance is a source of innovation that prevents the bourgeoisie from stagnating.

The schools that have developed through the years reflect this confusion. The perspectives of "social pathology," "social disorganization," "deviant behavior," and, to a large extent, criminology itself follow Durkheim in *The Division of Labour in Society*. Their topics of research and their research methodologies (especially the use of official statistics) are clearly inspired by the idea that crime is a disruption and a threat to the social order and by a desire for its prevention.[6] Similar to the Durkheimian conceptualization that "society is out there" and that we can learn about it by closely monitoring various indicators (e.g., types and rates of suicides), these schools closely monitor rates and types of deviant acts.

The "labeling," "phenomenological," and to some extent, the "value conflict" perspectives are much closer to Durkheim's statements in *The Rules of Sociological Method*. They concentrate on "soft" deviance and "victimless crimes" (prostitution, marijuana use, and homosexuality), implicitly underscoring the normality of crime. Like the Chicago school, they describe and largely identify with the inner, subjective social reality of the deviant himself. Their methods, however, are clearly non-Durkheimian. They consist mostly of participant observations and interviews (again, closely resembling the Chicago school), emphasizing the subjective and elusive nature of deviance.

The profound differences between these two approaches have also affected the distinction between deviance as a sociological concept and deviance as a reality. While the first approach took for granted its existence both as a reality and as an abstraction, the second approach challenged both assumptions. It blurred the demarcation between deviance and nondeviance in reality and created a theoretical chaos as well. Both approaches used "deviance" to describe an empirical reality and a sociological construct. To add further to the confusion, the same term is used by laymen and professional sociologists in very different contexts.[7]

Since Durkheim did not offer a solution for the paradox he created, it is incumbent us to resolve it. There can be two concrete solutions to the Durkheimian contradiction: a quantitative one and a qualitative one. The quantitative differentiates between levels of crime. Thus, a certain quantity of crime could be conceived of as beneficial and functional for society because it can promote change. Above (or below) that quantity, crime leads to rigidity. The second solution is to claim that the quality of the

6. This is so notwithstanding Durkheim's warning that "there is no occasion for self-congratulation when the crime rate drops noticeably below the average level, for we may be certain that this apparent progress is associated with some social disorder" (1938, p. 77).

7. It would, however, seem that the "street" usage of the term is fairly specific and the sociological use is more theoretical.

crime is the determining factor. Here we would have to differentiate among various types of crime, trying to show that certain types of deviance could contribute to change, while others create a chain reaction whose end result is more integration, cohesion, and rigidity. The qualitative argument implicitly includes the quantitative since various types of deviance could occur in different degrees and imply different consequences for the social system. My inclination is toward the qualitative argument because it subsumes the quantitative and because the quantitative solution is too broad to be meaningful.

Beyond this, sociologists should recognize that the Durkheimian dilemma relates to a very basic sociological problem: that of social stability versus social change. Rigidity and cohesion could, and should, be interpreted as social stability; flexibility could, and should, be interpreted as social change. Both are important aspects of the social system. Linking our dilemma to such central concepts enables us to integrate the subject of deviance into broader social processes and to conceptualize the idea (and reality) of deviance within a meaningful framework of general sociological abstractions. It follows from our previous description that if a comprehensive understanding of the phenomenon of deviance is to be attained, it must crystallize out of the Durkheimian contradiction. The questions we must deal with are, not only how to resolve the dilemma but how to integrate the solution into major sociological phenomena of social stability and social change. Answering these questions is the major focus of this work.

Deviance as a Relative Phenomenon

While "deviance" as a category is universal, a universal content of deviance is nonexistent. Deviance is essentially socially defined and is therefore always culturally relative (Goode 1978; Schur 1979). Thus, in order to understand a specific type of deviance, we have to understand its context within the social system and, in particular, the system's value structure. Depending on the sociohistorical context, some forms of deviance could either create rigidity or reflect an inflexible situation, while other forms could either create or reflect flexibility. Furthermore, the same type of deviance in certain circumstances could encourage rigidity and lead in other circumstances to flexibility.

Although it is easy to see how "soft" deviance is relative, it is not as easy to see the relativity of such crimes as murder and theft. Nevertheless, even these "hard" deviances are relative. A primary example of hard-core deviance is homicide. On the one hand, no known social system permits its membes to kill each other freely, making this act almost universally deviant.[8] On the other hand, in carefully defined situations, almost all social systems not only permit homicide but encourage it and provide ways and means for its efficient execution on a mass scale. Examples of such situations are war and genocide (the Jewish holocaust in Europe, the massacre of the Armenians). The norms regarding theft follow a similar pattern. Reflecting various degrees of sensitivity, almost all social systems have rules forbidding the taking of property by force. However, many so-called guerilla movements (which later came to power) not only allowed and encouraged but even sanctified theft, armed robbery, and burglary in order to secure the means for their activities. In the histories of these movements, such acts are justified and accounted for as acts against oppressors.

The definition of theft as a crime can be shown to be related to very basic assumptions concerning the sacredness of private property. Where private property does not exist, the meaning of theft will be very different. A contemporary example concerns fund-raising techniques among various "world-transforming" religious movements (e.g., the Moonies or Hare Krishnas). Bromley and Shupe have shown that fund raising becomes a central component of the individual member's role and a major focus of daily missionary activity. It is a sacred activity and is ideologically legitimized by being linked with the movement's goals, contributing to the salvation or spiritual improvement of all mankind. Many of the activities included in the fund raising, however, could be easily defined as deceptive, corrupt, and manipulative. These movements therefore have developed special vocabularies that allow members to neutralize the issues. The Hare Krishnas call such practices "transcendental trickery," and the Moonies call them "heavenly deception" (Bromely and Shupe 1980, pp. 231–33).

Deviance thus viewed is no longer a peripheral phenomenon, but a central element of any functioning social system. The analysis of social deviance thus becomes a crucial factor in an understanding of the social order itself.

A Macrosociological Conceptualization: The Social System, Deviance, Social Change, and Social Stability

In this book, I do not focus on a single type of deviance, but rather, in examining several, I delineate patterns of deviance as an integral part of a

8. Permission to commit murder can exist, however, under very specific circumstances, for example, self-defense or the custom of "blood revenge" in the Arab peninsula. How-

specific social order[9] or social system.[10] The conceptual framework used here does not therefore limit the discussion to a particular time and place.

An important and rewarding way to measure social orders or systems is by their complexity. The social order can be conceptualized as an information- and energy-processing organization.[11] One that processes a minimal amount of energy and information can be characterized as a simple society; one that processes large amounts is necessarily more complex. This is consistent with Thompson's view of an organization that utilizes energy and raw materials from its environment in order to survive and evolve (1967). Coon (1969) maintains that man has been converting energy into social structures at an ever-increasing pace, organizing himself into institutions of increasing size and complexity. Bellah, in a most intriguing attempt to interpret the concept of progress, suggested a cybernetic model of society and defined progress as "an increase in the capacity of a social system to receive and process information from within and without the system and to respond appropriately to it. Progress thus involves not merely learning but also learning capacity, an increasing ability to *learn to learn*" (1965, p. 170). Thus, in Bellah's terms, modernization should be conceptualized as an especially rapid increase in progress. In this context, deviance can be thought of as introducing new, additional information into the system, of presenting alternative forms of behavior.

We can apply this typology to more classical statements in sociology. In his *Division of Labour in Society,* Durkheim distinguishes between societies characterized by "mechanical solidarity" and those characterized by "organic solidarity." The first are similar to traditional, perhaps primitive, societies. The second would correspond to more differentiated, complex societies. Durkheim hypothesized that as population density increases in a society characterized by mechanical solidarity, it will evolve into a society characterized by organic solidarity. He also projected that with greater complexity in the division of labor, crime would also increase. Webb (1972) tested this idea and found that although the model is true regarding the correlation between increased division of labor and increases in crime, this is not related to population density.

---

ever, even under such circumstances, permission to deliberately take another person's life is a complicated issue.

9. For a thorough analysis of the concept see Eisenstadt (1968) Eisenstadt and Curelaru (1976).

10. For a broad view, the reader is referred to Parsons (1951).

11. See, for examples, Thompson (1967), Bellah (1965), Coon (1969).

To rephrase the Durkheimian model, we would maintain that societies characterized by mechanical solidarity are those that have a low utilization of energy and information. Constant increase in a society's ability to process information will eventually result in the development of organic solidarity. The crucial variable for this transformation is, not population density, but rather the increase in the society's ability to process energy and information. A related terminology was suggested by Tönnies (1957) in his discussion of change in social orientation from Gemeinschaft to Gesellschaft. While in both Tönnies's and Durkheim's discussions the emphasis is on the qualitative change, it is feasible to translate the idea into quantitative terms of a transition from low to high utilization of energy and information.

The solution for the problem of deviance in the context of the two types of societies suggested by Durkheim is a differential one, that is, it applies differently to different societies. It appears as if more traditional societies are less prone to change. Crime, or deviance, in this type of society would seem to define moral boundaries, enhance cohesion and rigidity, and preserve the social system. This is achieved merely by indicating what type of behavior is inappropriate. Some empirical examples are provided by Erikson's 1966 analysis of witchcraft accusations in Salem in 1692; Zablocki's 1971 analysis of the reactions to patterns of deviance in the Bruderhof, and analyses of reactions to assumed deviance (mostly political) during the Soviet purges (Bergesen 1977). In such societies, however, some patterns of behavior that are initially defined as deviant may sometimes provide a mechanism for change. At times, large-scale persecution of deviants is a good indication that profound social change is taking place. In order to differentiate between persecution that constitutes a societal redefinition of moral boundaries and that which constitutes either a need for change or actual change, one must analyze the system in which the particular pattern of deviance occurs. This is clear, for example, in the literature on insanity.

Cumming and Cumming (1957) describe how a whole community closed its ranks against induced changes in the perception and definition of mental illness. The researchers wanted to encourage change that would blur the distinction between "normal" and "crazy," a change that the people of the community were unwilling to tolerate. The experiment ended when the researchers were threatened with violence and were actually expelled from the community. This is a clear example of the maintenance of social stability through the sharp demarcation of that which is perceived to be deviant (in this case, mental illness) and that which is perceived to be nondeviant. A similar example is the persecution of the mentally ill described by Foucault (1967). In Europe during the Middle Ages, mentally-ill people were set adrift on special boats (Ship of Fools, *Narrenschiff*).[12] In later years, the "therapy" was to put them into special custody (jails), where they were chained and treated like animals. However, there have been many cases of mentally ill people who, because of their bizarre behavior, became very powerful in society, such as charismatic leaders, prophets, and oracles. In some periods, epilepsy was considered a sign of the influence of divine spirits (see Rosen 1969). Thus, reactions to a specific form of deviance—mental illness—could in one instance enhance mechanical solidarity and help sustain stability and, in another, introduce important elements of change.

Although our anlaysis indicates that in societies characterized by mechanical solidarity (i.e., low levels of energy and information processing) deviance creates and sustains stability, this is not always so. There is something in the very term "mechanical solidarity" that implies that deviance, in these types of societies, could serve another function. By mechanical solidarity we usually mean a cohesive and homogeneous society where little or no differentiation exists. For mechanical solidarity to develop and be sustained, however, people must be aware that they share similarities and a common cultural heritage. Every social system must invest resources to remind its members (through rituals, ideologies, and ceremonies) that a common ground actually exists. Acts that challenge this consciousness of likeness will most probably be defined as deviant and may lead to social change.[13]

Such acts, to use Durkheimian terminology, will directly threaten the "collective conscience," or in Shilsian 1975 terminology, the "center." They will either create social change or be vehemently counteracted in an attempt to restore society's moral boundaries. An analysis of power, class, and interest groups would probably allow a realistic forecast of the outcome. What Durkheim called the "collective conscience" is not a homogeneous entity; it exists on more than one level. The sociologist's task in each case is to determine what or who is being threatened by a specific act of deviance and thus conclude whether this act will foster

12. For recent challenges to this see Maher and Maher 1982 and Chap. 13 in the 1984 (2nd) edition of E. Goode's book on deviance.

13. While rituals were originally perceived as mechanisms that preserve continuity and stability, contemporary anthropological theory suggests that rituals may also be an occasion for change. More specifically, recent theories using Victor Turner's concept of "liminality" (1977) suggest that the social situation called "ritual" may be, simultaneously, a situation that emphasizes tradition and rigidity and a situation where change is initiated or emphasized.

change or enhance solidarity. Lofland defined deviance as "the name of a conflict game in which individuals or loosely organized small groups with little power are strongly feared by a well organized, sizable minority, or majority, who have a large amount of power" (1969, p. 14). Horowitz and Liebovitz affirm this definition: "Deviance is a conflict between at least two parties: superordinates who make and enforce rules, and subordinates whose behavior violates those rules" (1968, p. 282).

For example, both Erikson's analysis of the witch-hunt in Salem, Massachusetts, and my own analysis of the witch-hunts in Europe in the fourteenth to seventeenth centuries indicate how acts of deviance have accompanied and contributed to social changes. In both cases, guardians of the center failed in their attempts to restore the previous moral boundaries. In contrast, a thief's being tried, convicted, and punished strengthens and accentuates the existing boundaries of the social order. Such ceremonies re-emphasize the commitment of the system to particular norms and values (in this case, to the sacredness of private property). These examples, however, are somewhat extreme and oversimplified.

A multifaceted and well-documented area to examine is that of sexual deviance. Wheeler (1960) stated that laws concerning sexual behavior attempt to regulate the following four things: the degree of consent; the nature of the sexual partners; the nature of the sexual act; and the setting in which the act occurs. The laws stem from a specific value system. Phenomena such as "swinging," group sex, and prostitution are directly associated with the unique European marriage patterns that have developed since the fifteenth century (Hajnal 1968). Much of what we call sexual deviance provides alternative access to sexual services and gratification. Thus, it challenges very basic norms regarding the control of the sexual act and the utilization of sex as a means to viable, long-term social and economic arrangements (i.e., marriage). For many years, in more rigid and cohesive systems, various agents of social control condemned and tried to stifle acts of sexual deviance, preserving intact society's moral boundaries. However, as ideas concerning sexual behavior changed, it became exceedingly difficult to deal with behavior such as homosexuality and prostitution. It is conceivable that the institution of marriage itself will be transformed as sexuality is redefined. Under these circumstances, it is very likely that the meaning of sexual deviance will also change.

Societies that are characterized by organic solidarity are much more differentiated, process high levels of energy and information, and are often pluralistic. In such societies, values, norms, and moral boundaries are not given; they are negotiated. Therefore, the "negotiated order" is often a synonym for a pluralistic social order where conflict and consensus coexist. The diversity of life styles is emphasized, communicated, and legitimized. People must be made aware, then, that they share a common cultural heritage and a consciousness of likeness. To this end, a pluralistic social order employs various techniques (education), so-called secular rituals (Moore and Myerhoff 1977), symbols, and ideas (law, nation) that emphasize unity.

In the Shilsian view (1975), one could visualize a social system with a distinct center and a more-or-less identifiable periphery. By nature, a more complex and pluralistic social system is characterized by multiple centers, many of which compete with each other for legitimacy, resources, followers, and influence. These suggest alternative value and belief systems and advocate alternative life styles. Each of them can be isolated and defined and has its own more-or-less identifiable periphery. Modern societies are considerably different than simple societies, especially regarding the number of acceptable centers and their relative openness. The meaning of any "moral statement" thus becomes very problematic in a complex society. The more abstract such statements are, the more problematic they become. Douglas (1970) pointed out that in a monolithic social order, the meaning of such terms as "loyalty" or "traitor" is clear, but in a pluralistic society, the meaning of these terms is vague. Complex societies possess few geographically segregated cultural spheres and are described more accurately as having limited meaningful contacts and empirical knowledge. The social meaning of deviance in such societies becomes essentially (Rock 1973b) and situationally problematic, both to the members of the society and to the sociologist. Criminal law in a complex society, then, is increasingly relied upon as a formal mechanism of social control, integrating all those who live within its political jurisdiction (Hills 1980, p. 35).

Deviance is closely linked to and serves as a mirror image of conventional morality. Nevertheless, very little has been written about the complex interaction between the two. Thus Rock (1974) claims that the sociology of deviance has failed to study morality systematically and that if we are to understand deviance, we must first understand the moral order.

Some of the key concepts in this area were developed by scholars from the "labeling" school, by Howard Becker in particular. According to Becker (1963, chap. 8), in certain periods and places, people arise who, by virtue of their initiative, political power, influence, connections, skillful use of publicity, and success in neutralizing opposition, are able to force their interests and values onto society as a whole (see also Hills 1980, p. 35). Becker called these people "moral entrepreneurs," or "moral crusaders," and the process through which they shape societal policy he termed a "moral crusade."

The terms Becker used were based on research carried out by Gusfield (1963), who showed how the American temperance movement became a focus for the conflict between lower-class drinking urban Lutheran and Catholic immigrants and abstinent small-town, middle-class, evangelical Protestants. Defeat or victory in this conflict became symbolic of the status and power of the two opposing subcultures. For a while, small-town morality was ascendant and the prohibition laws were enforced in the United States (causing tremendous growth in organized crime). Later, prohibition was repealed. It is a clear example of where law does not reflect widespread consensus (Hills 1980, p. 37). Gusfield states that "what is at stake is not so much the action of men, whether or not they drink, but their ideals, the moralities to which they owe their public allegiance" (ibid., p. 177). Likewise, Gusfield stated (1981) that the development of the myth of the "killer drunk" has helped American society maintain the illusion of moral consensus (p. 167).

In 1972, the British sociologist Cohen published an analysis of the early 1960s' Mods and Rockers. The study utilized Becker's and Gusfield's terminology and added a new term, "moral panics." This phenomenon is evident in a recent example of a moral entrepreneur, Anita Bryant, who in Miami in the late 1970s conducted an intense campaign against homosexuals, using slogans such as "Save Our Children" (see Hills 1980, pp. 166–67).

Lidz and Walker explain morality as "the process of defining any object in the world as good or evil or any similar evaluative dualism (e.g., kind-mean, free-enslaved, smart-stupid)" (1980, p. 23). Morality is an important sociological concept, its main function being to orient and direct social actions toward specified goals. It not only determines social goals but defines the legitimate ways to achieve them. Morality, in any society, is represented by a complicated structure of symbols that establish and communicate the significance attached to various ethical factors and problems.

Morality and value systems are important for an understanding of the nature of deviance. In this sense, the differential damages attributed to various deviant acts (e.g., drug abuse, prostitution, homosexuality, and the like) are peripheral to the main offense, which is a moral one. Durkheim's keen observation that "an act is criminal when it offends strong and defined states of the collective conscience. . . . When [a crime] is committed . . . it is the common conscience which is attacked" corroborates this conclusion (1933, pp. 70–110). If crimes damage morality, then we have to ask whose morality? How powerful are the upholders of the offended system and to what extent do they feel threatened? Sometimes a moral challenge is perceived as far more threatening than an actual physical threat.

However, morality is far more complex than our definitions reveal. Becker (1967) noted that societies have "hierarchies of credibility," which in essence provide a stratification principle in the moral hierarchy. These hierarchies mean that specific members of society—by virtue of their social position—are perceived to be more credible than others. Furthermore, as Rock points out

> In complex societies, the distribution of deviant phenomena is closely linked to the distribution of power and life-chances. . . . A stratification system can also be viewed as a moral system: a major organization of beliefs about the rights, duties and moral properties of the members of a society. . . . A system of control based on authority rests, in part, on a recognition of the *moral* right of the authoritative to make decisions. . . . Thus, in a stable, but unequal society class position is often identified with moral position—the higher one's position in a stratification order, the greater is one's moral worth. (1973a, p. 47)

Rock's thesis establishes a clear relationship between moral status and social position. If a certain type of "deviant" occupies a lower social position, the probability increases of his being regarded as truly deviant and thus acquiring a deviant identity. A change in his social position could transform the moral meaning and the "threat" potential of his behavior.

The sociology of the law provides a most interesting illustration of the application of concepts such as moral entrepreneur and moral crusade. The law symbolizes and reflects different moral ideas in society. As sociologists know all too well, the law reflects the final outcome of a long process of interaction and negotiation among different interest groups, and it does not necessarily embrace the legitimate needs of large sections of the population. Marijuana laws in the United States today demonstrate this problem.

> "Marijuana has become the *new Prohibition* in contemporary American society, with upwards of 40 million persons having used this illicit drug, perhaps one third of them using it on a more or less regular basis. Effective enforcement of the law has become impossible. The use and sale of marijuana remain illegal, however, primarily because most of the older adult public are ideologically opposed to total decriminalization. Use of the drug is symbolically associ-

ated in much of the public mind with many kinds of activities, lifestyles, and moral and political beliefs that these dominant groups find repugnant (e.g., hedonism, sexual promiscuity, altered states of consciousness, radicalism, irreverence toward authority, and so on)." (Hills 1980, p. 38)

Religion, politics, medicine, the arts and sciences are other areas that define morality through complex sets of symbols of ethics and rituals. Morality thus renders a most important service to society through defining boundaries.

One must realize that competing moral crusaders and moral panics, all reflecting a "collective search for identity" (Klapp 1969), can be widespread phenomena in a society where morality itself is subject to negotiation. Such debates are usually carried out by politicians, law enforcement agents, lawyers, psychiatrists, social workers, and media people. Complex societies are morally heterogeneous and different sections of society present different moralities.

Durkheim was well aware of the problem concerning the moral structure of society.[14] Discussing his conceptualization of morality inevitably brings us back to what he felt was the very core of society, the collective conscience, which he defined as follows: "The totality of beliefs and sentiments common to average citizens of the same society forms a determinate system which has its own life; one may call it the *collective* or *common conscience.* . . . It is independent of the particular conditions in which individuals are placed" (1933, pp. 79–80). Thus, the collective conscience is the mechanism that defines the moral boundaries of society. It is the very essence of any social system, and it therefore is regarded as sacrosanct. Each individual's meaning of life is associated with his society's collective conscience. It follows that Shils's "center" is equivalent to the collective conscience. "The center . . . is . . . the realm of values and beliefs. . . . This central value system is the central zone of society" (Shils 1970, p. 1).

As noted earlier, in simple societies, the collective conscience (or center) is quite specific and plays a mechanical integrative role. In complex societies, the existence and role of the collective conscience becomes problematic.[15] There could exist a few competing centers, differing from

14. Durkheim (1973). For analysis of Durkheim's ideas, see Bellah's introduction and Wallwork's (1972) excellent integrative presentations. See also Durkheim's preface to the second edition of *The Division of Labour in Society*.

15. Durkheim (1933) himself recognized this possibility when he stated that each occupational group has its own collective conscience (i.e., different professional ethical systems) specifying meaningful values and conduct for that group.

one another in various degrees, or one collective conscience could be differentiated into various levels; yet society still maintains some form of integration.[16] In both simple and complex societies, the consciousness of likeness is a difficult issue. While it appears that simple, cohesive social systems are more characterized by stability, social change does occur there. In the same way, while change appears to be a hallmark of modern, pluralistic social orders, they also exhibit elements of social stability. In both types of society, deviance plays a crucial role.

To summarize, the discussion of deviance within the context of change and stability provides a resolution to the Durkheimian double bind and to some of the theoretical, as well as empirical, chaos in the sociology of deviance. Our analysis emphasizes two interdependent issues: the type of social system and the nature of its morality, that is, of boundaries. Deviance is the mirror-image of conventional morality and therefore of existing boundaries. In complex societies, where morality is continuously negotiated, the boundaries of society are constantly shifting. The problems of how, where, and when such negotiation takes place and what determines its outcome constitute a major interest for sociological research. Moral entrepreneurs, moral crusades, social power, and interest groups play a crucial role in these negotiations. The perceived threat of any real, imaginary, or assumed deviance is an important issue for its basic boundary-maintaining or boundary-changing functions.

Thus the answer to the problems raised at the beginning of this chapter is that the relativity of deviance has caused, in part, the fragmentation of its study. This problem has been further aggravated by the lack of a consistent solution to the Durkheimian double bind. My suggestion is that we analyze deviance as a relative phenomenon but within the general context of societal change and stability. This interpretation will not only provide a broader theoretical framework and focus for the study of deviance but can also give the subject a central role in sociology.

Plan of the Book

This book is addressed to the problem of deviance as a relative phenomenon in changing cultural matrixes.[17] What happens in the realm of

16. Support for this idea can also be found in Durkheim's discussion of the "non-contractual elements of contract." Despite the existence of different, or differentiated, collective consciences, there are still values and norms that are shared by all members of society that facilitate both variety and organic solidarity.

17. The theoretical and empirical discussions of deviance versus social change and stability in the literature are usually dull and incomplete. A few scholars, however, have

moral and social boundaries is of crucial importance. Most books on crime and deviance do not usually present the variety of cases chosen for this study. Therefore, an explanation justifying the choice of cases for this book is called for.

The first case provides a description and analysis of the European witchcraze. During the fifteenth through the seventeenth centuries, Europeans executed approximately half a million witches, mostly female. This was a time of transition in Europe. The old medieval order crumbled and a new moral-social order emerged. Society became more pluralized, differentiated, and complex. From a system controlled and supervised through a rigid religious mechanism, society moved to other types of social control, as profound changes in its moral boundaries took place. There were deep changes, not only in the social and political spheres, but also in the role of women and families. There were as well significant economic and demographic changes. The witchcraze, as a fabricated and collective form of deviance, is analyzed and interpreted within the context of societal transformation. It is shown that agents of the crumbling medieval order created the "crime" of witchcraft in a desperate attempt to redefine the moral boundaries of their rapidly changing society. This case is particularly interesting because it enables us to examine a specific

---

examined the relationship between deviance and social change with more attention. There seem to have been five major attempts in this regard. The first was the "social disorganization" perspective (Rubington and Weinberg 1971, pp. 47–79; Davis 1975), which developed in the early decades of this century. This perspective showed deviant behavior within the context of population movements, urbanization, and industrialization and suggested that social changes cause disruption in the social system, which then promotes deviance. The second was Merton's introduction (1938) of a typology in which the "innovator" and the "rebel" could be thought of as the deviants who introduce change. The third was Winslow's introductory text (1970) in which he attempted to examine deviance within the context of the Parsonian scheme and specifically within "social transition." The fourth attempt was by Sagarin (1977), who edited a volume of different papers dealing with deviance and social change. Unfortunately, this book does not provide an analytic framework for discussing deviance and social change together. With the exception of a short, general, and unconvincing introduction, no explanation is given for the selection of papers for the book. The fifth work is by Shelby (1981), who tried to analyze the complex relationship between modernization (social change) and patterns of crime. While the first, second, and fourth attempts are obviously more serious ones, it is evident that virtually no scholar has tried to analyze social deviance within the broader framework of social change and social stability, certainly not as an answer to either the Durkheimian double bind or the chaotic nature of the sociology of deviance itself. The few studies so far have concentrated on analyzing deviance within the more limited context of societal change. One must note, however, that some recent books on the sociology of deviance (e.g., Davis and Stivers 1975; Schur 1979, 1980) hint that deviance should be thought of as part of social change. Thus, the nature of the recognized relationship between deviance, change, and stability has remained obscure.

type of deviance within a simple society, characterized by a unique control mechanism.

The second case involves the modern revival of the occult and of science fiction, analyzing the rise of various esoteric and deviant quasi-religious movements and belief systems within a complex, constantly changing society. The rise of these phenomena is interpreted as part of an intricate system of competing centers in modern societies, each attempting to draw its own moral boundaries within the multidimensional control system. The concept of "elective centers" is used to illustrate how a variety of deviant belief systems can play an important role in processes of social change.

The final two cases examine the subject of deviance and science. The world of science and scientists is a complex social system geared to seeking truth and establishing certified knowledge, and thus, geared to change. Science, however, is also a stable system and uses many safeguards so that unjustified change can not be wrongly introduced. I make a distinction between deviant scientists and deviant sciences. The first category refers to scientists who report on observations that have never been made, frauds, and the like. Indeed, the structure and function of science itself are probably more conducive to deviance than what is usually accepted. Furthermore, the cases of known deviant scientists are used by the relevant disciplines to emphasize and draw the boundaries of their field and thus help maintain stability. Deviant sciences, however, are very different. They challenge—both substantively and methodologically—the boundaries of orthodox science and thus open the way for possible changes in science.

Each of the four cases presents a thorough analysis of a specific form of deviance. The analysis of each has two main focuses. The first emphasizes the problem of boundary maintenance, of change and stability within the different cultural matrixes where the specific deviance happens. The other emphasizes the natural history of the specific deviance, that is, how and under what conditions the behavior emerges, matures, becomes attenuated or dies out. This will enable us to understand better the form of deviance itself, and its relation to change and stability.

2

DEVIANCE WITHIN SOCIETAL TRANSITION

The European Witchcraze of the Fifteenth, Sixteenth, and Seventeenth Centuries

Introduction[1]

From the early decades of the fifteenth century until 1650, continental Europeans executed between two and five hundred thousand witches (according to conservative estimates), more than 85 percent of whom were women. We shall analyze this phenomenon from a macrosociological point of view, concentrating on several questions clustered along three axes. The first addresses itself to the problem of timing: Why did the witchcraze start in the fifteenth century? Why did it become so popular and widespread during the next two hundred years? Why did it end in the seventeenth century? The second axis addresses the question of content: Why the suddenly increased attention to witchcraft, black magic, and the like? How do we explain the emergence of a whole religious ideology about witches, who were perceived as the antithesis of "true" Christians? Why did this ideology culminate in persecutions of witches? The third axis questions the target of the witch-hunts: Why were women singled out as its main victims?

The answers suggested here are based on the convergence of several conditions: The vested interests of agents of the Catholic Church, such as the Dominicans and the Inquisition, and the collapse of the authoritative framework of religion and of the feudal social order explain questions related to the first axis. The dissolution of the medieval cognitive map of the world—which also gave rise to utopian expectations, magical beliefs,

1. The material in this chapter appeared in different form in the following two essays: "The European Witchcraze of the Fourteenth–Seventeenth Centuries: A Sociologist's Perspective," *American Journal of Sociology* 86 (1):1–31, © 1986 by The University of Chicago; "Problems Inherent in Sociohistorical Approaches to the European Witchcraze," *Journal for the Scientific Study of Religion* 20 (4):325–38.

and bold scientific explorations—relates to the questions clustered along the second axis. Changes in the economy, demography, and family, especially changes in the role of women—some of which were of catastrophic proportions—explain the target of the craze. The spatial distribution of the witch-hunt and its termination are a result of the presence or absence of these conditions in different parts of Europe during the period in question, and their disappearance everywhere at the end of the period.

The riddle of the European witchcraze is closely linked to specific changes in societal boundaries in different realms that took place between the fourteenth and seventeenth centuries. Thus, I suggest that medieval society was crumbling as new social, political, economic, scientific, and religious forms came into being. The boundaries of the old order were changing in a very significant way along more than one dimension. These changes brought about innovative institutional arrangements in all social spheres. As a result, new and positive reactions to the changes became possible, since old traditions, and limitations were broken (e.g., in the areas of art and science). However, there was also an extreme negative reaction, a ferocious witch-hunt aimed at restoring the old societal boundaries.

Before I begin my discussion, it is important to look at the witchcraze itself and to determine exactly which of its aspects require explanation. This requires a rather long description. It is well worth mentioning here that people of the period did in fact believe in the reality of witchcraft, demonology, and witches. Even men like Newton, Bacon, Boyle, Locke, and Hobbes—the greatest minds of the seventeenth century, the "century of genius," as Whitehead called it—firmly believed in the reality of witchcraft (Hansen 1969; Hughes 1952; Michelet 1965; Baroja 1965; Parrinder 1958). As Russell put it, "Tens of thousands of [witchcraft] trials continued throughout Europe generation after generation, while Leonardo painted, Palestrina composed and Shakespeare wrote" (1977, p. 79).

Witchcraft and Witch-hunts: The Phenomenon to be Explained

Early History

Witchcraft and witches have existed throughout history. Although the canonical books of the Old Testament virtually ignore the subject, one of the first places where witches are mentioned is in the story of the witch of Endor with whom King Saul consulted before his last battle (1 Sam.

28:9). Witchcraft is imbedded in the ancient Jewish law itself, in the divine command, "Thou shalt not suffer a witch to live" (Exod. 22:10; Williams 1959, p. 27). Throughout the Bible, the stories concerning witches are neutral, in that witches, devils, and demons are never elaborately conceptualized and the existence of a demonic world is never mentioned. The Old Testament, however, provides us with a most interesting account—that of the fall of Satan.

The story goes that the angels' leader, Semjaza (elsewhere called Azazel), together with his followers, bound themselves together by oath on Mount Hermon and descended to earth, where they took wives and begat giants. Their lust and cruelty wrought such destruction and wickedness that God sent the deluge. And so Semjaza and his band were sentenced to be buried under mountains till the Day of Judgment, when they were to be cast into the abyss of fire for ever and ever (Lea 1901, vol. 1). This theme will appear again in the Christian stories of the witchcraze.

In ancient Greece and Rome, magical processes were employed to produce rain, prevent hail storms, drive away clouds, calm the winds, make animals and plants prosper, increase wealth, cure sickness, and so on. But, it was also used to achieve other ends, for example, to ruin an enemy's crops or make his cattle sick. One could strike down an enemy as he was on the point of making a speech or taking an important part in a public ceremony. Death was quite frequently considered to be a result of witchcraft. These beliefs and practices were certainly not confined to specific strata of Graeco-Roman society but were dispersed throughout it (Baroja 1965, p. 18). The practice of magic for beneficent purposes was considered legal and necessary; only magical practices intended to do harm were condemned and punished. Beneficent sorcery was widely approved and even official and was commonly practiced by a great variety of people. The state supported those whose business it was to augur the future or make prognostications for special occasions and those who, in the public interest, discovered by divination what had happened or what was about to happen. For example, treatises on agriculture and medicine and the offices used by priests for certain cults and rites contained collections of spells (ibid., 1965, pp. 17–41).

As the Roman Empire became greater, more sophisticated and eclectic, the gods of each new conquest were included in a state pantheon that was—for all practical purposes—entirely outside the central control of the Pontifex Maximus. Here, in fact, is the very seed of its pluralistic, supernatural world. The Graeco-Roman religious universe was not divided—as were some other religions—into extreme good and extreme bad. In the Judeo-Christian religion, for example, God is the very image of good, and the devil of evil, but the gods of the ancient world, were subject to the same forces of evil and passion as men, and it thus is very difficult (and wrong) to conceptualize the Graeco-Roman deities in dualistic terms. The spirit world of Greece and Rome was all-embracing, so that even the most insignificant human actions were held to be the expression of something divine. As a logical consequence, nature could not be thought of as a separate entity. Thus there could never be an absolute dividing line between religion and magic. However, as Baroja (1965) reports, it is possible to argue that, in general, magic was connected with man's desire and will, while religion was more closely associated with feelings such as respect, gratefulness, submission. In this way, it was possible to combine a spell with a prayer. Probably the only real distinction that can be made in this respect is a distinction between white and black magic, good versus evil magic.

The nature of the Graeco-Roman expansion was such that, with each conquest, the conquered people could still go on and worship their local deities, but they had to accept one more—the emperor. This process was not a "one-way street," and the empire was itself influenced by those deities. As Hughes states, it was quite obvious that the Roman provincial firmly believed in the arts of witches—particularly the witches of Thessaly (1952 p. 39). The distinction between white and black magic represented an attempt to harness the power of the Unseen without the medium of the established priesthood. Magical practices and beliefs continued to be popular even after the disintegration of the empire. Thus the dates of the big festivals were those of the old hunting ceremonies and the times of the mating of animals (Hughes 1952; Baroja 1965). The famous Lupercalia (February 15) brought people from all over the empire to Rome. Young men covered their bodies with goat skins and danced in the streets.[2] Goats were sacrificed, and women were whipped with straps made from the hides. Masks were worn, images and balls were hung up on trees, and spells, repeated three times, were cast on enemies. Poisons and aphrodisiacs were manufactured, not always successfully. Lucretius, for example, is said to have died from an overdose of a love potion (Hughes 1952, p. 40).

From early Graeco-Roman times, there is documentary evidence of the existence over a very long period (possibly a few centuries) of the belief that certain people—usually (but not always) women—could

2. Interesting to note that much later, in the fifteenth century, the devil keeps appearing as a he-goat, not to mention the scapegoat in the Bible, which actually was a goat that was thrown from the mountain Azazael. Hughes (1952) reports that he found certain villages in Europe where goats still had a special semireligious meaning.

change themselves and others into animals at will, that they could fly through the air and enter the most secret and hidden places by leaving their bodies behind. There are two important points here. First, the sorcerer had a special, powerful position vis-à-vis the deities.[3] His knowledge of spells, charms, potions, and the like enabled him to force various deities into action they would not have otherwise undertaken. If you like, the witch had the "key" to activate deities. Thus, magicians became experts in a technological knowledge and magic became associated with "control." The second important point is the division between black and white magic we have mentioned before. The former was completely condemned and feared, the latter blessed and welcome. As Baroja shows, this distinction was formally laid down from the very earliest Roman times (1964, p. 40). Tacitus, for example, painted a brilliant picture of the terror in Rome when the spells that were believed to have caused Germanicus's illness were discovered. As we shall see, these two perceptions of magic changed radically during the fifteenth century.

O'Dea defines religion as "the manipulation of non-empirical or supra-empirical means for non-empirical, or supra-empirical, ends" In contrast, he defines magic as "the manipulation of non-empirical or supra-empirical means for empirical ends" (1966, p. 7). His approach recalls the work of Weber (1964), for whom witchcraft is a kind of technology. For Weber, the magician's main function is to cope with ad hoc interests and tensions. Magical powers can be "forced" to serve human needs through the magician's correct use of formulas. These, we believe, were the essential characteristics of European witchcraft until the witch-hunts of the late Middle Ages: its "technological" nature and its very specific goals (love potions, spells, love magic, and the like). There did not exist a developed, systematic conceptualization of a world opposed to our own and at war with it. The witch, so far, had a very special position vis-à-vis the gods (or deities): she could, with the correct "technological" use of spells, potions, and the like, compel them into specific actions.

In the fifteenth, sixteenth, and seventeenth centuries, however, witchcraft was transformed from a technology into an evil entity that created— rather than solved—problems. The distinction between good and bad magic vanished. Toward the end of the fifteenth century, a crystallized

3. Lucan asked how it was possible to force the gods to do something. Did they like obeying the spells of a sorcerer? Did the effectiveness of the spells lie in piety or was it the result of a mysterious power over the gods (Baroja 1965, p. 70). The questions Lucan asked were technical; he searched for specific answers to specific questions. To use Weber's terminology, here we have a "magician" looking for ad hoc answers (Weber 1964).

conception of magic and witchcraft as something purely evil became dominant. With the publication of the *Malleus maleficarum* (The Witch's Hammer) in the 1480s, demonological theories reached a peak, constituting an independent "quasi religion." To carry the point a bit further, they became "antireligion." Another important trait of ancient magic—the pluralistic conceptualization of the supernatural world—also disappeared (where it remained—for example, in Russia—the witchcraze was very weak and insignificant). During this period, the witch lost her special relationship with the deities, and her powerful ability to force them to comply with her wishes was replaced by total subordination to the devil. In short, the witch became Satan's puppet.

These changes in the perception of witchcraft were of crucial importance. Because witchcraft was regarded as a routine (almost personal) technology until the fifteenth century, witches were classified as good and bad depending on the objective of their magic. After the fourteenth century, witchcraft became a systematic theory—an analytical break—which enabled the Inquisitors and other individuals to legitimately persecute hundreds of thousands of witches.

The European Witchcraze

We have seen that the history of European sorcery and witchcraft extends well back into Graeco-Roman times. Witchcraft, however, as an elaborated belief system was a fairly new phenomenon, unknown as such before the fifteenth century.

> European witchcraft [between 1450 and 1750] was conceived of as a virulent and dangerous blend of sorcery and heresy. Sorcery is . . . anything that aims at negative supernatural effects through formulas and rituals. . . . The other element, heresy, . . . is the pact with the devil, the witches' sabbath in the form of a black or inverted Mass. (Monter 1969, p. 8)

There seems to be no argument among scholars that the main feature of the European witchcraze was the "witches' Sabbath," the climax of which was a huge orgy between the devil and witches.[4] There is no better

---

4. Lea (1901, 3:401–8) reports that in the teutonic tradition, there was a belief that witches were true cannibals, and, that once a year on the first of May or on Saint Walpurgis' night (probably a local god transformed to a saint), there was a nocturnal gathering of witches. At this gathering, called the trolla-thing the witches ate and sang. Lea suggests that the Dominicans inflated this theme. The idea of the witches' Sabbath and the notion that witches ride broomsticks or beasts at night to travel to the forest for the Sabbath or other black masses was partly created and partly crystallized by Dominican Inquisitors in the late 1400s.

way to introduce the reader to the atmosphere of the period than to read closely an account of the Sabbath rituals. Descriptions of this ceremony can be found in a number of texts, for example, Robbins (1959), Carus (1974), Murray (1962), Russell (1977), Trevor-Roper (1967), and Lea (1957). In the following discussion, I rely mostly on MacKay (1841) and to a smaller extent on Robbins (1959). The Sabbath was conceptualized as a ritual performed by the devil and his aids together with the witches. In the ceremony, homage was paid to the devil, the public profession of the pact was administered, and new witches were recruited and signed with the devil's mark. Furthermore, all Sabbath ceremonies had a few common characteristics: a banquet, dancing, and sexual intercourse.

It is said that the devil generally chose a place where four roads met as the scene of the Sabbath or, if that was not convenient, the neighborhood of a lake. Upon that spot nothing would ever grow afterward, as the hot feet of the demons and witches burnt fecundity from the earth. Witches from all over were supposed to arrive at this gathering place, riding on broomsticks in France and England and on the devil himself, in the shape of a he-goat, in Italy, Spain, and Germany. The back of the goat was supposed to have the miraculous ability of being longer or shorter, according to the number of witches he was desirous of accommodating. When all the witches had arrived at the place of rendezvous (anyone who did not make it was severely punished by demons), the infernal ceremonies of the Sabbath began.

Satan, having assumed his favorite shape of a very large he-goat, with a face in front and another in his haunches, took his seat upon a throne; and all present kissed the face behind. This infamous kiss, the *osculum infame* or *osculum obscoenum*, was documented in demonological literature again and again, and is featured by most authorities. Robbins quotes a contemporary lawyer, Jean Bodin, "There is no greater disgrace, dishonor, or villainy than that which these witches endure when they have to adore Satan in the guise of a stinking goat, and to kiss him in that place which modesty forbids writing or mentioning" (1959, p. 420). This done, a master of ceremonies was appointed, with whom Satan made a personal examination of all the witches to see whether they were stamped with his secret mark. Those who did not have it were stamped immediately. This done, they all began dancing and singing in the most furious manner. Then they stopped, denied their salvation, kissed the devil's back, spit upon the Bible, and swore obedience to the devil in all things. The dancing and singing began again. As the witches looked around, they were surprised to observe nearly all of their friends and neighbors, whom they had not previously suspected to be witches. With them, there were scores of demons, their paramours, to whom they had bound themselves by the infernal pact. And, above all of the feasting, dominating them all, was the imperious master, the god of their worship—the devil himself. Although usually he appeared as a he-goat, he also came in the guise of a big, black-bearded man or a great toad. His subjects danced to exhaustion while the macabre music of curious instruments—horses' skulls, oak logs, and human bones—kept playing.

Again, everybody kissed the devil, and having settled down (apparently they could get tired), they would usually recount the evil deeds committed since their last meeting. Those who had not been malicious and mischievous enough were severely punished by Satan (MacKay 1841, p. 471; Trevor-Roper 1967, pp. 94–95). Thousands of toads then sprang out of the earth, ready to Satan's commands, and standing on their hind legs, danced while the devil played the bagpipes, the trumpet, or some other instrument. This dance supposedly amused the witches very much. The toads could speak and entreated the witches to reward them for their exertions with the flesh of unbaptized babies, which the witches did. After that, they all settled down to a feast. In Germany, it was sliced turnips, parodies of the host. In Savoy, roast or boiled children. In Spain, exhumed corpses, preferably of kinfolk. In England, more sensibly, roast beef and beer. Sister Madeleine de Demandolx's confession (1611) states that "the meat they ordinarily eat is the flesh of young children, which they cook and make ready . . . sometimes bringing them thither alive by stealing them. After the banquet, the witches might partake in the magic cake, made of black millet mixed with flesh of unbaptized infants" (Robbins 1959, p. 421). But alas, these nice distinctions made little difference: the food, all agreed, was somehow too cold and quite tasteless. One necessary ingredient, salt, for some arcane reason, was never admitted (Trevor-Roper 1967, p. 95).

Having finished eating, and at a word from the goat, witches and devils threw themselves into promiscuous sexual couplings. Again, these orgies were not as pleasurable as one might have thought. Robbins mentions that sexual intercourse was indiscriminate (incest, bestiality, unnatural positions and acts, and the like), and according to demonologists, most witches found it quite painful. Robbins quotes from De Lancre, who gave the sworn testimony of sixteen-year-old Jeanette D'Abadie: "She said she feared intercourse with the devil because his member was scaly and caused extreme pain: furthermore, his semen was extremely cold" (p. 423). After the orgy, the dance began again, but not as intensively as before. The toads were called again, and the witches amused themselves by mocking the holy sacrament of baptism. The toads were sprinkled with some sort of filthy water, and as the devil made the sign of a cross, everyone cursed it. When the cock-a-doodle-doo was heard,[5] they all disappeared, and the Sabbath was over.

Witchcraft as a Counterreligion

What were the main characteristics of the European witchcraze ideology as it developed between the fifteenth and seventeenth centuries? Most important is the fact that this period witnessed the invention and crystallization of a demonical theory, unprecedented in quality and magnitude in earlier centuries. The totally negative description of the witch, as well as the whole new perception of witchcraft and demonology, was a dramatic change from the past. The kind of witches that Contemporary European demonologists referred to were qualitatively very different from their predecessors: witchcraft was losing its neutral technological character and acquiring the elaborate and complicated image of an "antireligion." This transformation in the perception of the witch, however, did not take place before the fifteenth century, when it was crystallized, authorized and accepted. This is a very important observation, since the following three hundred years witnessed the transformation of the concepts of witchcraft and magic from the technical realm to an ideological one.

What was this new conception of witchcraft? Above we used Monter's definiton of witchcraft, pointing to the central role of the Sabbath. However, there were three more important ingredients in this conception. First, the witch had lost her special position vis-à-vis the deities, and instead of controlling them, she became controlled by them. The witch was portrayed in demonological theories as purely bad, as Satan's puppet, as someone from whom no good whatsoever could ever come. Second, there can be little doubt that witches were identified with women. The *Malleus maleficarum* one of the most important contemporary books on the subject, specifically mentions that "witchcraft is chiefly found in women" because they are more credulous and have poor memories, and because "witchcraft comes from carnal lust, which is in women insatiable" (1487–89; Sprenger and Kramer 1968, pp. 41–48). Around 1435, Nider mentioned that "there were more women than men witches because women have a slippery tongue and tell other women what they have learned" (Robbins 1959, p. 541).

Third, the theory of witchcraft represented a reversal of Christian theology. In this context, both O'Dea's and Weber's definitions of magic

---

5. The description here is echoed in Saint-Saën's "Dance Macabre."

and witchcraft seem invalid. The witch myth, as it emerged and developed in the late 1400s, was in fact a kind of religion, or quasireligion. It was a whole, coherent, rationalized system of beliefs, assumptions, rituals, and "sacred" texts. The Dominicans, who more than any other contemporary group developed and helped popularize the conception of demonology and witchcraft, based their beliefs on a dualist view of the world as a battlefield in which a struggle between the godly sons of light and the satanic sons of darkness was being played out. Their fear was that Satan might win this battle and turn the world into hell. It is from this point of view that witchcraft was an antireligion. The stories and myths about the witches were the exact opposite of what was supposed to be the true faith, that is, Christianity. This perception was strongly reinforced by the confessions of some doomed witches.

In opposition to the central dogma of the Church, which states that something (neither alien nor opposed, but Utter Spirit) entered into the womb of a virgin woman, we have the stories about the perverted sexual practices of the devil and witches. Thus, in contradistinction to the idea of the holy birth of Jesus, the Dominicans tell us of a perverse and barren sexual intercourse between the devil and the witch. We are further told that the devil, appearing either in female form (succubus) or male form (incubus), would come before a human male or female in order to seduce them. However, because the incubus did not possess his own sperm, the woman had to steal it from her unsuspecting husband in order to copulate with the devil. There were also many reports that the succubus was in fact a revived corpse, who became a corpse again once her identity was discovered (see, for example, Robbins 1959).[6] Thus, instead of the birth of Jesus, the Son of God, from a pure union between a woman and the Holy Spirit, demonologists portrayed the loathsome intercourse of devil and witch.

Contrary to the day when Christians meet to pray, Sunday morning, the devil and his legions prefer the night between Friday and Saturday. Christians meet in a holy church; the devil and his minions in isolated and cold places. In the church, people kiss the cross; at the witches Sabbath, they kiss the he-goat's posterior. The symbols and objects used in the sacrament of communion are mocked at the Sabbath. Jesus is the pure good; the devil is the pure bad. The devil has his own baptism—a mark is

---

6. The explicit sexual overtones of the witchcraze myth cannot—and should not—be ignored. Demonologists went to great lengths to associate witchcraft with perverted sexual practices and with the seductive behavior of the devil's legions. Emphasis was particularly laid on the "insatiable" sexual appetite of women: the "incubus," for example, outnumbered the "succubus" by at least ten to one (Robbins 1959, p. 490).

imprinted on the witches, while filthy water is sprinkled, usually by stinking toads. Jesus is described with awe; the devil is described with fear. The music of the Satanic ceremonies parodied Christian hymns. In church, people tasted the holy symbols (wafers and wine), and at the Sabbath they feasted on unbaptized, roasted babies. Contrary to the joyful descriptions we have of people preparing themselves to go to church, we have the gloomy descriptions of witches preparing the orgiastic Sabbaths. The unbaptized infants who were aborted, strangled, or stolen from graves were destined to be the main course of the Sabbath feast. Semen was collected from unsuspecting husbands for use during the orgies. The host was saved from Mass and brought to the feast to be desecrated (MacKay 1841; Trevor-Roper 1967). All in all, overwhelming evidence points to the simple conclusion that the witch beliefs were a negative image—a dark reflection—of the so-called true faith.[7]

The Historical Development of the European Witchcraze

Monter states that "until the beginning of the 13th century . . . Church and State fought against 'maleficia' in the older, simple form. After 1230, the scholastic community investigated the possibility of a connection between humans and demons. . . . by 1430 this process was completed and the concept of a sect of sorceresses and witches gained ground" (1969, p. 59). Dating the witchcraze is not an easy task. Most researchers (Monter 1969; Kieckhefer 1976; Russel 1972; Robbins 1959; Cohn 1975; Trevor-Roper 1967) document its rise from at least the fifteenth century, although it had begun gaining momentum in the fourteenth, and see it ending in the seventeenth century. However, there are reports of cases as late as the eighteenth century.

After the disintegration of the Roman Empire and the rise of Christianity, the church made many serious efforts to convert European pagan tribes. Many Christian missionaries found that the "barbarians" already possessed quite a large spectrum of local deities (Lea 1901, 3:395). In the most sensible manner, the missionaries sought to convert these people by canonizing local idols so that the native population could continue to worship them as Christian saints. In this manner, not only were local deities transformed, but the old temples were converted into churches so that Mass could be celebrated in familiar places of worship (Michelet 1965; Eckenstein 1896, pp. 6–32, 484). The magical practices—whatever they were—were tolerated because it was felt that they would simply fall into disuse and be forgotten as the population became truly Christian.

---

7. For more aspects of the inverse nature of the witch myth see Clark (1980).

Thus, it seems quite clear that in Western Europe in the years between the fall of the Roman Empire and the beginning of the Renaissance, the Church remained tolerant of sorcery and witchcraft. Action was taken against sorcerers (if at all) only if their magic had resulted in a murder or the destruction of property (Lea 1901, 3:408, 485–96). In some cases, sovereigns not only punished sorcerers for wrongs they committed but rewarded others for using the craft to benefit their neighbors, much in the same manner as in Graeco-Roman times (Nelson 1971). This view gets more support from Michelet (1965, pp. 86–87) who states that sorcerers continued to be employed as well as feared at all levels of medieval society, especially among peasants.

Although the Church would have no doubt preferred to see the casting of spells, astrology, and the like abandoned, it did not persecute those practicing these arts. In particular, official Church policy held that belief in witchcraft was itself an illusion. This appears most clearly in the famous, but mysterious, *Canon episcopi*. The origin of this document is not entirely clear. Kors and Peters (1972) date it at 1140 and find it in the *Concordance of Discordant* by Gratian. Lea (1957 vol. 1, pp. 178–80, 494) attributes it to an obscure meeting, the Council of Anquira, held, perhaps, in the fourth century. Although there is no record of such a council, the statement on witchcraft was certainly adopted by later canonists as official policy in the matter.[8] The following passage of the *Canon Episcopi* is from the English translation in Kors and Peters 1972 (pp. 29–31).

> Some *wicked women*, perverted by the devil, seduced by illusions and phantasms of demons, believe and profess themselves, in the hours of night, to ride upon certain beasts with Diana, the goddess of pagans, and an innumerable multitude of women, and in the silence of the dead of night to traverse great spaces of earth, and to obey her commands as of their mistress, and to be summoned to her service on certain nights. But I wish it were they alone who perished in their faithlessness and did not draw many with them into the destruction of infidelity. For an innumerable multitude, *deceived by this false opinion*, believe this to be true, and so believing, wander from the right faith and are invaled in the error of the

8. The *Cannon episcopi* was attributed to the Council of Anquira, or Ancyra held, perhaps, in 314 by Regino of Prüm, Abbot of Treves, who was the first to present the text (about 906). The text was accepted, for many centuries, as the highest authority on the subject, and was incorporated into the *Corpus juris canonici* by Gratian of Bologna in the twelfth century and thus became part of the canon law (Robbins 1959, p. 74). Harrison (1973 pp. 119–20) also dates it in 314 and to the Council of Ancyra.

pagans. . . . *Wherefore the priests throughout their churches should preach with all insistence . . . that they know this to be false and, that such phantasms are imposed and sent by the malignant spirit . . . who deludes them in dreams. . . .* Who is there who is not led out of himself in dreams, seeing such in sleeping which he never sees [when] waking? . . . And who is so stupid and foolish as to think that all these things, which are only done in spirit happen in the body? *It is therefore to be proclaimed publicly to all that whoever believes such things . . . has lost his faith.* (Italics added)

For more than six centuries, this policy, namely, that witchcraft is an illusion, discouraged those in the Church who might have wanted to destroy the belief in witches and magic by sheer force. Furthermore, there can be little doubt that the *Canon episcopi* served as a very efficient brake on any sought-for change in this conception. No wonder that when in 1458 Jacquier Nicholas wrote his important book on witchcraft, he first had to tackle the *Canon episcopi*. As long as the document articulated Church policy, no mass witch craze could take place.[9]

Beginning in the fifteenth century, various writers started attacking, directly and indirectly, the policy endorsed by the *Canon episcopi* (see Robbins 1958, 1959). First, attacks were made on the authenticity and validity of the document itself. Second, it was claimed that contemporary witches were different from the ones to which it alluded. In 1450, Jean Vineti, Inquisitor at Carcassone, identified witchcraft with heresy. In 1458, Nicholas Jacquier, Inquisitor in France and Bohemia, identified it as a *new* form of heresy, radically different from anything described in the *Canon episcopi*. In 1460, Visconti Girolamo, Inquisitor professor, provincial of Lombardy, stated that defending witchcraft in itself was heresy, and in 1484–86 Sprenger and Kramer published the *Malleus maleficarum*, which developed the theory of witchcraft into the rigid pattern it kept for three hundred years. The crystallization of witchcraft ideology after 1450 culminated in the witchcraze itself, which lasted in Europe another two hundred years. It is important to note, though, that

The most spectacular witch, . . . Joan of Arc, was tried and condemned in France in 1431; three years before, Europe's first mass panic, or 'witchcraze', occurred in the bilingual Swiss Alpine land of Valais, when over 100 people were tried by secular judges for

9. However we must state here Midelfort's minority opinion (1972, pp. 16–19). Midelfort does not feel that the significance attributed to the *Canon episcopi* is justified. However, in view of the nature of the document, and especially all the other sources on the history of witchcraft, I tend to reject his argument.

murder by sorcery, for stealing milk from cows and ruining crops by hailstorms, for worshipping the Devil and using counter-magic against the *Maleficia* of other witches. Nor was the Valais panic the last. 110 women and fifty-seven men were executed in Dauphine for witchcraft between 1428 and 1477; three dozen people were tried in the *vauderie* of Arras in 1459 in Europe's first urban panic. (Monter 1980, p. 31)

As time went by, the witchcraze spread over Europe. "A French judge boasted that he had burned 800 in 16 years. . . . In Geneva . . . 500 persons were burned in 1515. . . . In Trevez 7,000 were reported burned during a period of several years" (Bromberg 1959). The *Malleus* itself reports "1,000 persons were put to death in one year in the district of Como. Remigius, an authorized Inquisitor, boasted of having burned 900 in fifteen years. . . . 500 were executed in Geneva in three months in 1515" (pp. 220–21). Midelfort provides some of the results of the witch-hunts:

> Between 1587 and 1593 the Archbishop-Elector of Trier sponsored a witch-hunt that burned 368 witches from just twenty-two villages. So horrible was this hunt that two villages in 1585 were left with only one female inhabitant apiece. In the lands of the Convent of Quedlinburg, some 133 witches were executed on just one day in 1589. At the Abbey of Fulda, Prince Abbot Balthasar von Dernbach . . . boasted of having sent over 700 witches to the stake. . . . At the *Fürstprobstei* of Ellwangen, ecclesiastical officials saw to the burning of some 390 persons between 1611 and 1618. . . . the Teutonic Order of Mergentheim executed some 124 in the years 1628–1630. . . . In just eight years Bishop Philipp Adolf von Ehrenberg executed some 900 persons including his nephew, nineteen Catholic priests and several small children. In the Prince Bishopric of Eichstätt some 274 witches were executed. . . . The Duchy of Braunschweig-Wolfenbüttel executed fifty-three between 1590 and 1620, while Duke August of Braunschweig-Lüneberg eliminated seventy between 1610 and 1615. . . . the Duchy of Bavaria probably executed close to 2,000 witches. (1981, p. 28)

In the Continental witch-hunts, children, women, and whole families were sent to the stake. The historical sources are full of the most horrible stories of the torture the "witches" went through, the lies they were told by judges and inquisitors. Entire villages were exterminated. As Hughes reports, the area we call Germany was covered with stakes, where witches were burning alive. "Germany was almost entirely occupied in building bonfires. . . . Travellers in Lorraine may see thousands and thousands of stakes" One inquisitor cried, "I wish [the witches] had but one body, so that we could burn them all at once, in one fire!" (Trevor-Roper 1967, p. 152).

During the 1580's when the Catholic Counter-Reformation began to reconquer the territories they had lost to the Protestants a decade or two earlier, the Catholics became dedicated witch hunters too. Many of the persons accused were Protestants who refused to flee or convert. In France, witches were found primarily in Huguenot areas such as Orleans, Languedoc, Normandy and Navarre. In Lorraine, Judge Remy boasted of having executed over a thousand witches. Along the Rhine in the 1590's whole villages were depopulated." (Ibid., 142–45)

In the later stages of the witchcraze, cruelty increased. According to Lea (1957, pp. 1088–1117, 1228–51) as many as one hundred were burned each year in villages in Bavaria. But, as Trevor-Roper (1967), Robbins (1959), and Lea (1957, 1901) report, the worst persecution of all was probably in Bamberg.[10] There, the prince-bishop was Joahnn George II Fuchs von Dornheim, known as the *Hexenbishop*, or "witch bishop." He built a "witch house," complete with a torture chamber adorned with appropriate Biblical texts, and in his ten-year reign (1623–33), he is said to have burned six hundred witches. One of the victims was the bishop's

10. In Bamberg, the witchcraze reached unimaginable "peaks." It was not only the prince-bishop Von Dornheim who committed atrocities. His cousin, Prince-bishop Philipp Adolf Von Ehrenberg (1623–31) also burned nine hundred witches. Trever, Strasbourg, Breslau, Fulda, and Wurzburg were also places where witches were severely persecuted at that time. The witchcraze reached Bamberg somewhat later than other German states, but, nevertheless, the persecutions there were most horrible. It started with Bishop Johann Gottfried Von Aschhaused (1609–22), who burned about three hundred witches, and continued with Von Dornheim. Small towns in the area did not lag behind. Places like Zeil, Hallstadt, and Kronch were persecuting witches too. In Bamberg, there were some cases of "political" executions since some of the accused were, clearly, from the town's elite (for example, Dr. Haan, Johannes Julius, and other burgomasters). The pace and rapidity of some of the trials were shocking. In the case of Frau Anna Hansen in 1629, the accused was arrested on June 17, put to torture between June 18 and June 28, and on July 7 (less than a month from her arrest) was beheaded and burned. It seems clear that the prince-bishop of Bamberg ignored orders from the emperor to release certain "witches." For example, Ferdinand's order to release Dorothea Block was disregarded as was his order to release Dr. Haan and his family because "their arrest was a violation of the law of the Empire not to be tolerated." Bamberg's witchcraze ended when King Gustavus of Sweden threatened the city (he invaded Leipzig in September 1630). This, along with local opposition to the torture the war and the death of the prince-bishop (1631) ended the mania (Robbins 1959, pp. 35–37.)

chancellor, Dr. Haan, who was burned as a witch in 1628 for showing suspicious leniency as a judge. Here, we have one of the most touching stories of the witchcraze. Under torture, Dr. Haan confessed to having seen five burgomasters of Bamberg at the witches Sabbath, and they too were duly executed. One of them, Johannes Julius, under fierce torture confessed that he had renounced God, given himself to the devil, and seen twenty-seven of his colleagues at the Sabbath. But afterward, from prison, he contrived to smuggle a letter out to his daughter Veronica, giving a full account of his trial: "Now my dearest child," he concludes, "you have here all my acts and confessions, for which I must die. It is all falsehood and invention, so help me God. . . . They never cease to torture until one says something. . . . If God sends no means of bringing the truth to light our whole kindred will be burnt" (Trevor-Roper 1967, p. 157).[11]

As Trevor-Roper points out, the wars of religion in the seventeenth century added fuel to the burning mania of the witchcraze and introduced the worst period of persecutions. Protestants and Catholics zealously accused each other of witchcraft, and the craze reached an unprecedented climax in the early decades of the 1600s. It also seems that the Thirty Years' War (1618–48) brought with it a vicious wave of witch-hunting, what Trevor-Roper calls the "épidémie démoniaque." In their most devastating form, the witch-hunts lasted until after the end of the Thirty Years' War. If the publication of the *Malleus malificarum* symbolized the beginning of the terror in the 1490s, we can symbolically date its end with the Peace of Westphalia (1648). In the end, as many as half a million accused witches may have found their torturous death by burning, drowning, or hanging. (Currie 1969; Kittridge 1929; Robbins 1959).[12]

Evidence indicates that the majority of the victims were women (Garrett 1977; Andreski 1982; Heinsohn and Steiger 1982). In one area in southwest Germany, females constituted 85 percent of all victims (Midelfort 1972, pp. 179–80). Monter (personal communication 1976) claims that a comparison of his research with that of Midelfort shows that nearly 90 percent of the victims were women. Lea reports that in Switzerland "almost every woman [was considered] a witch" (1957, p. 1079). In "[Weisensteig and Rothenberg], we find overwhelming proportions of women (90–100 percent)" among the executed (Midelfort 1972, p. 179). At the beginning of the witchcraze, we often find that accused witches

11. A good account of the case can be found in Robbins (1959).
12. Hsu (1960) estimates a minimum of 30,000 victims and a maximum of several millions.

were widows, spinsters, or "strange" old women. Later on, married women and young girls were persectued as well. Various historical sources reveal that neither social status nor age made any difference as the most crucial variable was the fact that most victims were women.

Jaquerius in 1458 stated that witches were women, and the *Malleus* specifically associated witchcraft with women because "all witchcraft comes from carnal lust, which is in women insatiable." Monter himself notes that "sex . . . seems to have been more important than wealth" (1976, p. 110). His data clearly undermine the notion that only poor, widowed, or otherwise strange women were persecuted. He notes that "compared to sex, poverty and other factors seem to be secondary" (ibid., p. 124). The major weight of empirical data supporting the view that witches were old, deviant women comes mainly from British cases (specifically from Thomas 1971). But the British witchcraze was very different from the European.

The witch-hunts did not affect all the countries or areas of Europe in the same way and showed a number of differences from area to area. The English witchcraze is notably different from that which occurred in continental Europe although Scotland highly resembled the Continental pattern.[13] It appears that the worst witch-hunts occurred in Germany, Switzerland, and France, and only to a much lesser extent in other areas. It has also been observed that the witch-hunts were conducted in their most intense form in those regions where the Catholic Church was weakest (Lea 1957). In areas with a strong Church, such as Spain, Poland, and eastern Europe, the witchcraze phenomenon was neg-

---

13. In England, the witchcraze started and ended later than in continental Europe and was much milder. A demonological ideology did not prevail there, and persons accused of witchcraft were considered to have committed crimes against men and not against God. It is very likely that the lack of inquisitorial machinery, the clear-cut relationship between Church and kingdom, and a strong monarchy rendered less painful the English struggle with the problems Europe faced. Furthermore, in England the judicial system was more humane than in Europe. It appears that during the late Middle Ages England was in many respects outside the dispute which tore Europe apart. Scotland, however, experienced much more religious turmoil, which affected the judicial foundations of the law and—together with King James I's personal encouragement—enabled the occurrence of a virulent witchcraze there. On the Scottish witchcraze, see Larner: "The Scottish witch hunt was arguably one of the major witch hunts of Europe. During its peak it was matched only by those of the German principalities and Lorraine" (1981, p. 197). On England's witch-hunt see Anderson and Gordon (1978), Currie (1968), Thomas (1971), MacFarlane (1970), Robbins (1959). On the European variations see Cohn (1975), Hughes (1952), Kieckhefer (1976), Lea (1957), Monter (1969, 1976), Robbins (1959), Russell (1972), Trevor-Roper (1967), Williams (1959), Midelfort (1972).

ligible.[14] Finally, we must realize that the description of the witch cult here is necessarily only partial and inexhaustive.

While there can be little doubt that such places as Germany, Switzerland and France suffered a most intense form of witchcraze, it is essential for my thesis to establish that in other regions, where a strong church existed, a witchcraze did not take place, or was negligible. There can hardly be a doubt that the church was strong in Spain, Portugal, Hungary, Poland, Bohemia and Italy. The research done by Lea (1975), Robbins (1959), Henningsen (1980a, 1980b), Monter (1980, p. 33), demonstrates that, indeed, in these regions witch hunting was rare and whenever it occurred, it did so on a small, virtually negligible scale.

The Scandinavian countries (Robbins 1959; Midelfort 1981) and Russia (Zguta 1977) present us with an interesting additional factor. In these areas, a strong pagan belief system existed alongside the Church, but there was a very low rate of witchcraft accusations and persecutions there. Taken together, these points imply that the coexistence of Christianity with widespread popular belief in demons and sorcery could conceivably counteract the persecutions or even prevent them. This conclusion, mind you, is against the view that in the witch hunt, sorcerers and paganism were fought against and eradicated. The Scandinavian and Russian cases strongly suggest that the witchcraft ideology—demonology—of the late Middle Ages was invented and was not necessarily aimed against existing popular witch cults or pagan groups.

To summarize, two observations can be made. First, where the Church was strong, witchcraft cases were rare. Second, the emergence of witchcraft cases in such countries was relatively late, and they were not persecuted with any force.

Witchcraft: Possible Explanations

The practice of magic, witchcraft, sorcery, and the like has long attracted the attention of historians, sociologists, anthropologists, and other scholars.[15] While anthropologists have traditionally focused their efforts in studying witchcraft in nonliterate, tribal, or traditional, social systems, other scholars have concentrated on its more modern aspects, in particu-

---

14. See (Lea 1975), Robbins (1959), Henningsen (1980a, b), Monter (1980). By this time, the Church was no longer a single unit, as evidenced by the religious turmoil in Switzerland and France. Nonetheless, when using the term "the Church," we refer specifically to Catholicism as the religious social structure that in essence held Europe together over an extended period of time.

15. For a recent comprehensive survey see Rose (1967) and O'Keefe (1982).

lar the European witchcraze, the Salem witch-hunt in New England, and today's revival of the occult. In the last thirty years or so, social scientists have become increasingly interested in the second of these phenomena and have attempted to integrate it into larger interpretative social schemes. Interest has concentrated on four main areas: anthropological explanations of magic and witchcraft, the history of psychiatry, the history of various scientific disciplines and more recently, power-play and the persecution of women in society.

Anthropologists who have studied primitive peoples tell us how widespread and common the belief in witchcraft is in these societies. Nonetheless, it is not a universal phenomenon. Aside from the early "armchair anthropoligists" (e.g., Frazer and Levi-Bruhl), the empirical work on witchcraft—most of it carried out in traditional societies—can be classified according to three major theoretical approaches. The first views witchcraft as serving certain "useful" functions, such as the alleviation of anxiety, integration, social control, and the creation of cohesion (Evans-Pritchard 1937; Kluckhohn 1967; Malinowsky 1955). The second is a structural approach, which sees accusations of witchcraft as part of the relation-network between different groups in a stratified society. A structural explanation might suggest that witchcraft accusations arise in times of rapid social change, that they are due to social inequalities or the struggles of various authority systems (e.g., Douglas 1966, 1967; Wilson 1951). The third approach analyzes the symbolic level of witchcraft rituals, focusing on the utilization, meaning, efficiency, and universality of various symbols used in magical practices (Lévi-Strauss 1963; chaps. 9, 10; Turner 1969). As a general rule, most anthropologists did not attempt to present an explanation for the European witchcraze since most of their work was done in small-scale social systems. Furthermore, the nature of that witchcraze renders much of these anthropological interpretations inappropriate.

Another influential theory is that of Margaret Murray (1921), who suggested that the witches of western Europe were the adherents of a once general pagan religion displaced by Christianity. Murray claimed that the target of the Inquisition's witch-hunt was the Dianic cult, a pagan cult with classical origins that had survived until the Renaissance. Murray's theory brings us to those people who actually believed in the reality and existence of the witches and the demonological theory behind them. Here we include contemporary demonologists. These writers were convinced that the varying frequency of trials reflected the balance of power between the forces of good and the forces of evil. Many modern-day writers on witchcraft also adopt this position (e.g., Summers 1956).

Another group gives credence to various medical-physical explanations of the phenomenon. Michelet (1956) believed that witches were
practitioners of traditional teutonic religion who had been incompletely
christianized, and he claimed that the wild dancing at the Sabbath was
actually produced by taking jimsonweed. He also believed that some of
the witches' fantasies, such as the belief that they fly, were produced by
hallucinogenic drugs such as deadly nightshade. Such scholars as Clark
(1921), Cohn (1975), Norman (1933), Harner (1972), and Forbes (1966)
suggested that some of the ingredients from which the witch's ointments
were made were highly hallucinogenic. The latest variation of a "medical" explanation was offered by Andreski (1982), who suggested that the
outbreak of the witchcraze coincided chronologically with a syphilitic
epidemic.

Writings on the history of psychiatry, highly influenced by Zilboorg's
pioneering works (1935, 1941) lead the reader to believe either in the
insanity of the witches (Anderson 1970; Neaman 1975) or in insanity of
the entire population that persecuted them. The first explanation appears
to be quite widespread. Schoeneman (1977, p. 331) reports that of
nineteen reputable textbooks of abnormal psychology, the majority
adopt this position. This psychopathological interpretation of the European witch-hunts is quite problematic, however, both in a logical and
substantive sense (Schoeneman 1977; Spanos 1978).

The other aspect of the psychological approach focuses on the behavior of the accusers, the witch chasers. Here efforts deal with the
accuser's emotional need to use the witch as a scapegoat, inferring that
the accusers—not the witches—were in need of psychiatric treatment
(Geis 1978; Szasz 1970; Rosen 1969).

The witch hunt has also been viewed as a group persecution for
political, social, or economic gains. The explanations offered are phrased
in terms of a political or economic struggle between different groups in
the social system. Such scholars as Lewis (1971), Currie (1968), and
Harris (1974) follow this line.[16] Typical is Harris's observation that the
"significance of the witch mania . . . was that it shifted responsibility for
the crisis of late medieval society from both Church and State to imaginary demons" (1974, p. 205). More recent studies tend to focus on the

16. Nelson (1971) suggested that the agencies for social control "created" witchcraft
and that the confessions were the result of loaded questions and torture. In fact, in a 1968
study, Currie had already suggested that the judges in the witch trials in Europe had a
personal profit (from the confiscations) in each conviction, while in England they did not.
This, in Currie's view, explains the weak form of the witchcraze in England. Unfortunately,
Midelfort's 1972 study refutes this claim.

status of women as a powerless group prone to persecutions.[17] A similar explanation is that offered by Sebald (1978, chaps. 11 and 12), which suggests that the culture in which witchcraft is embedded is pathogenic in itself.

Magic has been compared with science through the history and development of various disciplines, including medicine, physics, and psychology. Here we find such impressive scholarly efforts as those by White (1913) and Thorndike (1941), as well as those that explore the interlacing of science with magic and witchcraft, on the one side, and religion, on the other (e.g, Rattansi 1972; Ben David 1971; Hansen 1975). It has been pointed out that science resembles magic in that for both nature provides the background for experimentation and manipulation of environmental elements. The European witchcraze is thus seen as a prescientific revolution, and Kirsch even suggests that "the growth of demonology and of the witch hunt mania paralleled that of the scientific revolution. . . . The coincidence between the growth of the witch hunt and the rise of science was not only close, but almost perfect" (1978, pp. 152, 154).

One group of explanations worth examining are those suggested by various historians who have studied the phenomenon. Lea (1901, vol. 3) saw the craze as a period of darkness from which we have emerged and to which we will never return. Midelfort (1972) and Kieckhefer (1976) suggested that general fear, stress, and quarrels can cause mass persecutions of witches.

Finally, in this day and age, it is impossible to end this section without mentioning psychoanalytic explanations of the phenomenon. While Freud himself virtually ignored the European witchcraze, it contains elements to warm any analyst's heart: cruel and destructive persecutions, women, sex, and violence.[18] These could be easily integrated into psychoanalytic interpretations, emphasizing the projection of hostility, reaction formation, incestuous wishes, and impulses from the id. We might even trace a few ideas from "Totem and Taboo." Unfortunately, psychoanalytic examinations of the witchcraze are very rare. One example is Parrinder's 1958 study, which suggests that the witch-hunt had something to do with dreams of hostility and aggression against women (see also O'Keefe 1982).

17. See, for example, Garrett (1977), Nelson (1975), Anderson and Gordon (1978), Ehrenreich and English (1972), Matalene (1978), and Tucker (1980).
18. On some of the connections between sex, women, and the witchcraze see Midelfort (1972), Hays (1964), and Masters (1962).

The European Witchcraze: The Unanswered Questions

There are three main issues regarding the European witch-hunts that
have not been satisfactorily settled and that render most available interpretations useless (Ben Yehuda 1981). The first issue is that of timing.
Why did the persecution suddenly begin in the fourteenth and fifteenth
centuries? Why did it not take place before or after the given period?
Furthermore, why did it end when it did?

The craze's extended length and the large number of its victims are
also very disturbing. Why did no one challenge successfully the basic
theory behind the witch-hunts for nearly three centuries? Many researchers rightly state, again and again, that without the tremendous
popularity and intellectual support of the craze, it would neither have
begun nor have lasted so long. How do we explain this widespread
acceptance of great cruelty. Why did people who for centuries had
rejected demonological theories lend their support to the claims of the
Dominicans and others? What in those theories captured contemporary
minds? I feel that the issue of timing and the related issue of acceptance of
the witch myth are crucial to an understanding of the nature of the
phenomenon.

A second issue, largely ignored until now, is that of content. Why
witchcraft, or witches? While there is little doubt that the Inquisition was
very influential in shaping the witchcraft of the fifteenth through seventeenth centuries, that it in effect generated witches with its interrogations
and executions, no one has yet questioned why it diverted its attention
from more traditional scapegoats (such as the Jews, Moors, or other
contemporary heretical movements, like the Cathars or Waldensians) to
witchcraft and witches. Why did Catholics and Protestants persecute
witches with nearly the same zeal? Why were witches persecuted so
mildly in Spain or Portugal and so severely in Germany and France? In
short, how can we explain the content on which the hunts were based?

The third issue focuses on the direction and target of the witch hunts.
Although nearly all scholars agree that most victims of the hunts were
women, very few have attempted to consider why this was so. While
women did occupy an inferior status, they had never before been singled
out for persecution. This link between women and demonology has to be
sufficiently accounted for.

In light of these three very crucial issues, current interpretations of the
European witch-hunts in general, and socially oriented schemes in particular, are incomplete. In Table 1, I have classified the most prominent
interpretations along two main dimensions: the type of interpretation and

Table 1. Interpretations of the European Witchcraze

Type of Interpretation	Supported by	Sufficient Explanation		
		Timing	Content	Target
1. Belief in witches: Varying frequency of trials reflects varying prevalence of witches.	Medieval demonologists, Murray (1971), Michelet (1965), Summers (1956), Tucker (1980)	Partly[1]	Yes	Partly[2]
2. Medical view: Flying and other experiences of witches were side-effects of hallucinogenic ingredients in their ointment. Diseases explained as manifestations of witchcraft.	Forbes (1960), Harris (1974), Harner (1972), Diethelm (1970), Harper (1977), Andreski (1982), Heinson and Steiger (1982)	No	Partly[3]	Partly[4]
3. Psychiatric: Witches seen as mentally ill.	Sarbin (1969), Zilboorg (1935, 1941), Anderson (1970), Neaman (1975), Bromberg (1959), and textbooks on psychopathology and the history of psychiatry.	No	No	No
4. Psychiatric: Persecutors seen as mentally deformed. Society itself viewed as sick.	Szasz (1970), Rosen (1969), Senter (1947), Foucault (1967), Gies (1978), Connor (1975), Sebald (1978)	No	No	No
5. Hunts a result of social changes and upheavals.	Schoeneman (1977), Trevor-Roper (1967), Lea (1957)	Partly[5]	No	No
6. Hunts a variety of minority group persecutions for either political, social, or economic gains. Explanation phrased in terms of a political or economic struggle between different groups in the social system.	Lewis (1971), Nelson (1975), Currie (1968), Harris (1974), Ehrenreich and English (1972), Garrett (1977), Matalene (1978), Tucker (1980)	No	No	Partly[6]

Table 1. (*continued*)

Type of Interpretation	Supported by	Sufficient Explanation		
		Timing	Content	Target
7. Hunts and demonology part of the prescientific revolution.	White (1913), Kirsch (1978), Thorndike (1941), Ben-David (1971), Rattansi (1972)	Partly[7]	No	No
8. Historical studies that concentrate on establishing facts; eclectic explanations.	Monter (1976), Kieck-hefer (1976), Midelfort (1972), Cohn (1975), Russell (1972), Summers (1956), Lea (1901, 1957)	Partly[8]	No	No

Notes

1. It was believed that the devil's battle against God had come to a climax.

2. Various demonologists and Sprenger and Kramer in particular, went to great lengths to explain why women were on the devil's side of the battle. Tucker, for example, specifically states that "wise women" specialized in "white witchcraft."

3. The demonological theories could have been based on some people's reports about their hallucinations (one explanation today for UFO sightings is based on a similar hypothesis).

4. If women exclusively could be associated with the use of a hallucinogenic ointments (or other popular cosmetics), then this question has a partial answer. (This, for example, does not explain the unity or variations in the socioeconomic status of the accused witches confessions.)

5. The explanations use too broad terms and are not detailed enough.

6. See note 5 above.

7. Because the content is not explained, timing becomes a difficult issue to explain. Connections between the witch-hunt and the prescientific revolution are not made explicit.

8. Through the chronology of the phenomenon, a partial explanation is provided for the "timing" question. However, this "explanation" does not fully address the issue.

the extent to which it addresses itself to the three issues mentioned above. While the interpretations do, in fact, address themselves differentially to these issues, none concerns itself with all three (Ben Yehuda 1981).

The witchcraze of the fifteenth to seventeenth centuries was in many ways unique. It involved both accusations against people, especially women, of whom the overwhelming majority were probably completely innocent and the creation of a theological system in which witchcraft was of central importance. Most of the approaches we've discussed do not provide a full, satisfactory explanation for the phenomenon. While the theory of scapegoating fits, it does not explain the religious importance and intensity of the witch-hunts, their intellectual elaboration, the questions of timing, distribution, and the selection of women as its target. In the following pages, I attempt to identify the conditions that can explain these details.

Timing: Why Did the Witch Hunts Begin?

The witchcraft myth was largely created by the Dominican friars. As we have seen, until the thirteenth century, the Catholic Church's official policy regarding witchcraft was summarized in the *Canon episcopi*, which regarded beliefs in witchcraft as mere illusions. The Inquisition, an ecclesiastical court answerable only to itself, was founded in the thirteenth century in order to combat deliberate, continued, and public denial of the Church's doctrine, primarily by the Cathari and, to a much lesser extent, by the Waldenses. Thus, the Inquisition's primary objective was to single out and reconvert heretics (see Lea 1901, vols. 1, 2; Madaule 1967; Sumption 1978; Nelson 1971; Wakefield and Evans 1969).

In 1203, Saint Dominic first met the Albigensian heretics in southern France, three years after which he started a campaign to bring them back to the faith. In July 1216, Pope Innocent III, for whom he conducted his campaign, died, and his successor, Honorius III, finally formally sanctioned Dominic's new order, the Dominicans (December 22, 1216). The order was established with the express hope that it would successfully win back various groups of heretics to the Church. But the pope's expectations of the Dominicans were never realized, and they failed to bring the lost sheep back to the fold. The Cathari proved especially intractable. Between 1208 and 1213, Innocent III waged a crusade against heretics in southern France, against the Cathari in particular. The swift and bloody battle at Montsegur in 1245, for all practical purposes, marked the end of the Cathari movement as a serious threat to the Church. Most of those who remained were driven underground, and many of the French Cathari fled to Italy. Although the heresy lingered here and there through the fourteenth century, most of it faded in 1270s, and it finally disappeared altogether in the fifteenth century.[19] The Waldenses received almost the

---

19. See Madaule (1967), Peuch (1974), Turberville (1964). The Cathars, who flourished in Europe between the middle of the twelfth and middle of the thirteenth centuries, created a dualist religion based on the belief that "the material universe was created by an evil spirit . . . who still dominated it. But, . . . far from worshipping the Devil they were passionately concerned to escape from his clutches. . . . In the Catharist view souls are the angels who fell from heaven: they have been imprisoned in another, and they yearn to escape from the material world and re-enter the heaven of pure spirituality. . . . The morality of the Cathars . . . reflects their total rejection of the material world, imagined as a demonic creation" (Cohn 1975, p. 58). Rose (1962) and Maudale (1967) confirm this view.

same treatment. By the end of the thirteenth century, it was clear that
persecution had virtually eliminated the sect, and by the end of the
fifteenth century, the survivors were segregated, for the most part, in the
Italian and French valleys of the Alps.[20]

Although the Cathari and Waldenses were probably the most visible
and important heretics of the time, they were not the only ones (Loos
1974; Russell 1971; Runciman 1955; Turberville 1964). Other heretic
movements, prophets, and religious dissent groups were also active between the thirteenth and fifteenth centuries (Lerner 1970). For example,
there were the Hussites, who flourished from the end of the thirteenth
century to about 1430; John Wyclif (1330–1384); and later, the Lollards
(extinguished in 1431); the Flagellants, who flourished from about 1260
until the mid fifteenth century (their last persecutions and trials being in
1446–1481); (Leff 1967) and the dancing manias. (Rosen 1969) However,
by the 1250s practically no heretics were left to be pursued by the
Inquisition. (Lea 1901; Nelson 1971; Szasz 1970; Trevor-Roper 1967;
Turberville 1964). The two major heretic factions—the Cathari and
Waldensians—were in essence eliminated, while other groups were
either too small or more easily controlled. In order to justify the existence
of the Inquisition's machinery, the inquisitors began to search for new
apostates. "When the Inquisition had crushed the religious deviation . . . it had little justification to continue to exist. Its work was done.
The Inquisition, however, set about to introduce and develop the parallel
heresy of witchcraft, thereby widening its scope" (Robbins 1959, pp.
207–8). A campaign was also initiated in Rome to extend their jurisdiction to the Jews and the Moors of Spain.[21]

The inquisitors demanded, from the thirteenth century on, that their
authority be expanded to include witches they claimed to have found in
the Pyrenees and the Alps.[22] Their efforts were yielding results early in

---

The Cathars saw themselves as the authentic Christians and neither believed in a redemp-
tive Christ nor in the sacrament of Communion.

20. Rose explains that "the Waldensians . . . were . . . straightforward nonconform-
ists, Protestants before their time. . . . They rated morality and preaching above the
sacraments, and challenged the authority of the Church as not grounded in Scripture"
(1962, p. 235). See also Cohn 1975.

21. On late medieval heresies, see Loos (1974), Russell (1971), Runciman (1955),
Turberville (1964), Leff (1967), Lea (1901), Nelson (1971), Szasz (1970), Trevor-Roper
(1967).

The Inquisition in the Iberian peninsula kept persecuting Jews until the seventeenth
century (Roth 1971), which explains in part the virtual absence of witch hunting there.

22. As early as 1257, the Inquisition pressed the papacy, specifically Pope Alexander
IV, to extend its jurisdiction to sorcery (Trevor-Roper 1967, p. 103). The papacy resisted;

the fourteenth century with Pope John XXII's help. A fervent believer in the power and reality of magic, the pope himself gave the European witchcraze its impulse when he encouraged the Dominicans and inguisitors to persecute relentlessly all sorcerers, magicians, and other heretics, whose practices he feared were rapidly spreading.[23] In effect, however, as Lea 1901 notes, the actions of John merely reinforced already growing fears about witchcraft. In 1326, he issued his *Super illius specula*, which "authorized the full use of inquisitorial procedure against witches" (Trevor-Roper 1967, p. 103). There he specifically stated that

"some people, Christian in name only, have forsaken the first light of truth to ally themselves with death and traffic with hell. They sacrifice to and adore devils; they make or obtain figurines, rings, vials, mirrors . . . by which they command demons . . . asking their aid [and] giving themselves to the most shameful subjection for the most shameful of ends" (Robbins 1959, p. 288).

This document declared that all who used the services of sorcerers were to be punished as heretics and all books on the subject were to be burned.

The pope's efforts resulted in a small-scale witch-hunt in the Alps and the Pyrenees for more than a century and a half. Although scattered trials of individual witches had been carried out in 1245 and 1275, the early decades of the fourteenth century witnessed a tremendous intensification

---

indeed in the same year, Pope Alexander replied with the bull *Quod super nonnullis*, reaffirming that the *Canon episcopi* was still Church policy and urging the Inquisitors not to be diverted from their real task, the retrieval of heretics to the Church (Lea 1901, 3: 452–53). The bull was later reissued by Nicholas IV, and in response to similar petitions from Inquisitors, it became canon law under Boniface VIII in 1303. Its intent was to discourage the Inquisitors from hunting witches (although Boniface himself believed in them). However, Inquisitors did not rest their case and proposed that all witchcraft and sorcery were, by their very nature, heretical. In 1280, Bernard Gui drew up a handbook for the interrogation of sorcerers and a guide for the recognition of magical practices (ibid., p. 449). The handbook was modeled after the handbooks which various Inquisitors had produced to aid the persecution of the Cathars and other heretical sects they had dealt with in the past. Interesting to note that the interrogation procedure recommended by Gui outlines the Inquisitors' actual knowledge of occult practices at that time as well as their beliefs (Trevor-Roper 1967, pp. 100, 108).

23. Lea (1901, 3:450–54). This pope actually feared that there was a conspiracy against him and that conspirators intended to kill him through the use of witchcraft. He therefore maintained several special Inquisitors in his palace to search for witches. Thorndike notes that "Pope John XXII,. . . alarmed by attempts against his life made through sorcery and wax images by Hugh Geraud, Bishop of Lahors, the Visconti, and others, started the persecution of magicians in southern France which was continued by Benedict XII" (1936, 8: 687).

of attempts to stifle witchcraft practices, especially in France (Robbins 1959). The fifteenth century also saw the beginnings of many writings about witchcraft.[24] The most important and interesting of these, prior to the publication of the *Malleus maleficarum*, was Jacquier's *Flagellum haereticorum fascinatiorium* (published in 1458), which proved to be somewhat of a turning point in the perception of witchcraft.

In his book, Jacquier defined witchcraft—for the first time—as a new, evil heresey, claiming that witches were qualitatively different from the rest of humanity. Jacquier's problem was how to address the accepted view that beliefs in witchcraft were mere fantasies. His solution was swift and clear. In contrast to the *Canon episcopi*, he claimed that witches were real and were organized and flew to their atrocious Sabbath ceremonies, where they indulged in sexual orgies with the devil and feasted on unbaptized infants. Jacquier suggested that the existence of the "witch sect" demonstrated that contemporary witches were unlike their traditional counterparts. All this, however, was only the introduction. When between 1487 and 1489, the *Malleus maleficarum* was printed with the blessings of Pope Innocent's bull *Summis desiderantes*, the "art of witchcraft" had reached its peak, and the inquisitor's desire to control witchcraft was almost totally realized.

The *Malleus* appeared thirty years after Jacquier's book, and it was to become the most influential and widely used authority on witchcraft. It was written by two Dominican friars, Sprenger and Kramer. Monter states that it was "the single most important book in the history of European witchcraft" (1976, p. 24). Whether it contained accurate information or not is irrelevant because it was accepted as accurate, and as the most authoritative book on witchcraft. "The *Malleus maleficarum*, without a question [was] the most important work on demonology ever written . . . and, if any one work could, opened the floodgates of the inquisitorial hysteria" (Robbins 1959, p. 337).

The book is divided into three parts. The first section attempts to prove the existence of witches and devils. To be more accurate, this section proves by argumentation (rather than factual demonstration) that he who does not believe in the existence of witches is himself a victim of witchcraft practices—a clear departure from the policy of the *Canon episcopi* (Szasz 1970). The second section tells the reader how to identify a witch—what signs, techniques, and tests to use. If you like, this is almost

24. Robbins (1959, pp. 145–46) reports on sixteen different books on witchcraft in the fifteenth century. Midelfort (1972, p. 70) reports on the publication of thirty-seven such books in the sixteenth century in Germany alone.

as if, for example, Senator McCarthy had said that a Communist meets this or that particular description, and so now that we know what they are like, we can proceed to hunt them down. This is an important point since before the publication of the *Malleus* there had been no readily available, easy definition of a witch. The third section of the book describes the legalities of investigating and sentencing a witch. This goes into the legal technicalities and the technique of delivering a witch to the secular arm of justice for execution. The favorite way to destroy the devil was to burn his host "using green wood for the slow burning of the grossly impenitent" (Sprenger and Kramer 1968, p. 220). The text specifically encouraged the use of torture as means of eliciting confessions. The *Malleus* also explicitly connected witchcraft with womanhood.

The importance of the *Malleus* cannot be overestimated. Its enormous influence was practically guaranteed, not only because of its authoritative appearance, but also because of its extremely wide distribution. It was one of the first books to be published on the newly invented printing press (Trevor-Roper 1967, p. 101) and appeared in no less than twenty editions (Zilboorg 1941). It became the textbook of the Inquisition, and with the appendage of the *Summis desiderantes* as its preface, the last impediment to the inquisitorial witch-hunt was removed. The moral backing had been provided for the horrible suffering inflicted upon thousands of women.

In 1484, before the *Malleus* was published, Sprenger and Kramer petitioned Pope Innocent VIII to appoint them general witch-hunters in the Rhineland. In response to their petition, he issued the *Summis desiderantes* (Lea 1901, vol. 3, p. 540; Kors and Peters 1972, pp. 107–13). In this bull, the pope asserted official Church belief in witchcraft and the Church's duty—with the help of its tool, the Inquisition—to exterminate it. The *Summis desiderantes* itself explains the nature of witchcraft as follows:

> It has come to our ears . . . that . . . many persons of both sexes unmindful of their own salvation and straying from the Catholic Faith, have abandoned themselves to devils, incubi and succubi, and by their incantations, spells, conjurations, and other accursed charms and crafts, enormities and horrid offences, have slain infants yet in the mother's womb, as also the offspring of cattle, have blasted the produce of the earth, the grapes of the vine, the fruits of the trees, nay, men and women, beasts of burthen, herd-beasts, as well as animals of other kinds, vineyards, orchards, meadows, pastureland, corn, wheat, and all other cereals; these wretches furthermore afflict and torment men and women, beasts of burthen,

herd-beasts, as well as animals of other kinds, with terrible and piteous pains and sore diseases, both internal and external; they hinder men from performing the sexual act, women from conceiving, whence husbands cannot know their wives nor wives receive their husbands; over and above this, they blasphemously renounce that Faith which is theirs by the Sacrament of Baptism, and at the instigation of the Enemy of Mankind they do not shrink from committing and perpetrating the foulest abomination and filthiest excesses to the deadly peril of their own souls, whereby they outrage the Divine majesty and are a cause of scandal and danger to very many. (Sprenger and Kramer 1971, pp. xlii–xlv).

Lea (1957) and Zilboorg (1941) both provide vivid and accurate descriptions of the various deceptions used by Sprenger and Kramer in order to authenticate their book. Apparently the authors did not take for granted the general acceptance of their demonology, especially by the academic community, and were therefore eager for the *Malleus* to appear authoritative. Before releasing the handbook, the authors sought the endorsement of the entire faculty of the theological school at Cologne, one of the most prominent schools of theology in Europe at the time. Lea (1957, vol: 1, pp. 338–45) reports that nearly all of the faculty refused to endorse the *Malleus* and did not want the name of the school associated with it. Sprenger and Kramer then forged the endorsement they desired and published it along with the *Summis* at the front of the book. They were careful to omit their forgery from the copies destined for Cologne, but the deception was soon discovered, nevertheless, and the theologians were furious. But to no avail. The book was already widely distributed and accepted as official despite their protests. For the sake of historical accuracy, we have to bring Zilboorg's version of the matter as well, which stands in sharp contradiction to Lea's description.

Almost two and a half years after the issuance of the papal bull [Sprenger and Kramer] submitted the *Malleus* to the Faculty of Theology at the University of Cologne. On the nineteenth of May, 1487, Dean Lambertus de Monte called a faculty meeting. The Dean affixed his signature to the indorsement of the *Malleus*. Four out of seven professors concurred in similar manner. The lack of unanimity was not acceptable to the Inquisitors. They persisted and prepared a new letter of indorsement, and, whatever their powers of persuasion, these powers must have proved sufficiently intimidating, for the remaining members of the faculty finally signed the document. The two Inquisitors were now in possession of both spiritual and academic authorization. (1941, p. 151)

The two inquisitors also secured a special document from Maximilian, the king of Rome. The document, issued from Brussels on November 6, 1486, with royal signature and seal duly affixed and in perfect order, took official notice of the *Summis desiderantes affectibus* and gave official support to Sprenger and Kramer in the discharge of their sacred duty (Zilboorg 1941, p. 151). By 1490, therefore, the Inquisition found itself in possession of a potentially very powerful judicial machinery. It was authorized specifically to uncover and punish offenders whose crime was, by its nature, unobservable and unprovable except by the offenders' own confession, which could be readily obtained through the use of torture. This clearly links the beginnings of witch-hunts to the vested interest of the Dominicans and the Inquisition. They had a professional interest in the discovery of problems and populations on which to exercise their specialized theological expertise and their investigative skills. The fact that they showed much less interest in witches in such places as Spain and Portugal than in other countries of Western Europe is consistent with this hypothesis. In the Iberian peninsula, the persecution of Jews and Moors provided them with plenty of intellectual challenge and employment.

The End of the Medieval Order

The professional concerns of the Inquisitors explains why they began to take interest in the witches as early as the thirteenth century. But the transformation of this interest into an elaborate demonological theology did not take place until the fifteenth century, and only at that time did the general public begin to share the interest of the Inquisitors in witches. What were the conditions of these two fateful developments? The answer to this question requires a broad perspective on the social, institutional, intellectual, and emotional changes that prepared the ground for these and other developments that began in the thirteenth century and reached their culmination between the fifteenth and the seventeenth centuries. During this period, the medieval social order underwent a series of significant changes, which completely altered the dominant European outlook.

According to Pirenne (1937), the growth of cities and of an industrial form of production started in the Low Countries and in England in the twelfth century, and from there reached down the Rhine in the thirteenth century, reaching a peak in the fourteenth (Nicolas 1976). Among the changes of this economic expansion were a significant increase in population size, perfection of the monetary system, and the mapping of new lands. The expansion of commerce was not limited only to central

Europe; ore-mining began in Poland (Molenda 1976) and Mediterranean trade flourished at the same time (Ashtor 1957, 1976; Abulafia 1981). Pirenne is not the only one to describe this economic development, and the dramatic industrial, commercial, and monetary developments are corroborated by many other scholars.[25] Cipolla (1976, 1978) called it a commercial revolution, "a sort of Industrial Revolution."

This economic development brought with it increased trade, expanded urban industry, standardization, exports, division of labor, and specialization (Bernard 1972; Griggs 1980; Thrupp 1972; Le Goff 1972, 1980, pp. 43–52). By the end of the thirteenth century, "the development of industry and commerce had completely transformed the appearance and indeed the very existence of society. . . . Continental Europe was covered with towns from which the activity of the new middle class radiated in all directions. . . . the circulation of money was perfected. . . . new forms of credit came into use" (Pirenne 1937, pp. 189–90). All this was only the beginning of a process that peaked in the period we call the Renaissance. These centuries proved not only a turning point in commerce (Bogucka 1980; Lane 1932) but also in geographical discoveries and their utilization. (Postan and Rich 1952; Pounds 1979). "The exploration and exploitation of non-European areas by Europeans during the 15th and 16th centuries form one of the greatest phenomena of the Renaissance" (Penrose 1962, p. vii), no doubt forcing "a re-evaluation of the idea of Europe as a model Christian society" (Rattansi 1972, p. 7).

These extreme and relatively rapid changes made deep inroads in the hierarchic structure of feudal society sanctioned and legitimized by the Catholic Church. In the medieval tradition, the moral boundaries of society were clearly defined. Christendom was ruled spiritually by Rome and structured in a uniformly conceived hierarchic feudal order, firmly embedded in the finite cosmic order ruled by God. This order was threatened by the Jews and Moslems, but their faiths were in many ways related to the Christian tradition and the relationship to them was clearly defined: they had to be converted and saved, and if recalcitrant, fought

25. See, for example, Thrupp (1972), Le Goff (1972), Bernard (1972), Earle (1969), Lane (1932, 1933), Lopez (1972), and Hicks (1969). Carus-Wilson (1941) describes a thirteenth-century industrial revolution centered in England. Van der Wee (1975) reports on developments in the Netherlands, Stromer (1970) tells of the commercial growth of Nurnburg, and Irsigler (1977), of Cologne. Nate (1978) describes changes in Europe generally, and Malawist (1974) compares the expansion in central and eastern Europe. On the growth of cities and the credit system, see Le Goff (1972) and Russell (1972). Postan and Rich (1972) and Pounds (1979) are useful on the age of exploration.

and suppressed. But the changes we have described above were not so easily categorized. The late medieval order was threatened by the rise of an urban society that did not fit into the feudal hierarchy, by the increased contact with non-Christian people who did not fit the conversion-conflict model, and by the resultant autonomy of economic and political transactions from theological guidance. Indeed, this was all part of what Brown (1969) describes as the disengagement of the sacred from the profane.

The stress and confusion created by these circumstances were further aggravated by external catastrophes, especially the devastating epidemics of plague and cholera that decimated the population of Europe and lasted throughout the fourteenth century. Even the physical climate underwent severe changes in those fateful centuries, "affecting . . . central and eastern Europe . . . by changes in temperature. . . . The coldest time began in the 13th century with the onset of the Little Ice Age which, with exceptions of occasional periods of warmth, lasted until well into the 18th century" (J. C. Russell, 1972, pp. 51–52; see also Lamb 1982; Leroy 1971; Robock 1979). To add to the confusion and distress, in 1456 Halley's comet was clearly visible in the sky. The appearance of the comet was often interpreted as a bad omen and created much anxiety, fear, and unrest.

Furthermore, Griggs points out that the massive population growth in the thirteenth century was not paralleled by technological developments (especially in agriculture).

> All writers believe that populations had grown beyond the technology and resources of the period. . . . We can conclude then that by 1300 population densities in *some parts* of western Europe had exceeded the optimum density for the technology, resources and institutions of the time, that there may in some regions have been a Malthusian crisis . . . by the late thirteenth century symptoms of overpopulation were appearing: prices and land values were rising, in many regions there was little left to bring into cultivation, holdings were small. (1980, pp. 81–82)

All this, obviously, created more stress and contributed to the feelings of sadness and of an impending doomsday (Anderson 1970).

Rosen describes the contemporary atmosphere, the "feeling of melancholy and pessimism which marked the period. A sense of impending doom hung over men and women, intensified by a belief that the end of time was approaching and that the last days were at hand" (1969, pp. 154–55). In such a period, madness was not unusual:

Within this context madness, through its linkage with the revelation of religious truth, became a means of achieving knowledge. Madness was a primitive force of revelation, revealing the depths of menace, destruction, and evil that lurked beneath the illusory surface of reality. Unreason revealed the unbearable, the things in the world upon which one could not otherwise bear to look. . . . This theme of cosmic madness is a major element in the art and literature of the fifteenth and sixteenth centuries. (Ibid., p. 155)

Foucault adds a most picturesque description:

Up to the second half of the 15th century, or even a little beyond, the theme of death reigns alone. The end of man, the end of time bear the face of pestilence and war. What overhangs human existence is this conclusion and this order from which nothing escapes. (1967, p. 15)

Stress and confusion, however, were only one aspect of these developments (Holmes 1975). There was confusion about the moral boundaries of society and the cognitive map of the world; frequently there was fear of impending doom. But there was also an opening up of new possibilities, a rise of standards of living in the wake of the great catastrophes of the fourteenth century. Those who survived the epidemics inherited the wealth of the deceased, and even those who had to maintain themselves by their work could obtain far better wages than before because of the shortage of manpower.

Thus the fifteenth century was a time of great enterprise, bold thought, innovation, as well as one of deep confusion and anomie, a feeling that society had lost its norms and boundaries and that the uncontrollable forces of change were destroying all order and moral tradition. These developments allowed many contemporary thinkers to overstep the boundaries of reality and enter the realm of magic, fancy, and make-believe. "The disengagement of the sacred from the profane opened up a whole middle distance of conflicting opportunities for the deployment of human talent compared with which the society of the early Middle Ages appears as singularly monochromatic" (Brown 1969, p. 135). Thus during the period between the fifteenth and seventeenth centuries, there was frequently no clear demarcation between rational science and magic.

The Inquisitors were forming their demonological theories in the early years of the scientific revolution, (Ben-David 1971; Rattansi 1972) when pseudo-science was rarely distinguished from other forms of science (Thorndike 1941; White 1912; Shumaker 1972). There was great preoccupation with so-called secret (or esoteric) knowledge, namely, the Hermetica. "The [Hermetica] focused attention on . . . extraordinary and marvelous virtues. . . . The aim was to grasp the hidden powers of nature and the mysterious forces" (Rattansi 1972, p. 5). This explains why "the growth of demonology and of the witch hunt mania paralleled that of the scientific revolution" (Kirsch 1978, p. 152). A rise of interest in social uptopias and "ideal societies" in the early decades of the fifteeneth century (Cohn 1961; Graus 1967) was another reaction to the dissolution of the cognitive and moral boundaries of the medieval world. The expansion of horizons, more flexible social conditions, the Reformation, the beginnings of the scientific revolution, Renaissance art and humanism were all results of the disappearance of traditional norms and social-moral boundaries. The creation of greater cultural diversity and freedom gave rise to a new, infinitely more differentiated society than that of the Middle Ages. The witchcraze was a negative reaction to this emerging culture in the sense that its purpose was to counteract and prevent change and to re-establish traditional social-moral boundaries and religious authority.

Talcott Parsons's (1966, 1971) views on the development of modern European society are worth considering at this point. In his analysis, Parsons contends that the traditional feudal system began to differentiate during the eleventh century, starting a process that led—by the seventeenth century—to an increasing autonomy of the religious, governmental, and economic institutions. This new social order replaced a rigid, religiously defined, and more-or-less unified social system. The social change affected the very "center," or the "collective conscience," of society, or to use Parsons' own term, the definition of the "societal community."[26] Parsons notes that the Renaissance was the first era to give rise to a highly developed secular culture differentiated from the religious matrix. In simpler terms, this means that there was a newly felt need for the definition of the moral boundaries of society. The European witch-hunts should be considered in this context. By persecuting witches, society, led by the Church, attempted to redefine its boundaries. This was one of the numerous instances in which deviance served the social functions of emphasizing and creating moral boundaries and enhancing solidarity. In fact, this was fictitious deviance, created for those purposes.

Until the Renaissance, the Catholic Church was at its peak of power. All problems were treated as theological or theosophical, and there were no serious threats to its authority and its well-defined norms. This is the reason that during the so-called Dark Ages, we have hardly any record of

---

26. Parsons notes that the societal community is "the salient foci of tension and conflict, and thus of creative innovation" (1971, p. 121).

a witchcraze. As the results of the differentiation process became visible in the fifteenth century, and a sharp decline in the Church's authority was noticeable, it "began to need an opponent whom it could divinely hate" in order to affirm old standards (Williams 1959, p. 37). The differentiation of the societal community vibrated the structure of the medieval order and directly threatened the Church's authority and legitimacy. For a highly rigid system, one can hardly imagine a greater danger. Thus, the major "social stress" was the differentiation process itself.

It is obvious why the church "needed" an opponent. But it needed a very special type of deviant-opponent to redefine its legitimacy. The opponent had to be widely perceived as a threat to society itself and to the Christian world view. What could do this better than witchcraft? This helps us understand why only the most rapidly developing countries where the Church was weakest experienced a virulent witchcraze. Where the Church was strong hardly any witchcraze worth mentioning occurred, even in rapidly developing societies such as the Italian city states. Although this was not the first time that the Church had been threatened, this development, culminating in the Reformation, was the first time that it had to cope with a large-scale challenge to its very existence and legitimacy (Elton 1963).

Nevertheless, Protestants persecuted witches with almost the same zeal as the Catholics, despite many objective differences between them. Protestantism might have been a result of the differentiation process, but this is not to say that Protestants were capable of either mastering or steering the process itself. Both Protestants and Catholics felt threatened by the process and by each other. "The Reformation shattered the unity of Christendom, and religious conflicts . . . the Wars of Religion . . . destroyed the illusion of the perfect Christian societies" (Rattansi 1972, p. 7).[27]

This interpretation makes plausible the choice of such a strange and esoteric phenomenon as witchcraft for elaboration into a myth in the

27. Luther himself believed in witches and believed that his mother had been bewitched. He "often felt sick when he visited Wartburg and attributed this to spells cast by his adversaries there" (Lea 1957, 3: 417). Calvin was more skeptical of the Dominican witch beliefs than was Luther. He believed that the devil could do nothing without the permission of God and that he could never conquer the faithful. Nevertheless, he was an alert and an energetic enemy (ibid., 1: 428). In 1545, Calvin led a campaign against witchcraft in Geneva that resulted in the execution of thirty-one witches (Szasz 1970, p. 296). Calvinist missionaries succeeded in spreading the craze to Scotland in 1563. When James VI of Scotland, a Calvinist, became king of England, he revised the lenient statutes dealing with witchcraft and wrote his own handbook for witch-hunters, *Demonologia* (Trevor-Roper 1967, p. 142).

early modern era. Dominican theory portrayed witchcraft and witches as the negative mirror-image of the "true faith." As Clark (1980) points out, in a social world generally characterized by dualism, the Dominican theory made much sense. It was possible to attribute all the undesirable phenomena associated with the anomie of the age to the conspiracy of Satan and the witches against Christianity. By associating everything negative, bad, and vicious with witchcraft, the ideal components of the true faith were highlighted. In his *Daemonologie* (1597), King James gave this idea direct expression: "Since the Devil is the verie contrarie opposite to God, there can be no better way to know God, than by the contrarie."[28] In this sense, the witchcraze could be called a "collective search for identity," (Klapp 1969) and the authors of the *Malleus maleficarum* were what Becker (1963, pp. 42–163) called "moral entrepreneurs" taking part in what Gusfield (1967) termed "moral crusade," striving to restore the integrity of the old religious-moral community. Witches were the only deviants who could be construed as attacking the very core of the social system.

This explains, not only why a number of theologians and intellectuals found in demonology a satisfactory diagnosis of the moral ills of their time, but why this abstruse theory became so readily accepted by the masses. "The individual was confronted with an enormously wider range of competing beliefs in almost every area of social and intellectual concern, while conformity-inducing pressures of a mainly ecclesiastical sort were weakened or discredited" (Rattansi 1972, pp. 7–8). The existential crisis of individuals—expressed in terms of anomie, alienation, strangeness, powerlessness, and anxiety—created a fertile soil in which the Dominican solution could flourish.

What could better explain the strain felt by the individual than the idea that he was part of a cataclysmic struggle between the "sons of light" and the "sons of darkness?" His acceptance of this particular explanation was further guaranteed by the fact that he could help the sons of light to trap the sons of darkness—the despised witches—and thus play a real role in ending the cosmic struggle in a way that would bring salvation nearer. Thus the differentiation process threatened, not only the macroinstitutional level, but also the microlevel—each individual's cognitive map. In such a case, a redefinition of moral boundaries and a restructuring of cognitive maps would be more than welcome: for this reason the witchcraze won such extensive popular support.

28. Quoted by Clark (1980, p. 117).

Witchcraft as an Ideology

The demonological theory had all the characteristics of what would be considered today an effective ideology. I refer of course to Geertz's (1964) concept of ideology. Although Geertz limits his discussion to situations in which the need for cognitive and moral reorientation is the result of the emergence of an "autonomous polity," namely, the differentiation of the political from the religious sphere, widespread need for such reorientation is caused by every process of significant institutional differentiation, which creates a disturbing discrepancy between what is and what is believed. The function of ideology is to provide authoritative concepts capable of rendering the situation meaningful and "suasive images" by which this meaning can be sensibly grasped, which can arouse emotions and direct mass action toward objectives that promise to resolve the strain.

The existence of widespread strain due to the inadequacy of traditional concepts, especially in the religious-moral sphere, has been documented above. However, it is also possible to show that much of this tension was focused on women, which explains why witches—usually female ones—could become such effective symbols in a new ideology. How women became symbols of fear can be followed through three processes: structural and functional changes in the family, changes in the status and role of the woman, and demographical changes.

Aries (1962) points out that the medieval family was a property-holding unit, and "the home of the early Middle Ages was the heart of the industrial life of the community" (Goodsell 1915, p. 207). In this home, the woman possessed a central role, both as a housekeeper and mother and as a breadwinner. (Chojnacki 1974; Herlihy 1971) For example, "in the 7th century the textile industry was wholly carried on by wives and daughters of the family. . . . Such was the case prior to the 12th century when weaving [increasingly became] a skilled craft in the hands of the men" (Goodsell 1915, p. 208). Goodsell's book leaves the reader with a firm impression of the medieval wife's hard life.

According to Jarrett (1926), the main functions of married women were (a) to provide male heirs for the family's property and (b) to make their husbands richer by the treasures brought as dowry (see also Bullough 1974, Goodsell 1915) and by their labor. Jarrett's main theme is the subordinate status of medieval women.

The social position of medieval women is a problematic issue, and researchers have only recently begun to seriously explore it (e.g., Bridenthal and Koonz 1977; Gies and Geis 1978; Herlihy 1971;

Morewedge 1975; Power 1975; Stuard 1976). Power (1926, 1975) states that the social position of medieval women was far from clear; indeed, it was the subject of an ongoing dispute between the Church and the aristocracy. She claims, however, that everyone seemed to accept the subordination of women, and that the prevailing attitude toward them was one of possession. Women thus had very little control over their fates. There were those who regarded women as superior beings (as in the Virign Mary cult) and those who believed them to be seductive and dangerous.[29] Lemay (1978) reports that in the thirteenth and fourteenth centuries, it was taught in universities that women were biologically inferior to men and extremely dangerous. The lecturers emphasized that menstruating women kill little children, that women insert chemicals in the vagina in order to wound the penis of a sexual partner, that they feign virginity and conceal pregnancy.

Despite these negative and limiting images, Herlihy (1971) pointed out that the general inferior status of women was changed many times, owing to the frequent absence of men who went to fight wars. This process, peaking in the eleventh century, enabled many women to gain almost total control over the family property and thus improve their status. Later, as the Geises point out (1978, p. 29), the rapid growth of commerce and city life added to women's status. It is also important to notice that several other studies in addition to those mentioned above (Bainton 1971, 1973; Chojnacki 1974; Coleman 1971; O'Faolain and Martines 1973) generally tend to corroborate the conception of the subjugation of medieval women, but they also point to specific instances, periods, and situations in which women successfully raised their status.[30]

Toward the end of the thirteenth century, many families moved from the rural areas to towns, changing their economic outlook and shifting from producing and exchanging goods to a purely cash economy. This shift had a number of consequences: (1) the family could hardly afford to support ill, unemployed, or unproductive members; (2) it changed from a property-holding, working unit to a consuming unit; (3) as a result of the great number of peasants coming to town, the worker's real wages remained very low, and any fluctuation in business caused severe survival problems.[31] This situation understandably produced considerable in-

29. Obviously, women from different classes and families were not regarded in the same ways.
30. Policelli (1978) even points to a case where an influential Franciscan friar preached that women should have more rights than they did.
31. Garraty (1978) describes the disastrous effects of the mass immigration of peasants to cities in the fourteenth century.

security among the new city-dwellers (Cohn 1961; Helleiner 1967); consequently, male employees in large-scale enterprises (textiles, flour mills, mining) subsisted close to the starvation level and could not afford marriage. Moreover, guild members who had not reached master status were forbidden by the guild to marry. "Marriage of the artisan depended on admission to masterhood, and this in turn depended on conditions which favored the masters of the guild. Guild regulations prohibited admission of married apprentices" (McDonnell 1954, p. 84; also see Wrigley 1969).[32]

These factors created very strong pressures upon women to enter the job market, either to support their families, if they had any, or to support themselves, if they were alone. The fate of the unmarried girl was more or less sealed. (Goodsell 1915, p. 210) Some were sent to convents, an alternative provided "for those women who were prevented from fulfilling their 'natural calling'" (McDonnell 1954, p. 83). In Germany and Belgium, for example, these convents "were charitable houses for unmarried and widowed women" (ibid., p. 88). Unmarried women could also stay with their families and help with the work. In the cities, however, women without mates, without families to support them, or with no chance of entering a convent usually worked in spinning and weaving. Some also resorted to prostitution (McDonnell 1954). Certain documentation (although not very substantial) indicates that the number of prostitutes increased quite significantly at the very beginning of industrial development, especially in growing cities. Other sources (Bullough 1964; Henriques 1963; Sanger 1937; Scott 1936) attest to the sharp increase in the number of prostitutes in the urban industrial centers of the fourteenth and fifteenth centuries. La Croix (1926, vol. 2) points out that cities along the Rhine and in Alsace Lorraine (where new industries were developing) had instituted numerous laws against prostitution by the end of the fourteenth century. (These places, incidentally, were also characterized by a high degree of witch-hunting) It hardly seems coincidental that Sprenger—one of the authors of the *Malleus*—came from Cologne, the principal industrial and commercial city on the Rhine. (Nelson 1971, p. 25) During this period, numerous rich families attempted to establish secular convents to which they could send their unwed daughters, but they deteriorated rapidly and were later turned into hospitals and poorhouses (McDonnell 1954, pp. 82, 84; Nelson 1971, p. 25).

32. This rule, essentially, was an attempt by those in power to keep it. As Marx pointed out, this development, together with the insecurity of the new city dwellers, also gave rise to a permanent proletariat.

Women responded to these pressures by entering various newly industrialized spheres. Consequently, during the thirteenth and fourteenth centuries, the woman's dual role as part of the traditional family structure and as an unmarried worker became very problematic. An initial reaction to this dilemma was to glorify her old role. Women thus became objects of worship, appreciation, adoration, and admiration (Nelson 1971). Lea (1901) and Warner (1976), report on the growing support generated by the cult of the Virgin (in which the Virgin was worshipped as the ideal woman). However, this attitude did not last very long, and the image of the woman soon changed.

The Fourteenth Century: New Patterns Emerge

During the fourteenth century, Europe experienced severe demographical changes that bore directly on the concentration on women as victims of witch-hunts. In particular, the Black Death (1347–51) had devastating and far-reaching effects. Although the major epidemic abated in 1350, the disease reappeared intermittently in various localities until the end of the century. The mortality rate was particularly high in cities because of the density of population and the absence of hygienic conditions. Those who ran from the afflicted cities back to the villages only spread the disease to the rural areas as well (Helleiner 1967). Lea (1901, vol. 2) reports of certain places where, out of each 1,000 people, barely 100 survived. McNeill (1976, p. 149) estimates that at least one third of the total population died.

This constituted a turning point in the demography of Europe (J. C. Russell 1972; Borrie 1970; Wrigley 1969). The population had grown with relative rapidity since the tenth century (Grigg 1980). Various cities had reached populations of 50,000 to 100,000. "Central and northern Europe . . . saw a threefold growth in the pre-plague period with its most rapid advance from about 1150–1200 to 1300" (J. C. Russell 1972, p. 40). Griggs (1980, p. 77) adds that "in the early fourteenth century the populations of Florence and Venice were not far short of 100,000, of Paris about 80,000 of London and Ghent about 50,000. North of the Alps and the Danube, Europe's urban population had probably reached 2 million" (1980, p. 77). J. C. Russell (1972) also indicates that until the fourteenth century, there had been more males than females in the population, although it is not clear exactly when a better female/male ratio was achieved later. Griggs states that "There is . . . some evidence of overpopulation in some parts of Western Europe by the end of the thirteenth century" (1980, p. 70). The effect of the plague on the population was thus devastating. "Two thirds or three quarters or five sixths of the inhabitants of Europe fell vicitm to the pest" (Lea 1901, 2: 378–79). It can be assumed with a fair degree of certainty that between thirty and fifty percent of the population was annihilated by this disaster (Bridbury 1973; Cipolla 1974; Griggs 1980, p. 54; Langer 1964; J. C. Russell 1972; Usher 1956; Ziegler 1971). Postan (1950), for example, reports that the decrease in population size was so sharp, with no corresponding increases during following centuries, that almost sixty percent of the land was deserted in Denmark, Sweden, Norway, and Germany.[33]

While Griggs indicates that parts of Europe "must have had a very low standard of living in the early fourteenth century" (1980, p. 67) after the major plagues had passed, the peasant and wage-laborer survivors found themselves in a highly favorable and advantageous position. As a direct result of the shortage in manpower, (Spengler 1968, p. 433) their real income was tremendously increased, food supplies improved, and job security magnified. In addition, many survivors had inherited large amounts of wealth from their deceased relatives (Langer 1964). Chojnacki (1974) notes in particular that women enjoyed increased economic success and wealth and that "their determination to keep control of their enlarged wealth also increased" (p. 198). Thus he documents the fact that following the end of the plague, women became increasingly active in the economy and gained much economic power.

Under such favorable conditions, one might expect an increase in the population size, but this did not occur (Nelson 1971, Spengler 1968, Deevey 1960, Helleiner 1957). The real increase in population did not take place before the sixteenth or seventeenth centuries (Helleiner 1957, Langer 1964, Wrigley 1969). This phenomenon can be explained in part by the sporadic, unpredictable reappearance of disease, as well as by the continuation of the Hundred Years' War. But the essential reason lies elsewhere. The fact that the population did not increase and the birth rate decreased in the second half of the fourteenth century was due to the massive use of contraception and infanticide (Helleiner 1967, p. 71). Why these techniques were used can be easily understood.

Because part of the population was—quite suddenly—exposed to a high standard of living because of an increase in real income, these people did not want to undermine their new prosperity by raising large families.[34]

33. Although the plague hit England quite hard, the country's large population counterbalanced some of its effects and probably affected the emerging patterns of witch hunting in England (see, for example, Bridbury 1973, 1977; Postan 1950; Usher 1956; Gottfried 1978).

34. The Geises (1978, p. 230) report that in the fourteenth century life expectancy rose sharply for women, so that it is possible that they outnumbered men.

Furthermore, the economic, monetary, commercial, and urban revolutions that accompanied the Renaissance and Reformation probably also gave a powerful stimulus to the rise of individualism and egoism.[35] Those who married took care to limit the number of their offspring, while those who did not marry made efforts to prevent pregnancy. (Spengler 1968, pp. 436–37, 440) The Church bitterly complained of the widespread use of *coitus interruptus*, by married and single persons alike, as a means of preventing pregnancy (Himes 1936; Noonan 1965; Wrigley 1969, p. 124). Although historical research on infanticide is still itself in its infancy and cannot yet provide us with reliable numbers concerning the actual scope of the phenomenon in the twelfth through fifteenth centuries, a growing number of scholars have suggested that the rate and scope increased sharply and significantly during the period under question. "Widespread infanticide and abandonment of children were responsible for the spread of foundling homes in the late Middle Ages" and for extensive legislation by the Church to fight this practice (Trexler 1973, p. 99).[36]

Coleman notes that "many children were left abandoned at a church's door; and they were accepted in order to prevent their death at the hands of their parents" and that "the purpose of . . . infanticide was to regulate children, not eliminate them" (1976, pp. 57, 69). It was exceedingly difficult to prove the crime of infanticide; indeed, "the unwed mothers and the presumed witches . . . were to bear the brunt as examples and admonitions" (Langer 1974b, p. 350).[37]

It is quite clear that the fifteenth and sixteenth centuries brought with them one of the most severe demographic changes Europe had ever experienced (Midelfort 1972 pp. 184–86; Noonan 1968; J. C. Russell 1972; Spengler 1968; Wrigley 1969). Hajnal demonstrates how the patterns of European marriage date roughly from this time: "The marriage pattern of most of Europe as it existed for at least two centuries up to 1940 was, so far as we can tell, unique . . . in the world. . . . The distinctive marks of the 'European Pattern' are (1) a high age of marriage and (2) a high proportion of people never marry at all" (1965, p. 101; see also

35. See, for example, Brown (1969) and Colin (1972).

36. This problem began before the fourteenth century. By the end of the twelfth century, Innocent III had established a hospital in Rome "because so many women were throwing their children into the Tiber" and "there were as many infanticides as there were infants born out of wedlock" (Trexler 1973, p. 99). See also Spengler (1968), Himes (1936), Noonan (1965), Wrigley (1969), Coleman (1971), Davies and Blake (1956), De Mause (1974), Goodsell (1915), Helleiner (1967), Helmholtz (1975), Langer (1974a, b), Radbill (1974), and Webster (1979).

37. Langer also examined the court and prison records of Nurnberg from 1513 to 1777 and found that during this period about eighty-seven women were executed for infanticide.

Spengler 1968, p. 1433, and Wrigley 1969, p. 90). Hajnal notes in particular that "the proportion of singles among women [was] high. . . . The marriage pattern is tied in very intimately with the performance of the economy as a whole [and] wealth may . . . cause late marriage. It was suggested . . . that people married late because they insisted on a certain standard of living . . . as a prerequisite of marriage. More single men married late because they could not 'afford' to marry younger" (1965, pp. 117 132, 133). He suggests that the origin of this marriage pattern lies "somewhere about the sixteenth century [and] became quite widespread . . . in the general population . . . in the seventeenth century" (ibid., p. 134; see also J. C. Russell 1972, p. 60). Litchfield (1966) gives us additional figures that exemplify changes in the family structure and functions. He reports that the age of marriage for males rose to twenty-five and more. He also indicates that among the upper middle class in Florence in the sixteenth century, larger dowries were required for marriage. This both delayed marriages and motivated more of the ruling classes in Catholic countries to send their daughters to convents, which required smaller dowries. (pp. 202–3). The rise of Beguins reflected new arrangements concerning marriage and the status of women in the fifteenth and sixteenth centuries. The parallel development in Protestant countries was an increased number of spinsters. Midelfort reports similar facts, and he adds that in some places, the age of marriage for women rose to twenty-three and even twenty-seven. He also reports that the proportion of those remaining single rose from five to fifteen or even twenty percent (1972, p. 184). Wrigley notes that "between two fifths and three fifths of the women of childbearing age 15–44 were unmarried" (1969, p. 90).[38]

These figures indicate a definite shift to late marriage which was the focus for the crystallization of the nuclear family on the one hand, and marriage by choice on the other (Noonan 1968, p. 468). The significance of a high proportion of unmarrieds is tremendous in a society that attaches a stigma to being single. In particular, the appearance of a large number of unmarried women produced serious problems, and it is probably no coincidence that a significant number of the witches were either widows or spinsters (at least when the persecutions started). Later on, however, married women and young girls were persecuted as well. (Midelfort 1972).

---

38. These changes took place progressively over Europe. In many areas they began in the fifteenth and sixteenth centuries; in others, they may have been present as early as the fourteenth century (Wrigley 1969; Herlihy 1965).

It is evident from all this that, beginning in the twelfth century and throughout the entire period with which we are concerned, the social role of women was in constant flux. Urban industrial life compelled them to step outside their traditional roles. Women entered a market characterized by lack of manpower. Their assumption of "male" employment, particularly in cities, where the job market was tighter produced a virulent misogyny (Bainton 1971, pp. 9–14; Kelso 1956; Midelfort 1972, p. 183). Two centuries earlier women could not get married because men could not afford marriage, in the fifteenth century, they were unable to marry because of men's reluctance to marry.

There were other deep changes in women's social roles as sexual partners and mothers. As we have seen, there was widespread use of contraception and infanticide, which the church strongly and fiercely denounced as most evil. Trexler notes that "child-killing has been regarded almost exclusively as a female crime, the result of women's inherent tendency to lechery, passion, and lack of responsibility. . . . "Infanticide was . . . the most common social crime imputed to . . . witches . . . by the demonologists (1973, pp. 98, 103; also see Lea 1957, vol. 1; Murray 1918; Sprenger and Kramer 1968). Furthermore, Piers (1978) notes that as large waves of immigrants came into the newly establishd towns, many of them extremely poor, women had no choice but to sell themselves. Many times, they also followed armed forces who traveled throughout Europe fighting numerous wars. Because of the low pay, prostitutes had to have masses of customers. They thus became bearers of various veneral diseases. Even the higher-status job of a servant meant that a woman was at the disposal of her master's (or his friend's) sexual appetite. Piers points out that the servant's unquestioning sexual availability was, many a time, the only thing that stood between her and plain starvation. All these conditions obviously created countless cases of pregnancy, which many times ended in infanticide.

But infanticide was not only a result of the fact that many children were born out of wedlock. Many rich women either could not breast-feed their offspring or did not want to. Consequently, wet nurses were sought. There are indications that many wet nurses were poor women who hired themselves after their infants either died naturally or more often, were killed (Piers 1978). Trexler suggests that it is quite possible that in many cases, becoming a wet nurse was a planned course of action. It was a safe, comfortable living. No wonder, then, that midwives were among the chief suspects of witchcraft (Forbes 1966; Heinsohn and Steiger 1982). The Dominicans suspected—and probably rightly so—that midwives were experts in birth control and no doubt helped and cooperated in infanticide. This suspicion was explicitly voiced in the *Malleus:* "No one does more harm to the Catholic Faith than midwives."[39]

Under the chaotic circumstances described above—large numbers of unmarried men and women, sexual license, sinful contraception, infanticide—the relationship between the sexes must frequently have been one of mutual exploitation fraught with deep feelings of guilt and resentment.[40] Because of the powerlessness of women under secular and religious law, and their inferior status, it was convenient to project on them all the resentment and guilt. The ideology of the witch-hunt made use of these emotions. It made it possible for men who indulged in sex that proved unhealthy for them to accuse women of taking away their generative powers. Those who were party to contraception through *coitus interruptus* could project their guilt on women for stealing their seed. The fantasies about the unlimited sexual powers and depravity of women might have been a reflection of the fear engendered by the large number of unmarried women not subject to the authority of fathers or husbands, as, according to prevailing standards, they ought to have been.

It is thus clear why women were the principal victims of witch-hunts. The witchcraze paralleled profound changes in women's roles and in the structure of the family. The tensions reflected in the images of demonology must have been very widespread among men, who presumably in large numbers took advantage of the prevailing sexual freedom. Among married women, who probably did not or could not indulge in illicit sex, there must have been strong feelings against "bad women" who might have "bewitched" their husbands and sons. Therefore, the female witch, using sex to corrupt the world, was a "suasive image" of great power in an ideology that aimed to rid the world of Satan's power, of all the effects of social change, and to restore its moral boundaries.

Timing: Termination of the Witchcraze

How did the European witchcraze end? In their most devastating form, the witch-hunts lasted until the seventeenth century, or to be more accurate, till the end of the Thirty Years' War in the Peace of Westphalia (1648). A few factors contributed to the end of the craze. First, the invasion of foreign armies from the north halted the persecution of witches in many cases (Nelson 1971; Robbins 1959). Second, the sheer

39. Reported by Parrinder (1958, p. 109), who quotes from the 1928 English translation of the *Malleus*.

40. Payer (1980) describes how hard the Church tried to control and regulate even marital sexual relationships.

terror, scope, and nature of the witchcraze helped undermine the process itself.

> The terrible persecution of the 1620's caused a crisis within the very order which did so much to direct it: the Jesuits. Already in 1617, Tanner, a Jesuit of Ingolstadt [had raised] very elementary doubts. . . . Another Jesuit, Friedrich Spee, was more radically converted by his experience as a confessor of witches in the great persecution at Wurtzburg. That experience . . . turned his hair permanently white [and] convinced him that all confessions were worthless." (Trevor-Roper 1967, p. 158)

Third, the number of executions and the organization they demanded was quite a burden, both economically and socially. The witchcraze caused havoc in Europe, whole villages were destroyed, commerce was inhibited. "Germany was almost entirely occupied in building bonfires. . . . Switzerland had had to wipe out whole villages in order to keep them down" (ibid., p. 152). It seems very clear that the cost of the craze began to be too high, too many people were burned, a substantial part of the population was eliminated, and the atmosphere it created was increasingly unbearable.[41] Fourth, although there were critics of the witchcraze, such as Weyer, Scot, Spee, Tanner, and Paracelsus, none doubted the existence of the devil and witches. Their main criticism was leveled against the use of torture. During the sixteenth century, it was understood that the Church was engaged in a life and death struggle with Satan. In the seventeenth century, this central dogma was under attack. By 1624, such people as Episcopius and Greve had begun to doubt the central dogma of the persecutions. "Men revolted against the cruelty of torture, against the implausibility of confessions, against the identification of witches" (ibid., p. 172).

The witchcraze was thus attacked at its foundation. As Midelfort (1972) shows, the fact that secular courts were used for judging witches also undermined the craze. This happened mainly because of changes in the law itself in the seventeenth, and later in the eighteenth, century. It included breaking accusations of withcraft into parts. For example, poisoning was viewed as a different kind of murder, and infanticide was separated—legally—from witchcraft. Eventually, "witchcraft" as a category for trial disappeared.

41. Solzhenitsyn (1975) and Connor (1972) point out that in a similar craze, the Stalinist persecutions in the USSR between 1936 and 1938, the economic problem was solved by the slave work the prisoners did. In the Russian case, the patterns of repression were successfully constructed so as to decrease the economic pressure associated with the persecutions. The witchcraze, on the other hand, was—economically and socially speaking—disastrous.

Thus, the ideological basis for the witch-hunts was clouded by growing doubts as to its legitimacy, and the various "technologies" and tortures used to hunt and isolate witches were meeting with severe criticism. Eventually, power was taken away from the courts, the inquisitorial machinery was dismantled, and persecution of witches came to an end. This is consistent with the idea that once the differentiation process was well under way and people had begun adjusting to the new situation, the persecutions ended.

The coincidence of the termination of the worst of the craze with the close of the Thirty Years' War is not just chance. The Peace of Westphalia gave official recognition and legitimacy to religious pluralism and symbolically ended the struggle to redefine the moral system of Europe. The stresses, insecurity, and instability experienced by persons living in war-stricken areas provided fuel to the burning furnace of the final phase of the witchcraze. But once stability was achieved and religious pluralism accepted, the witch-hunts weakened, finally disappearing altogether.

It is thus evident that by the seventeenth century, new cognitive maps and new institutional arrangements had emerged. There was a demarcation between science, magic, and religion, recognition of autonomy of government and economy in England, and settlement of secular and spiritual relationships elsewhere in a way that recognized supremacy of the political sphere. A new social order had visibly and triumphantly been created. The age of "reason" was at hand within its model of the "rational man." It was the era of emerging nation states, where man's loyalty was to his state and not to the Church. This was part of a more general secularization of society. When the differentiation proeess came so far, the basis for the witchcraze was, in fact, eliminated. The reasons for its beginning and duration ceased to exist. A new definition of societal borders was taking shape, the societal community was already fractured, and the witch-hunt had no purpose whatsoever.

Were the persecutions successful in restoring the religious boundaries of medieval society? Obviously, the answer to this question is negative. Medieval society was not reconstructed or restored and probably could not have been restored. The attempt to do so was futile, and the sacrifice of innumerable human lives could not be justified even in any instrumental terms. Whether participation in witch-hunts helped people psychologically to survive the period of uncertainty and transition is a different question. Even if it did, it was at the expense of the lives of many for the passing gratification of some, and it certainly did not make the persecutors into better Christians, which was its avowed purpose.

Generally speaking, it appears, then, that when a community so vehemently and desperately tries to restore its moral boundaries, it is doomed to fail. It is possible that the very attempt is in itself a symptom that profound change is taking place, that it is impossible to "go back," so to speak. In this sense, the persecutions can be interpreted as a symbol of incapacity, of a system's failure, as "death throes," if you wish, and they might be viable proof that the previous equilibrium cannot be recaptured. The European witchcraze, and the witchcraft trials of Salem, Massachusetts, (especially Erikson's 1966 analysis) seem to be sound proof of this.[42]

Concluding Discussion

In the previous pages, we examined a specific phenomenon of deviance, albeit an invented deviance, and the societal reaction to it. Generally speaking, we analyzed the witchcraze as a by-product of the European transition to modernity. In the theoretical terminology developed in the first part of the book, medieval society was characterized by mechanical solidarity, low usage of energy and information. It was an undifferentiated and simple society undergoing significant changes. This process was neither short nor easy; it started in the Renaissance and was established in the seventeenth century. We have here, therefore, a case of deviance within a prolonged societal transition process. On the one hand, the transition period was characterized by various innovative movements in the scientific, political, and religious realms. These innovations, branded more than once as heresy and deviance, introduced essential elements of flexibility and, in the final analysis, created and reinforced a new society. On the other hand, there was the witch-hunt, a clear attempt to redefine the dissolving boundaries of medieval society. This attempt introduced an element of rigidity to the system. The witch-hunt represented a futile effort to keep previous moral boundaries intact and prevent the changes that the medieval social order was going through. The dual nature of the transition and of its "deviants" thus fit the theoretical framework laid out in chapter 1.

Within this context, we interpreted the European witchcraze on several levels, suggesting that it occurred because of the convergence of a

---

42. In 1692, a witch craze broke out in Salem, Massachusetts, and lasted for about one year. Only a few dozen people were involved, and even fewer were executed (see Erikson 1966; Demos 1982; Weisman 1984).

few key factors. Having described the elements of the craze, we isolated the following questions:

1. Timing: why did the witchcraze start when it did, why did it end when it did, why was it so widely accepted, and why was it distributed the way it was?

The witchcraze began in the late fourteenth century because the inquisitors and the Dominicans had a vested interest in it. They had to either find new goals for themselves or remain without purpose and slowly lose power and disintegrate. However, that in itself is not enough of an explanation. During the fifteenth and sixteenth centuries, Europe experienced the painful birth pangs of a new social order. We referred to this as a differentiation process. The confusion and sense of powerlessness and anomie experienced by contemporary individuals were further aggravated by severe climatological and demographical changes and by hitherto unimagined geographical discoveries. Nevertheless, the dissolution of the medieval cognitive map of the world also gave rise to utopian expectations and bold scientific explorations. These conditions created a widespread need for a redefinition of moral boundaries. This need explains the popular acceptance of the craze, as a desperate attempt to recapture and restore the previous moral social order.

2. Content: why a *witchcraze* and not something else? How do we explain the emergence of an antireligious ideology, focusing on the witches? The answer to this question lies precisely in the antinomian character of the ideology. By emphasizing the negative, the bad, an implicit finger was pointed at what should have been. Only demonology and witches could serve this purpose since no other heretical group— imaginary or real— threatened the Christian legitimacy. The elaboration of witchcraft theories into a complex religious ideology was a direct result of the need for a theoretical construct to explain the turmoil and anomie of the period. This ideology culminated in the actual persecution of witches, first because it was devised for that purpose, and second, because the trials and executions represented the endeavor to redefine moral boundaries. Demonology provided the theoretical justification for the craze; persecutions were its manifestation. We also examined the efficincy and success of the witchcraze ideology. Neither in early modern Europe or in seventeenth-century Massachusetts did the persecutions fulfill their primary function and prevent, or reverse, social change.

3. Target: why were women the major victims of the craze? Our analysis of changes in the economy, demography, and the structure of the family, especially changes in the role of women, clarified the nature of the target of the craze. It is evident that the increased number of unmarried

women, the incidence of prostitution and infanticide, and the use of contraception formed a salient complex of problems likely to arouse strong feelings. These conditions explain the suitability of a female symbol, such as the witch, to become an effective and central element in a demonological ideology. Furthermore, women offered a safe, weak target for the emotional zeal of the craze. Women had an initially inferior status to begin with, and their lack of power and organization (Lewis 1971) rendered them easy victims of widespread persecutions.

The witchcraze ended when the conditions for its inception were no longer in existence. The spatial distribution of the witch-hunts (and its termination) were direct results of the presence or absence of all or part of the conditions described above. The witchcraze occurred in those countries and areas where the crisis was most deeply felt and where the Church was weak. Where the Church was strong or where progress was not marked, (or both) hardly any witchcraze occurred. The disappearance of these conditions everywhere in the seventeenth century inevitably meant the end of the craze.

3

DEVIANCE WITHIN A MODERN, COMPLEX SOCIETY
The Revival of the Esoterica

Introduction[1]

In the past decade, social scientists have witnessed a growing popular interest in the occult, science fiction, and fantasty.[2] I focus in this section on these phenomena, first characterizing them and second analyzing their timing, content, and meaning.

The major thrust of the interpretation is that both the occult and science fiction should be understood as forms of alternative, or "elective," centers used by adherents to recenter, revitalize and redefine their world views. Both science fiction and the occult, as two different varieties of deviant subcultural belief systems, flourish in a pluralistic, complex society, offering a variety of ways to redefine and change not only one's subjective outlook but societal moral boundaries.

The Revival of Interest in Science Fiction, Fantasy, and the Occult: The Phenomena to be Explained

We can interpret the phenomena on two interdependent levels: the cognitive (What is its content?) and the social (Who is involved?).

Modern Occult

In the last decade, occult-related phenomena and the "black arts" have become a major area of activity. Book, TV series, films, and the reading

---

1. This chapter appeared in different form as "A Quest for the Beyond and Recentering the World: The Revival of the Occult and Science Fiction," *Journal of Popular Culture*, forthcoming.

2. We define occult as things beyond the realm of conventional knowledge that are usually regarded as secret.

of horoscopes have become an integral part of everyday life. Blumberg (1962), Truzzi (1972, 1974), Greeley (1970a, 1970b), Tiryakian (1972, 1974), Staude (1970), Marty (1970), Hartman (1976), Eliade (1976), Galbreath (1971b), Singer and Benassi (1981), all report similar findings. The phenomenon is not restricted to the United States alone but is evident in other countries as well (Tiryakian 1972, Shepherd 1972).

Hartman estimates that "every U.S. city with a population over 100,000 has some occult activity; and every metropolitan center probably has an involvement of between 100 and 2,000 persons. . . . A comparison of the 1969 and 1974 Subject Guides of *Books in Print* reveals that the number of books dealing with non-fictional aspects of the occult grew from 519 to 2,240" (1976, p. 169). Truzzi confirms Hartman's finding: "We are in the midst of a widespread boom of things occult" (1972, p. 16). Eliade calls the phenomenon "the occult explosion of the seventies." He argues that interest in the occult is very common in Europe and the United States and that "at least 5 million Americans plan their lives according to astrological predictions," that an "estimated 40 million Americans have turned the zodiac business into a $200-million-a-year enterprise" using computers to cast the horoscopes (1976, pp. 58–59). Occult beliefs have thus become a viable part of the Western cultural heritage (Singer and Benassi 1981).

Almost all sources agree that the modern "occult explosion" is generally characterized by mystery, claims to specific "forbidden knowledge," the creation of belief systems, and has an antiscientific flavor. The existence of many sects and communities created by an interest in the occult and esoterica, however, clearly undermines a point made by Marty (1970), and shared by Hartman (1976) and Truzzi (1972), that the occult revival lacks the "communal impulse" and fails to generate what can be called "social communities." Among so-called occult communities, we find the Church of Satan in San Francisco and other, widely publicized satanist groups. Then there are cults such as the Builders of the Adytum, whose spiritual life is based upon hermetic and kabbalistic traditions; the Church of Light, which professes a mysterious belief in the supernatural; the Church of All Worlds, based on a science fiction novel by Robert Heinlein; the Feraferia, a neopagan movement; the Scientologists and others.[3] These small-scale social organizations give further credence to

3. See Alfred (1976), Moody (1974), Bainbridge (1978), and Ellwood (1973). For discussion of other occult groups operating as communes, see, for example, Larsen (1977), Ellwood (1979), Robbins (1979), Adler (1979). For analysis of "deviant religions" see, for example, Richards (1978) and Stoner and Park (1977).

the idea that the occult can be an important source for personal as well as social change.

What are the main ingredients of the revival? Astrology, of course, plays a central role. Various occultists believe in PSI and ESP (i.e., parapsychology and its variants),[4] "life energies" and the physics of paranormal phenomena, automatic writing, trances, seances, astral problems, telepathy, hypnosis, natural and spiritual healing, reincarnation, the afterlife, clairvoyance, sexual pursuit of spiritual fulfillment, tarot cards, kabbalah, numerology, metoposcopy, chiromancy, ghost invocation, poltergeists, possession, exorcism, (Pattison and Wintrob 1981) and various witchcraft technologies (i.e., love potions, charms, and spells).

Involvement in the occult comprises a large spectrum of behaviors. The nature of one's involvement is, sociologically speaking, an important issue. The nature scope and subjective meaning of this differential involvement, however, has not been theoretically or empirically researched yet. The lack of empirical data in this area is disturbing. We lack data pertaining to who practices what, to what extent, and even how widespread the phenomenon really is. The revival appears to rest, first of all, on a great amount of published material, newspapers, movies, and other manufactured paraphernalia (charms, tables, and the like). Second, this social movement is typically represented by America's urban middle classes and by people in their mid twenties to late thirties. Third, as suggested, participation assumes many forms. Some people's involvement is confined to reading their horoscopes or books, others subscribe regularly to various journals, and still others change their life style completely in order to join satanic or esoteric groups, cults and covens. (See, for examples, Tiryakian 1972, Greeley 1970b, Moody 1974, Hartman 1976, Ellwood 1973, 1979, Bainbridge 1978, Alfred 1976, Robbins 1979, Eliade 1976.) Fourth, it appears that there is a correlation between expressed interest in the occult and various occupations. The revival seems most popular among white-collar workers and those of high educational achievement. It is interesting to compare these findings to others that indicate that although beliefs in the paranormal are widespread in the general American population, American college and university professors' attitudes toward parapsychology are particularly positive (Wagner and Monnet 1979). Fifth, it appears that a significant majority of

4. Singer and Benassi (1981, p. 49) report that belief in ESP is consistently found to be moderate or strong in 80–90 percent of the U.S. population. In one study, it even ranked as the most popular supernatural belief, surpassing stated beliefs in God in both strength and prevalence.

those who are expressly interested in the occult but do not practice it have no religious affiliation.

The last point is important: Contrary to past interest in the occult, which was generally passive, modern occultists are in many cases actively engaged in a search for events that by their nature cannot be rationally explained.[5] Truzzi gives a succinct example: "Years ago, few would dare enter the [haunted] house; all would whisper in fear about it. Now such an allegation would bring a rush of inquisitive teenagers who desire to spend the night there just to see the ghost" (1972, p. 29). Truzzi also argues that, contrary to the past, "being labelled a witch today is hardly stigmatic. In much of today's middle-class society, a witch is viewed as a highly glamorous figure. Announcing that you are a witch today is more likely to get you invited to a party than burned at the stake!" (1974, p. 633). Roszak (1981) agrees that post-Christian, postindustrial society is engaged in an active, intensive search for the miraculous.

Eliade (1976) and Greeley (1970a) both note that a boom in science fiction and fantasy literature—books, magazines, and movies—has paralleled the "occult explosion." Greeley notes, "There also exist some rather strange relationships, to which I must confess a lack of complete understanding, between science fiction and various neo-sacral movements" (1970a, p. 133).

Science Fiction and Fantasy

Science fiction and fantasy are anything but new phenomena. Sam Moskowitz characterized science fiction as "a branch of fantasy identifiable by the fact that it eases the willing suspension of disbelief on the part of its readers by utilizing an atmosphere of scientific credibility for its imaginative speculations in physical sciences, space, time, social science, and philosophy" (Nicholls 1979, p. 160). Science fiction and fantasy stories usually include a fantastic voyage, encounters with alien beings or experiences, and technological or magical inventions, contact with the "ultimate" usually within the endless vastness of the universe, and a very strong sense of wonder. Niven's, Clarke's, Herbert's, Pohl's, and Lem's stories (to mention only a few) all demonstrate this point vividly. By its nature, therefore, science fiction mystifies the world and creates a sense of awe. Rose (1981) states that the key for understanding the tremendous attraction of science fiction must be the fact that it always leads to an

5. Greeley (1970a) reports that when he taught at the University of Chicago, one of his students—a responsible Methodist turned agnostic—reported to him that he had been in contact with the devil. He states that the student was "visibly shaken by his experience with the diabolic" (p. 140).

encounter with the unknown. He feels that science fiction is both a
displacement of esentially religious concerns and a mirror of various
aspects of the alienated sensibility of the modern era.

The genre as we know it today is a product of the mid nineteenth
century. Among the writers who helped shape the form were Wells, Poe,
Verne, Hagrad, and Stevenson. It is the legacy of these men, especially
Verne and Wells, that we see today. Science fiction books, journals, and
movies have appeared regularly since the 1920s.[6] However, despite two
small-scale booms—one in its "golden age" in the 1930s and another in
the 1950s—nothing approximates the tradition's present popularity.
Even dissertations and research entirely devoted to science fiction are
being produced (Tymm, Schlobkin, and Curry 1977). Aside from such
well-respected journals as *Analog,* and *Amazing Science Fiction,* the last
two to three years have witnessed a flood of science fiction and fantasy
publications (e.g., *Cosmos, Destinies, Isaac Asimov's Science Fiction
Magazine, Omni*).[7] Advertisements for such journals even appear on
commercial TV stations. Two journals—*The Bulletin of the Science Fiction Writers of America* and *Locus*—admit that the present boom is
beyond their wildest dreams and hopes, and they had wild dreams indeed. John J. Pierce notes that "the Golden Age is really *now*. More
people are reading science fiction than ever before. . . . Today we have
milions of viewers willing to accept a world with double suns, bizarre
aliens, . . . Galactic Empires [Science fiction] is entertainment for people who *think*" (1977, p. 158). An editorial in *Analog* adds that "science
fiction has . . . become more popular, more flexible and various, much
of it more literary and more sophisticated. It has spread internationally,
through most of the technologically developed nations" (Williams 1978,
p. 15). The annual science fiction conventions have become popular
spectacles.[8] Awards ceremonies ("Hugo," "Nebula") attract the atten-

6. See Ashley 1975, Tuck 1978, Nicholls 1979, Knight 1975, Scholes and Rabkin 1977.

7. Many of these journals appeared for only short periods; others have been much more
successful and are thriving.

8. The thirty-seventh World Science Fiction Convention, held in Brighton, England, in
August 1979, had an official attendance of 2,300 with a registration of about 5,100. The
thirty-eighth World Science Fiction Convention, held in Boston, Massachusetts, had an
official attendance of about 5,900, the fortieth World Science Fiction convention held in
Chicago in 1982 had an attendance of 4,325, and the forty-second convention, held in Los
Angeles in the summer of 1984, had an attendance of 8365 fans. The European convention,
held in May 1980 in Stresa, Italy, had an attendance of only about 1,000 participants. From
the lists of conventions, it seems that a small science fiction convention is being held at least
once a month somewhere in the U.S. or Europe. Apparently, the boom in science fiction
has not been restricted to the United States only.

tion of millions all over the world.[9] Hundreds of books—both new and old titles—are being published, and movies are being constantly manufactured or reissued.[10]

As a popular phenomenon, there can be little doubt that the science fiction subculture exhibits some distinct features. In the popular sense of the term, science fiction usually means books, movies, and magazines. On a more involved level, it includes specialized fan clubs, newsletters, jargon, fanzines, regular regional, national, and international conventions, specific and specialized areas of interest, and intense social interactions. On a still more involved level, one can find groups of people who make science fiction the center of their lives. For example, in 1961, a group of young people established the Church of All Worlds, a community founded on a science fiction novel, *Stranger in a Strange Land*, written by Robert A. Heinlein. The novel describes a person from Earth who is educated by Martians and later returns to Earth. He starts spreading the Martian philosophy, based on such concepts as love, peace, and unity with the universe. In Ellwood's description, "the principal purpose of a Martian's life is to '*GROK*,' to intuit the 'fullness' of something completely from within." The church itself began to operate in 1961. Before its establishment, the group experimented with living according to ideas developed by Ayn Rand and Maslow, and they only later discovered Heinlein's book. That book was "seized with ecstatic sense of recognition" (Adler 1979, p. 271). Ellwood adds: "This book was one of the bibles of the youth of the sixties, for in a real sense they felt they were Martians on Earth" (1973, p. 201). The church grew and expanded in the

9. Since 1953, the "Hugo" has been awarded every year by fans at world science fiction conventions for the "best" creations of the preceding year in various categories (book, short story, movie, and art). The "Nebula" award has been given by the science fiction writers of America since 1966.

I myself have always been a devoted fan of science fiction. When I came to study at the University of Chicago in 1974, I went immediately to the Kroch's and Brentano's bookstore in downtown Chicago to look for some literature. The store then had a modest, but good, section of science fiction literature. In 1977, when I left Chicago, Kroch's and Brentano's had quadrupled the space devoted to science fiction. Moreover, bookstores specializing only in science fiction have appeared in large numbers in the United States, England, and Europe.

10. Books and journals dating from the 1930s are now being sold as "collectors' items." As concerns modern movies, it is interesting to note that science fiction fans do not readily consider them "good" science fiction. Bova, former editor of *Analog*, states, for example, that neither *Star Wars* nor *Close Encounters* can be regarded as science fiction, that "in fact, they bear the same relationship to science fiction as the Nazi treatment of Poland bore to the Ten Commandments" (1978, p. 10).

late 1960s (it even published a magazine called *Green Egg*). By 1978 it had "nests" all over the United States.

Another social movement clearly inspired by science fiction is Scientology. Scientology is important for our purposes for it illustrates the way in which science fiction can be transformed into a scientific-religious theory. As Wallis (1977) points out, Scientology succeeded, not only because of an excellent organization, but because it presents itself as both a form of therapy and a religion. In its first years, it was known as "Dianetics." Dianetics itself, a system of axioms for mental as well as physical therapy, was introduced in 1949 by L. Ron Hubbard in a science fiction story published in the magazine *Astounding Science Fiction*. In 1950, the magazine published a lengthy paper on Dianetics, which "was boosted as a form of psychotherapy which could achieve almost miraculous results in sweeping away all the dross that encumbered ordinary minds, leaving the superman that is latent in us all" (Nicholls 1979, p. 167). In the next few years, the system attracted many people. Although originally it was presented in a novel, people took it seriously, and Dianetics developed into a large-scale movement. Hubbard understood the goldmine he helped create, and in a series of long legal as well as social battles he was able to win complete and exclusive control over this movement. In 1952, he changed the name of the movement to "Scientology." By that time it was well established. Today Scientology, with a large international organization, offers religious and scientific explanations of the "true" nature of the world, as well as various mental and physical therapies. Evans (1973) calls Scientology "the science fiction religion," and according to Bromley and Shupe, "Hubbard has consciously or unconsciously concocted science fiction to supplement Dianetics' neopsychoanalysis and is selling it as psycho-spiritual snake oil to the gullible" (1981, p. 49).

"Fans," or "fandom," in science fiction goes beyond passive or irregular involvement and usually refers to the active readership of the genre. This group maintains national and international contacts through fanzines and conventions. Originally fandom started in the United States in the late 1920s, when readers of the first science fiction magazines contacted each other. Fans have specialized language and jargon, and they sponsor numerous conventions. The yearly Hugo awards are given by the fans. Most are young, white, single males. (It appears that in their late thirties and forties, many lose interest in the field.) Most have changed their religious affiliation at least once since childhood and are employed in professional or managerial positions that rate above average in terms of prestige scales and salary. A large portion have at least an M.A.

degree, and they major in "hard" sciences (i.e., engineering, physics, chemistry, and the like). IQ studies reveal that fans average 127–40 points and that their reading habits are very intensive (see Finer 1954; Waugh, Libby, and Waugh 1975; Berger 1977; Bainbridge 1976; Schmidt 1981; Waugh and Schroeder 1980). How many of the fans' life-style changes are a direct result of science fiction, and to what extent, is very difficult to assess. However, here too it is evident that there are various forms of involvement and commitment.

In summary, four points are worth mentioning. The first is that both the occult and science fiction clearly constitute deviant subcultural belief systems (and life styles) in societal definitions of content, quality, and size. The extent to which deviant subcultures are tolerated, ridiculed, ostracized, or even persecuted varies as a function of the society in which they appear. Adherents to these belief systems—as far as their membership becomes known to their social environment—usually have to do a lot of explanating. Second, one has to notice the similarity in the social and demographic characteristics of adherents to the occult and to science fiction. Third, the lack of good, empirical data prevents us from providing a more comprehensive overview. It is not entirely clear when and what kind of functions the phenomena discussed here serve for their followers: plain entertainment, serious activity, or a central life interest. Fourth, it is important to note that these phenomena are revivals of older themes. Undoubtedly, the novelty of this revival centers in its scope, place, and timing. Consequently, the sociological questions we must ask ourselves concern its timing, meaning, and content.

Explanations of the Phenomenon: A Critical Discussion

Douglas (1966, 1967), Blumberg (1962), Henslin (1967), Gmelch (1978), and Singer and Benassi (1981) claim that magical beliefs and practices exist in those sections of the social system characterized by insecurity and uncertainty. The modern occultists' active quest for the unknown cannot, however, be sufficiently explained through a description of uncertain, irrational, or uncontrollable circumstances. Marty (1970) claimed that people's adherence to the occult stems from the way in which it enhances their quality of life. The idea is confirmed by Truzzi, who suggested that "for most Americans, the involvement in the occult is a leisure-time activity and a fad of popular culture, rather than a serious religious involvement in the search for new sacred elements," (1972, p. 29) an observation that clearly contradicts some facts mentioned earlier.

Greeley (1970a,b) and Staude (1970) claim that people resort to the occult out of alienation, and that with its divination, mysticism, and bizarre cultist groups, the occult explosion is a form of neosacralism. Greeley mentions that the occult helps people find meaning, community, transcendental values, and conduct norms. Galbreath (1971) and Shepherd (1972) support this view and emphasize the experiential aspects of the phenomenon. Tiryakian (1972) expands the concept of the occult explosion into what he called the "esoteric culture," namely, "those religio-philosophic belief systems which underlie occult techniques and practices" (p. 499). He suggests that the occult is "a seed-bed culture source of change and wide-ranging innovations in art, politics, and even science" (p. 446).

Eliade (1976) claims that the revival indicates a deep dissatisfaction with traditional Western religious institutions (why such a dissatisfaction should exist, to begin with, is not explained). Hartman (1976) suggested that it constitutes a new direction of religious commitment, a point alluded to earlier by Stark and Glock (1968). Slater (1975) used the phenomenon to level a strong attack on both the scientific establishment and contemporary American culture.

While there is a relatively large amount of literature on the modern occult explosion, less exists regarding possible explanations of the boom in science fiction and fantasy. Landsman (1972) and the Panshins (1981) suggest that science fiction provides modern society with a mythology and a strong sense of transcendence (alas, no indication is given as to how [or why] can science fiction does it). Ebel (1978) claims that the revival in science fiction signals that Western civilization is experiencing a shift to a new theology. According to Greco (1978), the popularity of science fiction rests on a millenarian fantasy that protects the believers from deeper anxieties: for example "at the deepest level, *Close Encounters* is an Oedipal fantasy revealing repressed incestuous wishes for both the mother and the father" (p. 508). Claus applies a Lévi-Straussian analysis to the TV series "Star Trek," claiming that "myth and *Star Trek* provide a model of real society in which the conflicts of life can reasonably be solved . . . by adhering to values transcending nature" (1976, p. 30).

The explanations surveyed thus far lack specificity. They do not explain the timing, content, or sociological meaning of the phenomenon.

Toward a Sociological Conceptualization

a. Background

It is clear that rather than dealing with a new phenomenon, we are faced with a revival (Truzzi 1972, Jorgensen and Jorgensen 1982). Modern occultists have added practically nothing to occult practices, theories, or notions, which have existed for hundreds of years. Saler (1977) notes that the category of the "supernatural" itself has been part of Western culture for many years. Science fiction too is an old story; not as old as demonology perhaps, but it has been with us since the 1920s, (the fantasty has been with us even longer than that).

An interesting contrast is provided by the European witchcraze of the late Middle Ages, in which the witches' myth was invented and crystallized during the fifteenth century. The "new" dimension of the modern occult is the revival itself, its intensity, vast popularity, and wide coverage by the mass media. In former times, the occult and science fiction attracted the attention of only a few; recently, however, these phenomena have become the focus of attention for thousands, perhaps millions of people all over the globe.

It is important to notice a few common characteristics of these phenomena. Common to all manifestations of the modern occult and science fiction is the attempt to grasp and arrive at the ultimate "entity" that defies all empirical expressions and explanation. The world described is one in which laws and technology alien to the positivistic Western mind prevail. In this sense the occult explosion is, not only religious, but it also negates both conventional religion and science. It presents us, not only with a complete belief system, but with an interesting form of nonpositivistic "science" as well.

O'Dea (1966) defines religion as "the manipulation of non-empirical or supra-empirical means for non-empirical or supra-empircal ends," and positivistic science as the manipulation of empirical means for empirical ends. As we saw in chapter 1, his approach closely recalls that of Weber (1964), for whom magic and witchcraft is a kind of technology. From the various definitions, it appears then, that the closest proximity exists between positivistic Western science and magic; both seem in opposition to religion as it is presently defined. A table of such a theoretical formulation would go as follows:

		Means	
		Empirical	Nonempirical
Ends	Empirical	SCIENCE	MAGIC
	Nonempirical		RELIGION

The fourth cell is the problematic one. Perhaps the appropriate categories here would be science fiction, fantasy, and various modern myths.

Several studies have already demonstrated that magic and science are in fact very similar. Frazer (1963), White (1913), and of course, Thorndike's prestigious work (1941) argue that magic is necessary for the development of science. Kirsch (1978) even states that the growth of demonology paralleled that of the scientific revolution. Once magic becomes reality, it is no longer magic, it is science.[11]

The rise of modern magic, however, is in many respects unique. First, the modern occult consists of a sophisticated technological system capable of telling its orthodox adherents exactly how to get what. If love is desired, a specific potion is prescribed;[12] if a spirit of the dead is wanted, given rites summon it; if success is called for, certain charms are used. Second, this technology is usually anchored in a wider belief system, which maintains that the orthodox, correct use of the various spells, rites, potions, or sacred symbols allows the magician to "force" the deities to do as he wishes. The fact that the modern aherent believes he has power over the deities through such instruments means that modern occult involvement and practice is described in almost the same terms as positivistic science. The modern occultist's position is further strengthened because, not only does he aim to use supernatural forces, but he also claims to understand why and how they operate. Singer and Benassi (1981) also note that modern occultists and occult practices offer an ability to increase both control and predictability. The mythical heroes of the modern fantasy, such as Elric of Melnibone, the albino; Moorcock's legendary prince; or some of Niven's fictional heroes, who command a perfectly astonishing scientific-technological knowledge, are some cases in point. Darth Vader of *Star Wars* probably epitomizes control over both scientific knowledge and the black arts of the Jedi knights. Third, the occult-technological system is described almost as science. In this sense, it

11. This position is very specific. However, other scholars maintain that while science attempts to understand reality (or, in the positivistic tradition, even to predict and control it), technology is the application of a scientist's knowledge. In this sense, magic is associated more with control and manipulation and less with explanation. Religion can also be conceptualized as the creation of models—in an increasing order of abstraction—to explain reality. I adopt the approach of Weber (1964) and O'Dea (1966), as stated. In dealing with the modern "occult explosion," it is very apparent that the debate regarding distinctions between science, religion, and magic loses much of its intensity as the phenomenon itself is a blend of the three.

12. The technology of manufacturing such a potion—and other potions or charms—is not simple. It requires knowledge, skills, raw materials, and must be precisely made according to secret recipes and formulas that date back, perhaps, hundreds of years. The slightest deviation from the instructions, of course, could be crucial and would be regarded as a valid explanation for the failure of the object to act.

is close to science and competes with it. The underlying ideological assumptions at stake here constitute a belief system that also resembles and competes with religion.

The occult differs from both, however, in substance. Although the modern occultists demonstrate a fundamental craving for basic scientific ideas (and by doing so, accept part of the positivistic method), they nevertheless reject the substance of the ideas. For example, many would claim that the universe is limitless and, therefore, everything is possible, including witches, materialization of science fiction, and the like.[13] That there is a gap separating the "possible" from the "actual" does not appear to bother the zealots very much. Another example is their rejection of cause-and-effect relationships, of reproducibility and the description of a phenomenon, or the empirical method. This type of "logic" is expressed in a very simple question typical of many of my students during discussions about the occult (see Greeley 1970a as well). Very often, in discussions comparing science (empiricism) and magic, a student would ask, "Can you *prove* that while talking with you, I have not been in New York (Chicago, the moon, another universe) and back again?" This, he would claim, can be done using "unknown" powers, and indeed, no empirical test can ascertain that he has *not* been there.

This is, perhaps, the place to note that the scientific method has severe difficulties coping with such negative claims. The problem of reproducibility is also not an easy one. Although, in general, occultists do cling to a technology based on reproducibility (i.e., whenever using charm x, spell y, or ritual z, a certain constant effect is expected), many modern adherents of PSI, science fiction, and the occult challenge ideas of reproducibility. In an editorial entitled "Irreproducible," Schmidt (1979) suggested that a whole class of phenomena might exist (e.g., ESP, music, art) that cannot be reproduced and whose observation calls for a fundamentally new methodological study.

This, in part, explains why the modern occult threatens clergymen and scientists alike. It tries to be and competes with both science and religion. The phenomenon is unique. Beyond any shadow of a doubt it is anti–established religion and antiscience: "The recent tide of anti-scientific and pseudo-scientific irrationalism threatens to drown us in sheer nonsense and may ultimately threaten the social climate within which the pursuit of objective knowledge is advanced" (Frazier 1978, p. 40).

13. Modern cosmologies, especially those inspired by quantum mechanics, seem to give strong popular support to these ideas in general and to the idea of the existence of multiple universes in particular (e.g., Davies 1980, 1982a).

Etzioni describes a case in which "186 scientists issued a statement expressing concern about the rapid spread of astrology and warning the people about its false pretences" (1978, p. 47; see also Jerome 1977). Singer and Benassi (1981) also express concern about this matter and state that the strength and extent of the occult revival constitute a challenge to the validity of science and to the authority of the scientific community. Does all this mean, as Shepherd (1972) and Tiryakian (1972) suggested, that we are witnessing the creation of a new scientific paradigm (Kuhn 1962)? While later I shall try to provide an answer to this question, we have to realize that this challenge is aimed at transforming and changing the conventional boundaries of science. It is a clear attempt to redefine what is, and what is not, scientific and to reshape both the focus and methodology of science.

The Timing of the Phenomenon

The first question is, Why does the "occult explosion" exist today? Almost all explanations suggest that people resort to magic and the occult in situations of uncertainty and alienation. They are searching for new meanings and identity, for transcendental values and an experience of the ecstatic, the supernatural. They want to take part in social change and find expression for their dissatisfaction. They seek new forms of religious commitment. It is obviously difficult to add new elements to this rather long list. I suggest, therefore, a new conceptual framework for the timing problem based on the terms "revitalizing" and "recentering." These concepts are used here to illustrate how the occult and science fiction can be thought of as introducing change into modern society. The challenge of these deviant subcultural belief systems is aimed at the social order at large, and specifically at science and conventional religions. Both science fiction and modern occultism constitute elective centers and offer adherents the possibility of recentralizing and changing the moral boundaries of their worlds.

In the following analysis, I shall compare science fiction and modern occultism as elective centers, pointing to how they should be understood within a process of recentralization. The analysis addresses seven factors: (1) the cultural conditions that engender the quest for the beyond; (2) the degree to which science fiction and modern occultism are consciously recognized as elective centers; (3) the degree of structure they manifest, (4) the degree to which science fiction and modern occultism emerge spontaneously or are sponsored; (5) the "site" of the elective centers; (6) their mechanisms of recruitment; and (7) the possibility that science fiction and modern occultism serve as a foundation for a new institutional and moral order.

The first factor forces us to note a few general characteristics of modern, complex, and pluralistic societies. Modern occultists and science fiction fans are not overwhelmed by an incomprehensible environment to which they respond passively by developing various supernatural and superstitious belief systems. On the contrary, they are usually well-educated people, quite capable of coping with their complex environment. However, they do find themselves, by the very nature of their social position, within the midst of what Keniston (1969) calls "chronic change." Landsman (1972) notes that Western society is devoted and committed to the concepts of progress and change and is thus a future-oriented society. The division of labor, specialization, and differentiation does not enhance modern man's quest for harmony and completeness. It is in this light that the social upheavals experienced recently around the globe must be seen. Relevant here are the emergence of new communities—earlier the hippies, beatniks, and later the drug and "pop" subcultures—various youth movements, a multitude of religious (and social) movements, the student revolts in the 1960s, protest movements, civil rights movements, and mass tourism.

Furthermore, there are two links in this chronology of cultural beliefs in America that need more explication. The first is that much of the sixties counterculture reflected themes familiar in the occult and science fiction and other modern myths. These included rejection of materialism, attack on rationality and science, interest in Eastern philosophy, and revival of bohemianism. Thus, the subjects and the social movements discussed here are, in a way, an extension of a few aspects of the sixties. Second, the late sixties and early seventies witnessed the decomposition of the political part of the counterculture (i.e., the failure of the sixties optimism). This failure led to increased interest in the "self"—human growth, self-awareness movements, consumer issues—and to MacIntyre's claim (1981) that the modern world is characterized by total lack of moral consensus. Lasch (1979) gloomily describes the self-centered modern person: closed, atomistic, and vacuous. Marty (1981) indicates that even religion in the modern world becomes more individualized, and Peters (1980) supports this, claiming that religion may well become another "choice" commodity for consumer-oriented Western society. Berger (1979) notes that the modern world is saturated with what he calls "rational skepticism" and that people can choose a specific type of transcendance. However, such a choice—in itself—is both difficult to make and difficult to maintain. Choice always means implicit doubt, which might later erode the decision and adherence to a too specific system.[14]

This analysis is consistent with that presented by Berger and Luckman (1967) and Berger et al. (1973) in which they point out that in the modern world, construction of social realities is a very complicated process. This process has at least five very important functions. First of all, it helps the members of a social system interpret and understand their differential experiences. Second, it tells them how to behave in different situations and thus defines accepted norms of conduct. In this way, ideology can control behavior. Third, it prevents difficult existential questions from being raised and permits members to take for granted many aspects of their social and physical environment. Fourth, it makes certain aspects of one's world more salient than others. Fifth, constructions of social realities, much like religion and various other so-called secular ideologies, address themselves to the problem of meaning. Subjective definitions of reality are determined to a very large extent by objective social conditions. In this way, subjectivity is, in fact, determined by social objectivity. As Berger and Luckman put it, "The individual's *knowledge* of the world is socially derived and must be socially sustained" (1967, p. 66).

There can be no doubt that throughout history, religion has played a major role in both construction and maintenance of social realities and subjective universes. However, while from the individual point of view the functions of reality construction are objective, these same functions, from the societal point of view, are subjective. Therefore, all social realities have the essential element of consciousness that constitutes the individual's world view (Berger 1973). This world view, in modern society, is characterized by what Berger and Luckman term the "privatization of belief," meaning that all individuals have their own, private "religious universes" and, therefore, also their own "private realities," since they no longer depend so much on institutions or religion to provide much needed, ready-made, definitions of reality. The meaning of social complexity is also that each individual, within very short periods of time, moves from one social role to another—some complementary and some contradictory. The movement from one social role to another, and there are many such roles, also means that subjective interpretations and definitions of social realities also undergo many changes within short periods of time. Berger refers to this phenomenon as the "pluralization of social life-worlds": "This quest for more satisfactory private meanings

14. Robbins and Anthony (1981) review some of these choices.

may range from extramarital affairs to experiments with exotic religious sects" (1973, p.64).

Thus in a complex society, not only do we have different social groups that define reality in different, sometimes contradictory, ways (and who hold different world views), but we also have individuals possessing within themselves large arsenals of alternative realities and world views. This, obviously, creates not only a high level of social uncertainty but also much tension, because playing even a few roles could well mean contradictory performances. Thus, modern society is characterized by a multiplicity of "private universes" that define reality in numerous ways and enable the existence of Lasch's "self-centered" man.

This state of affairs has brought a few scholars to make comparisons between the mentality of the late Middle Ages and what Lasch calls the "waning of the sense of historical time" in modern societies. Lasch points out that as we approach the end of the twentieth century, a conviction that many other things are close to an end grows as well. The twentieth century has been characterized, among other things, by the Nazi holocaust, the threat of a nuclear winter and total annihilation, depletion of natural resources, and threats of ecological disaster. Thus, many twentieth-century people seem to share a keen sense of imminent doom. After the political turmoil of the sixties, expecially in the United States, many people retreated to purely personal preoccupations: psychic self-improvement, health food, jogging, and hedonism in its many varieties.

Nevertheless, the trend toward radical secularization, contrary to dire prognoses of men like Weber at the beginning of the century, does not dominate the late modern world. The contemporary era presents the curious spectacle of a world whose Judeo-Christian foundations have been thoroughly shaken, but rather than becoming an Eliotean wasteland, it swarms with a variety of competing soteriologies, promising salvation from nihilism in a wide variety of ways. These new directions cover an extremely broad spectrum—from various forms of new political radicalism, communitarianism, drug and rock subcultures, new religious sects, to renewed popularity of orthodox religion. They offer what could be called competing and alternative centers, suggesting various forms of change. Each of them, with varying degrees of intensity, offers its adherents a new way to recentralize their world. The recentering of one's world, even in its collective manifestation, is essentially a personal one—it is a quest for an elective center. Kavolis, when referring to postmodern, atomistic man, stated that the "decentralized personality" is one "in which no set of activities is perceived as particularly important for the maintaining of personal integrity and in which the functions of the personality are not arranged in a hierarchical pattern" (1970, p. 439). On the personal level, such decentralization is the major implication of radical secularization.

Most people are satisfied with a superficial involvement in the occult, with amateurish, perhaps even irregular, reading of horoscopes and science fiction or with mildly superstitious behavior. For them occultism and science fiction provide excellent entertainment, escapism, and plenty of intellectual stimulation. For others, who join cults or become full-time science fiction fans, a serious life-style change is introduced. This suggests that the real question is not "Who is attracted to what?" but "To what degree?"

Interviews I conducted in Israel from June through August 1982 with, among others, science fiction fans, Jews who had returned to orthodox Judaism, members of different cults (Scientology, Hare Krishna, Moonies, and some others), consumers of astrology journals, and palm readers indicate clearly that such people gravitate constantly among various centers, looking for "something." Furthermore, it is quite possible for some to become members of a specific, even overpowering, belief system and still retain older, noncongruent beliefs. For example, in one interview, a "returnee" to orthodox Judaism told us, to the apparent amazement of his guide (who was present throughout the interview), that he still believed in some of the "things" of the previous cult he belonged to (in this particular case, "Ananda Marga").

These interviews suggest that such people maintain a rather superficial level of interest (e.g., dabbling in the occult activities or science fiction fandom), then may gradually shift to more involved levels until they are actual participants in a cult or commune or are converted. Members can (and often do) gravitate from one occult group to another as well. Bird and Reimer's 1982 study corroborates this observation, which Greeley (1981) calls "religious musical chairs." Thus, the tension between personal decentralizaton—a reflection of a centerless world—and the quest for elective centers determines the basic dynamics of the various attempts at "recentering the world" and changing some, or all, of its aspects.

The second factor with which we are concerned is how far science fiction and the modern occult are consciously recognized as elective centers. In its most intense forms—for example, a satanic group or the Scientologists—the elective center is very explicit. It is somewhat less explicit if one's involvement is concentrated in the medium level of such activities as science fiction conventions, fan clubs, or spiritualism. The other possibility is to have an implicit elective center, that is, those centers that constitute quite vague common notions, uniting adherents into a rather diffuse subculture without real or explicit direction of orientation, attitude, and behavior. In their most popular and widespread form, science fiction, fantasy, and modern occultism are probably implicit. Most adherents read horoscopes, like to watch a science fiction movie, read a science fiction book, or even subscribe to journals. This superficial involvement provides them with an almost instant gratification, a clear and strong sense of the "beyond." In this way, most can have, even daily, a small and controllable excursion into a revitalizing elective center. This escape is necessarily limited in terms of time, ecology, and geography, and it is not unlike taking some psychoactive substances, like marijuana and alcohol, for leisure-time experiences and purposes.[15]

Third, both science fiction and the modern occult can provide different degrees of structure for their adherents. When one joins such groups as the Church of All Worlds, LaVey's church of the devil, one obviously has to subjugate one's whole life and self to a new, rigid, and comprehensive structure. This, however, is hardly the typical case. The terms that best describe the structure introduced by both science fiction and modern occultism are harmony and liminality. While occupying oneself with science fiction or occultism is certainly considered somewhat deviant, the behavior still possesses some legitimacy, for it represents the pursuit of desires and needs through the social order, which after all, provides and nourishes science fiction and occultism. Dabbling in such deviant activities will therefore usually not be met with extreme resistance, provided that one does not get drawn in too deeply. On the most popular, widespread level of the phenomena, harmony exists between the demands of the social order and individual needs and desires as they find expression in transitory, controlled interest in science fiction and occultism. The sense of awe and bewilderment experienced repeatedly in science fiction and occultism necessarily brings one very close to what O'Dea (1966) called existential "breaking points," or to a liminal situation, that is, a state of existential transit (Turner 1977). It becomes impossible to encounter either science fiction or occultism and remain indifferent to them, unless one is well shielded by some other strong belief. While in most

15. In testimony (August 16, 1982) before the Israeli government interministerial committee on cults in Israel, a representative of the kibbutz movement in the country indicated that the representation of youth from kibbutzim in cults is way beyond their relative demographical proportion in Israeli society. Furthermore, he indicated that almost all of the young "kibbutzniks" who are attracted to cults regularly go through a "route" starting with drug abuse (usually hashish), and leading to cults. That is, they are engaged in an active search for alternative centers.

cases, these situations are short lived, the tremendously large world of science fiction, fantasy, and occultism enables anyone to find in them his own private sphere and to delve more intensely into it, if he so wishes.

Fourth, we have to examine the extent to which science fiction and the modern occult emerge spontaneously out of the common quest of individuals or are sponsored by various entrepreneurs who initiate and build them up, out of spiritual or commercial motives. Clearly, cults and more involved consumers of science fiction and the occult are driven by both spiritual and commercial motives. However, for the most popular level of these phenomena, the argument is more complex. Let us take science fiction first. That there has been increased popular interest in and demand for science fiction since the early 1970s can hardly be debated. This need translated itself into two developments. First, tens—and perhaps hundreds—of science fiction fan clubs sprang up like mushrooms after the rain. The creation of these fan clubs, their fanzines, specialized jargon, and interests were, no doubt, a spontaneous development of the common quest of individuals who shared similar views and interests and who wanted to spend time together. These fans not only volunteered time and effort toward creating extensive personal networks connected by news-letters and more paraphernalia, but organized numerous conventions, including the annual World Science Fiction Convention. Second, because the field comprises authors, writers, artists, organizers, the movie indus-try, tourism (for conventions), and publishers, we find that it has many deeply rooted commercial interests. Publishers of science fiction books and magazines have high stakes in this field, and they are usually more than willing to contribute support and organize various activities (includ-ing the conventions and fan clubs). In a sense, therefore, the need for more activity in science fiction was met on the one hand through spon-taneous activity by fans and, on the other, by the sponsorship of various agencies and institutions who have real, undeniable, commercial in-terests in this area.[16]

The modern occult scene presents a similar panorama. There too, spontaneous organizations of clubs reflected individual demands. However, it seems that the scope and intensity of activities in these clubs have always been much lower than in science fiction. Therefore, spon-sorship by commercial firms, agencies, and interests is clearer and stronger here. There are specialized stores, magazines, and books people can buy to "get into the scene." Most prominent, of course, is astrology.

16. The USSR seems to support science fiction at least in part because it is felt that it encourages young people to get into technological careers (personal communication with Professor Joe De Bolt, June 1982).

Our fifth concern is the "site" of the elective center: in the past, the future, outside or inside the individual or society. Clearly much of the modern revival of the occult, if not all of it, looks for its origins in the past, attempting to establish a link with times and places where magic "really" worked (e.g., the myth of Atlantis). In this way, many occult aficionados boast of having "secret" ancient knowledge. Many techniques utilized in various modern activities are said to be remnants, or direct descendants, of ancient knowledge. Science fiction, clearly, is much more future oriented. It thrives on the question of "what if," and some of the speculative "breakthroughs" described in it are really stunning. There are, however, two streams within science fiction that constitute exceptions. The first deals with so-called alternate histories. In these stories, authors send their heroes back in history to prevent certain events or to act in such a fashion as to change (or prevent change of) history as we know it. For example in her book *Shadow of Earth*, Phyllis Einstein assumed that in 1588 the Spanish Armada won the battle against the English fleet, conquered England, and assured Spain's domination of the world for centuries. Such stories (see Hacker and Chamberlain 1981 for an exhaustive survey) blur the distinction between past and future. The other stream is fantasy. While many fantasies take place, conveniently, in "alternate realities," not all do, and some of the adventures take place in Earth's past (e.g., some of Moorcock's stories).

Both science fiction and occultism are more private, oriented toward an inward experience, than public. A regular excursion into an alternate reality for a specified period of time is probably what a large part of the "science fiction experience" is all about: a controlled encounter with the ultimate. This, basically, is an internal quest through a fascinating, enchanted, and marvelous world (or, if you like, to the end of the time and the universe). In a sense, the science fiction experience is a mystical one; it puts romanticism back into cold technology.

Occultism, in some ways, is similar. On the popular level of reading one's horoscope or a book or journal, the occult experience greatly resembles the science fiction experience. What is different are encounters with such "real life" phenomena as ghosts, possession, reincarnation, trances, seances, automatic writing, and the like, which are usually not found in science fiction. In this sense, occult-related phenomena can have a deeper, more pervasive experiential impact on an observer than science fiction.

It seems that in both occult and science fiction, the establishment of communes or satanist cults provide examples of attempts to go beyond modern society to new forms of moral order. However, it is important to note that there is a difference in the basic ethos of these two alternative centers. The occult (and in a similar fashion, fantasy as well) presents adherents with alternative rationality, life styles, belief systems, in many cases very different from conventional beliefs of modern pluralistic, moral orders. One of the major points in this regard is the fact that the occult reintroduces enchantment, mysticism, and romanticism into one's world view. In this sense, it is truly "outside" modern society. Science fiction, on the other hand, takes various elements of modern society, or assumed and hypothetical technologies, and makes an extrapolation. In this sense, it presents various scenarios of "What if?" While it too falls outside modern society, in a strange fashion it is also an extension of it.

The sixth of our seven issues involves mechanisms of attraction and recruitment to these elective centers. The amount of attraction a specific alternative center has for any person depends on many factors: the needs and personality of the decentralized individual, the type of demands and benefits the center has and offers. From my interviews with cult members and science fiction and occult fans, it appears that many of them move from one alternative center to another. The reasons for these moves are very different, and in some cases, the move itself becomes the pattern. The choice of a center seems to indicate more the level of commitment one wishes to make than the specific content of that center. For example, many adherents of EMIN and Scientology in Israel seem also to have been science fiction fans and highly interested in the occult as well.

At the popular level, it is easy to get into both the occult and science fiction—all one has to do is enter a bookstore, kiosk, or even take a course in high school, a university, or local community center on these topics. These entries are widespread and easily available. Getting more involved, however, demands more skill and effort. To plug into the vast network of science fiction fans, reading a book or watching a movie will not suffice. As a minimum, one needs to buy or subscribe to a science fiction journal or magazine. There, references can be found to local and national fan clubs, times and places of meetings and conventions. Attending meetings opens the way for deeper involvement. Almost the same applies to occult-related activities. Other mechanisms include simple advertisements in local newspapers and in the electronic media. In the case of communes or cults, other patterns emerge. Probably the most important mechanism is one described by Stark and Bainbridge 1980: the recruitment through personal networks on the one hand and, on the other, the cult or commune's ability to give significant direct rewards to new members, not only in spiritual terms, but also in such earthly terms as food, shelter, clothing, and possibly a career and a sense of purpose.

Finally, one has to examine the possibility that both science fiction and modern occultism will serve as foundations for a new institutional and moral order. It is noteworthy that Shepherd (1972), Tiryakian (1972), Heirich (1976), and Collins (1977) have all suggested that the occult can provide a fertile "seed bed" for new ideas in both science and society at large, thus generating a process of social change.[17] Obviously such groups as the Church of all Worlds, EMIN, satanists, and Scientologists aim at transforming the world and creating a new system. Its many small-scale organizations attest to the fact that the occult can be an important source for personal and social change. Ben David (1971), Rattansi (1972), and Kirsch (1978) have pointed out that the scientific revolution itself developed out of many Renaissance occult practices. Under what conditions do modern transformative efforts develop? There are groups that demand a total change in life style, communal life, various restrictions of food, sex, and entertainment. They require that members disconnect themselves from their families, friends, original community reference groups and nationalities. One relinquishes control over one's private life in return for a career and an alternative vision. Such groups have as explicit goals the recruitment and total conversion of as many members as possible. They are usually international in nature and profess a messianic ideology. In general, the science fiction and modern occult subcultures do not fit this description. For most people, being part of the science fiction or occult subculture, even at a relatively high degree of involvement, means the enjoyment of an alternative center toward which they can orient themselves whenever they so wish, with very little risk to their otherwise usual and conformist life styles.

When these subcultures do have an institutional focus, it is usually close to one of their areas of interest. For example, science fiction fans like to think of themselves as supporters of space exploration programs. Many modern occultists support research into astrology, parapsychology, reincarnation, and the like. Although the nature of these subcultures is such that hardly any type of institution building takes place, there are two exceptions. The first consists of groups or movements, such as Scientology with many institutions, functioning as a bureaucratic church. The second exception includes the organizers and founders of fan clubs, conventions, study centers, associations, and groups dedicated to the dispersing of occult or science fiction ideas.

Most of these groups, however, do not aim at transforming the world,

17. Jorgensen and Jorgensen (1982) suggested that the occult did not represent a serious challenge to science or religion. However, their study was based on a rather limited type of occult activity—tarot—and this particular conclusion, I feel, should be taken with caution.

and the institutions built by them are geared toward the needs of their members. Thus, weak as they are, the existence of these institutions affect recruitment positively and makes the attachment of older members more meaningful. They give members a sense of the history of the elective center (which is strongly emphasized in both science fiction fandom and in occult movements) and therefore strengthens their sense of belonging and of purpose.

The Content and Meaning of the Phenomena

Traditionally, it has always been religion's role to help man cope with difficult existential problems. It is every religion's function to explain the uncertainty of life, man's inability to exercise full control over his environment, and the fact that goods, values, and services are scarce. Furthermore, religions provide meaning, a basis for community, establish contact with the sacred, and prescribe conduct norms (O'Dea 1966; Greeley 1970a,b). Viewed in this light, Weber's suggestion about the demystification (and possible secularization) of the world becomes very problematic (Bell 1977). With the exception of only of few, almost all sociologists have predicted the disappearance of religion, citing "secularization" as the phenomenon's strongest empirical indicator. What I wish to argue here is that "religion," in the classical, conservative connotation of the term (Christianity, Judaism), while doomed to a problematic existence in the future, cannot be forced to disappear. Despite tremendous technological progress and a changing environment, which threaten "classical" religions by the mere fact that they render the existential, ready-made answers of those religions almost useless, the problems that religion once addressed must still be met. Of these, the need for transcendental experience and contact with the beyond are perhaps the most pressing. Sapir (1960) suggested that mankind copes with a hostile and indifferent environment through an identification with "what can never be known," and thus the experience of the sacred, and of the "beyond," can be interpreted as an efficient tool protecting the human consciousness. In this sense, religion cannot "disappear"; particular religious forms might, but not the ideological structure that answers various existential problems. "Religion," as a system of related ideas dealing with basic human needs, will always remain.

This brings us to an interesting and important connection between modern occultism and neopaganism on the one hand and science fiction and fantasy on the other hand. Adler (1979, pp. 24–38) notes that all neopagans and modern occultists agree about three main themes: (1) Animism, implying a reality in which all things are imbued with vitality; (2) Pantheism, a world view that emphasizes that divinity cannot be separated from nature and is always part of it; (3) Polytheism, an attitude and perspective much broader than religion. This third view emphasizes that reality is multifaceted, complex, and heterogeneous and that there are many deities, or spirits, controlling or influencing various aspects of reality. It necessarily implies the possible existence of parallel universes, of humans' potential ability to maintain a dialogue with various deities and even to force certain deities to comply with specific human wishes. A modern occultist view of the world also involves some form of control over certain aspects of that world. For science fiction and fantasy fans, the concepts described above, and ideas about "multiple realities," "alternative worlds," and "parallel universes" in particular, are of central importance.

That such ideas flourish in modern society can hardly surprise us. A society such as ours has a strong commitment, almost a religious one, to the existence of a negotiated, multidefinitional approach to social reality. Thus, almost by definition, a pluralistic society provides fertile soil for the growth and dispersion of neopagan, occult, science fiction, and fantasy cults and groups. The characteristics of the specific population attracted to such phenomena support this conclusion. They are usually young, educated, sophisticated people in large urban areas who are highly exposed to multiple definitions of reality. Furthermore, the neopagan, occult, or fantasy world view emphasizes the enchanted quality of the "parallel universe." One need only read Silas's *The Panoramic Egg*, Pratt and de Camp's *The Compleat Enchanter*, Ann MacCaffrey's *World of Pern* (The Dragonriders of Pern series), or Heinlein's *Glory Road*, to mention only a few, to realize how fantastic are the worlds described there. The pagan did not need to create an enchanted world, he lived in one. Modern people, however, live in a world that is totally disenchanted, and thus to imagine an enchanted parallel universe (not to mention actually spending some time in one every now and then) can become an irresistible prospect. This hypothesis also entails the observation that many people shift their commitment and interest from various neopagan activities to science fiction and fantasy and vice-versa.

In recent years, social scientists have witnessed various phenomena aimed at meeting some of the needs previously met by "classical" religion. For example, the drug subculture (especially hallucinogenic use) has been interpreted as an attempt to get in touch with the transcendental (Timothy Leary—the "LSD prophet"—perhaps best exemplifies this). The quest for community had been met by hundreds of quasi-religious and secular settlements; meaning has often been found through involve-

ment in business, science, and politics. However, none of these attempts
give holistic answers similar to those provided by traditional religion.
What traditional religions apparently lack is the flexibility to cope with
what Keniston termed "chronic change." Specific answers formulated
hundreds of years ago cannot sufficiently answer the problems and needs
of today. Two examples that come to mind are the 1969 moon landing and
advances in genetic engineering. These tremendous technological
achievements challenge the old religious idea of modesty before the
creator. The moon conquest implies that there is no limit to what the
human race can do. Genetic engineering could very well mean that the
human race will actually create totally new forms of life. In strictly
orthodox religious terms, this idea is sheer blasphemy. Other, perhaps
less philosophical, examples, include the Catholic church's attempts to
cope with birth control, the agonies that the state of Israel must face while
attempting to reconcile religious demands with modern life (and technology), and the orthodox Islamic outcry against modernization in Iran. The
scientific revolution of this century has generated and reinforced other
problematic trends too. Along with it came an unprecedented stress on
personal choice and the fashioning of individualistic lifestyles. Urbanization and frequent moves from one dwelling place to another have helped
to break the hold of traditional religion on its constituents.

Modern Americans, especially the well-educated and young, seek
immediate solutions to existential problems. This appears to derive more
from popular expectations of science and technology than it does from
traditional religion, with the latter's emphasis on the proper "living of
life" in hope of divine intercession. Furthermore, the crisis we experience
is, not only "religious" by nature, but scientific as well. In past decades,
especially during the 1940s and 1950s, Western science and the scientific
establishment believed they had answers to all questions, be they technical or social , and encompassed all aspects of human existence in so-called
scientific rationality. This pretension was shattered (see Holton and
Morison 1979) during the 1960s and 1970s as, for example, various
ecological groups pointed out some of the disastrous effects of industrialization and advanced technologies and as it became increasingly clear
that science is incapable of solving existential dilemmas. The modern
crisis, then, is science's inability to provide answers to all questions and to
satisfactorily relate to issues that go far beyond its range.

In sum: (1) Mankind must cope with fundamental existential problems; (2) both traditional religion and the scientific community fail to
cope with these problems; and (3) the reason for this failure is rapid
social change, which is anchored in various technological innovations.

How can we understand the occult explosion against this background? I maintain that the occult and science fiction are capable of answering fundamental existential problems and, moreover, that nothing else apart from them is capable, at the moment, of doing that, for the specific population they attract.

The occult explosion is embedded in an eclectic belief system. Its various technologies spring from a quasi-scientific conceptualization of our cosmos and supposedly allow human adherents the power of enlisting different deities (or forces) to do things for them. Humans, in this sense, are not "puppets" of the devil; rather, they can use supernatural powers to benefit both the world and themselves. Alas, the kind of "science" professed by these occultists is always antithetical to positivistic science. It uses PSI powers, unmeasurable results, nonempirical means, irreproducible experiments. The new occultists seek solutions for ancient existential problems by resorting to ancient legends, alternative universes, and magic. They look for the transcendental, for community, for meaning, and they find them in science fiction, in witchcraft, in myth.

This is no coincidence. In many cases, the new wave presents a necessary alternative to science and conventional religion. Contrary to some traditional societies, who fear its subversive potential, Western societies put few restrictions on the accumulation and diffusion of various types of knowledge. In modern societies, there is a growing socioeconomic differentiation within what Shils calls their centers and periphery. This development is connected to changed relations between different types of rationality in modern society. As Eisenstadt posited (1971), perhaps the major transformation accompanying modernity was the growing secularization of the centers, and "opening up" of their contents, and consequently, a growing interpenetration and interdependence between centers and periphery. The creation of numerous "elective centers" only continues this process. Thus, modern societies are continuously faced first with the basic problem of how to redefine cultural tradition and then with how to legitimate it. The development of science and technology plays a crucial role in these complex processes as their incorporation into modern societies has its effect on the formation and mastery of the continously expanding cultural and social orders (Eisenstadt 1971, pp. 39, 41).

Science fiction and modern occultism present a variety of deviant belief systems, in the form of elective centers. The degree to which one chooses to immerse oneself in any of these elective centers is totally up to one's wishes. The young, educated, and sophisticated persons who are the zealots of these social phenomena face fundamental existential problems, in part because they are at the forefront of various social-technological innovations. Traditional religion's failure to cope successfully with their questions, especially in large urban centers where social change and technological innovations are so visible, has also not escaped their attention. It is no coincidence that the science fiction boom and the occult explosion generally characterize larger cities, where there are frequent attempts to compare contemporary "scientific" phenomena with phenomena of a "cosmic" nature. The believers hide their cosmologies behind a quasi-scientific cloak, using an "alternative" scientific paradigm—science fiction. This phenomenon is unique in history. It constitutes the abuse of Western positivistic science, the rediscovery of ancient "scientific" paradigms, and the dependence on an eclectic belief system.

The most commonly heard criticism of science fiction literature is that it lacks multidimensional characterization, that the description of its heroes is shallow, and that the real hero of the genre is technology. Considering that science fiction is a reflection of a future oriented society, committed and devoted to change, then it stands to reason that the real societal hero is change, the future, technology, and not the human factor. The "occult explosion" also represents the more individualistic search for immediate solutions to problems—perhaps best exemplified by the modern-day ethos of "How to . . . in ten easy lessons"—it is fostered by the very processes of differentiation and specialization that have been overwhelming traditional religion. The world today is characterized by supremacy of technology, science, empricism, but it also leaves the individual perplexed. The scientification of the world does not provide him with essential answers to his existential problems. Reactions to this scientification thus present antiscientific ideas as an alternative vision. The reaction is widespread both because science's ability to answer fundamental problems (psychiatry, perhaps, being the sole exception) has been proved false and because traditional religions find themselves facing problems with which they cannot cope.[18]

In this sense, the occult movement definitely works against what Weber called the "demystification" of the world. We have seen the rise of the modern occult, science fiction, and modern myths against the back-

18. Science fiction has been used, more than once, to post alarming warnings about the future. For example, the dangers of genetic engineering, an all-out nuclear war, depletion of natural resources, and environmental abuse have all been portrayed in science fiction. We have even been warned of social dangers by science fiction, for example, the possibility of an irreversible totalitarian regime, of what could happen if a specific age group gained societal control or if society allowed regular use of mind altering drugs. Thus, Sontag (1967) argued that science fiction is a screen on which modernity projects its deepest fears. However, while these alarmist themes were very salient in the 1960s, they diminished significantly in the 1970s and are certainly not a major characteristic of science fiction today.

ground of the demise and failure of previous movements to cope with this problem. Eisenstadt (1971) comments that a major theme of protest that develops in modern society is the "antirational" and the creation of tendencies of widespread antinomianism. He specifically mentions that this type of protest is not limited to a small, closed intellectual group, but that it is commonplace and widespread among novices and aspirants to intellectual status. The fact that modern occultists are willing to encounter spirits, demons, possession, or poltergeists in their pursuit of the unknown should not really surprise us. In contrast to medieval demonologists, they do not shy away from supernatural phenomena. They believe in them, want to prove their existence, and most important of all, to control them. Modern occultism offers something traditional religion does not have—an alternative scientific paradigm coupled with a "scientifically" controllable belief system.[19]

Modern science fiction no longer describes the old 1950s hero from Earth who somehow finds himself in an alien world. Rather, authors imagine alternative universes and galaxies where unknown laws of nature and superadvanced technologies prevail. Asimov's famous trilogy, Larry Niven's "known" universe, Robert Silverberg's worlds, Frank Herbert's *Dune* series, and others have all brought the art of "creating" new universes (even to the small details of geography, weather, social customs, countries and regimes) almost to perfection. Eliade's note that "the discovery that your life is related to astral phenomena does confer a new meaning on your existence. . . . the horoscope shows how you are related to the universe" exemplifies the point (1976, p. 61), because our culture worlds away from any order of cosmic unity (Landsman 1972, p. 991).

The growth and spread of the modern occult and of science fiction should be taken as an indication of a cultural-institutional vacuum. Moreover, these deviant elective centers should not be thought of as being either esoteric or marginal, as they are associated with major, macrosociological processes: the diffusion of knowledge from the centers to the periphery (and the growing interdependence of the centers and the periphery) and the creation of existential needs out of social change. The vacuum is precisely the condition that enables the coexistence of both science and religion with that which is neither. In a sense, the search for the beyond is a manifestation of what Wilson (1979) called "the return of the sacred." The adherents of the occult and of science fiction seek answers that can integrate both science and religion. It is thus my suggestion that science fiction and the modern occult as elective centers, can

19. This is not a rerun of older arguments of science versus religion (e.g., White 1913; Eister 1978) but a new and unique blend.

provide a meaningful, attractive, and controllable scientific-religious paradigm. Furthermore, by participating in these deviant elective centers, adherents gain, not only a sense of the transcendental, but also a deeper, more powerful understanding of their individuality within the complex collectivity of modern society (Lynch 1979).

The phenomena discussed above constitute an attempt, mostly on the part of young people, to introduce an element of change into a complex society, to refocus and recenter the world. Although science fiction and the occult are main ingredients in this recentering, they are not the only ones. Such social phenomena as drugs, deviant cults, Eastern-inspired religions (Rice 1980) also play a crucial role. These various social movements clearly provide meaning for the two Durkheimian views. They are reactions to change, and they also create much needed flexibility and point the way for possible social chnages, although the impact of science fiction and the modern occult on policy, science, and religion is not very clear at the moment. However, the personal impact of such phenomena in terms of creating identities and sustaining specific world views is much more marked. It is clear that the science fiction subculture supports what it feels is the culture of the future or, alternatively, tries to warn against some of the dangers in technology and thus supports specific social changes. In many respects, modern occultism resembles the turmoil of the prescientific period during the Renaissance. Thus, it is quite possible that the modern revival of the occult is a necessary byproduct of the development of new forms of science and theology.

Thus, both the occult and science fiction serve in a lengthy process of social change and the redefinition of moral, social, scientific, and religious boundaries. On the other hand, in their reactions to deviant centers, both institutional and personal, religion and science tend to reinforce their moral boundaries. The scientific and religious literature devoted entirely to debunking various occult claims is abundant testimony. Nevertheless, the reactions to these phenomena provide both the scientific and religious community with a golden opportunity for self-reflection. Both communities use this opportunity quite effectively. In our terminology, the revival of science fiction, fantasy, and the occult serves both the adherents and the opponents for recentering their own worldviews.

Concluding Discussion

We have documented the revival of modern occultism and science fiction and interpreted this phenomenon along three lines. First, the timing of

the phenomenon can be explained by using the concept of recentralization. Our century has been characterized by a rapid process of social
change, a scientification of the world, which is anchored in, and stems
from, various scientific-technological innovations. This rapid change creates many fundamental problems for modern man for which the old
solutions posed by traditional religions are clearly inadequate. The revival of the modern occult, science fiction, and fantasy can be understood
as an attempt to recenter the world, find new meaning and order in what
otherwise seems to be meaningless. This analysis is strengthened by
Berger and Luckman's 1967 theory of the "privatization of belief," which
suggests that in modern society each individual has his own private
"religious universe" and therefore also his own "private reality" since
individuals no longer depend so much on institutions and religions to
provide definitions of reality. Berger (1973) feels that these phenomena
can be described as a "pluralization of social life worlds" (p. 64). Thus,
the complex and pluralized matrix of modern society enables its members
to actively search for "privatized beliefs and realities." The quest for
alternative centers and actors' efforts to recentralize their world views
and redefine boundaries are essential and vital phenomena in such
societies.

The second theoretical concept that can be of help in this analysis is the
concept of revitalization. Wallace (1966), who suggested the term, had in
mind religiously-oriented movements, aimed at creating a more satis-
fying culture. He points out that revitalization movements find clear
expression in various rituals and function as a source of cultural diversity.
Without them, cultures are apt to disintegrate, providing no outlet for
identityless (or decentralized) people and no vehicle for social change.
Both science fiction and fantasy and the modern occult provide not only
elective centers but essential and cherished individual revitalization experiences as well. Although they have the potential to create an all-
embracing movement of social change, it seems that both types of elective centers—at their present levels of popularity—are oriented more
toward individual inward experiences and less toward large-scale
changes.

The second question we had regards the specific content of the phenomenon—Why the occult and science fiction? The revival of these areas
is a unique blend of science, technology, and religion. It competes with
both Western positivistic science and traditional religion. The revival can
be seen as a reaction to the contradictions of the scientification process of
the world, on the one hand, and as a response to the lack of scientific and
religious answers to the problems created by this process on the other.

Our third question relates to the meaning of the observed phenomena. I maintain that the revival of the occult and science fiction constitutes a search for the beyond, for a universal pattern, by educated young people in large urban centers. The revival involves a search for scientifically controlled and explained involvement. This search is reinforced by the existence of a multitude of "individual universes" within the population and by societal acceptance and legitimation of these privatized world views.

The occult and science fiction challenge both science and religion, suggesting new ways to recenter the world. We must thus assess how successful these challenges will become. A few factors have to be considered. First, although the occult and science fiction represent "antimystification" trends, their search for the beyond, requires encounters with supernatural phenomena. Above all, the modern occultist wants to control such phenomena. This aspiration in essence further demystifies the occult. Someone who looks for the mystic, the beyond should, at least theoretically, not want to control it. Once full control is achieved, the phenomenon stops being magic and becomes science, pure and simple. The paradox here is that while the modern occultist seeks the novel, the irreproducible, the genuine supernatural experience and knowledge, the scientific means used to achieve this goal will eventually render the solution useless and defeat its original purpose.

Second, together with the revival of the occult and science fiction, social scientists have observed other social movements that could be thought of as presenting alternative centers (see, e.g., Glock and Bellah 1976). The next question is thus "What type of people choose what type of elective center." Unfortunately, we don't have sufficient data to answer this question.

Taking into consideration all these factors, we must conclude that these deviant subcultures are here to stay. Certainly the specific needs they meet will continue to exist. The shape and style of the answers to these needs cannot be specifically delineated, for they will grow out of future social contexts, as yet unknown. No doubt, however, that they will include traditional religions, perhaps remnants of the occult revival, other Eastern inspired belief systems, and possibly, a religious orientation Bell describes as "a return to some mythic and mystical modes of thought" (1977, p. 445). The future of science fiction and fantasy is, perhaps, easier to predict. There, at least, part of the revival is based on commercial considerations and the question simply is, How many people can afford, for how long, to support the science fiction industry. It is very likely that in the near future the commercial boom in science fiction will go down, but it will certainly remain on a much higher level than its pre-1970 level. While both science fiction and the occult are here to stay, they will no doubt experience a less intensive existence and popularity in the future than today.

One of the major points of this section has been that the occult and science fiction challenge both traditional religion and science. Modern occultists and science fiction fans search for a "scientific" base for their claims. They are interested not only in problems of credibility but present what they feel is an alternative scientific paradigm. The question of the viability and validity of their claims becomes a crucial one. Neither, I feel, are very high. Essentially, the problem for the occult is whether it really works, whether it produces desired effects. From various sources, it appears that it generally lacks strong empirical influence, that is, one that can be measured and replicated. Mostly, the occult and science fiction affect social definitions of reality and thus, no doubt, human behavior. Nevertheless, many scientific disciplines and traditional religions are faced with attempts to break old boundaries. The occult and science fiction make the borderline between science, religion, and magic obscure, and with the emergence of "speculative science," the border becomes almost nonexistent, for it itself is under attack. It is well worth stressing that while science's core activities solve intellectual and some-times practical problems, its margin may answer profound spiritual needs. These needs seem to be whetted rather than satisfied by marginal (or deviant) science, which makes even more fertile the grounds of various deviant belief systems and practices. The challenge of the occult and of science fiction to science certainly deserves a more thorough discussion. The next chapter of the book is devoted to the problem of "deviant sciences," and there this specific question—together with some others—will be examined.

4

DEVIANT SCIENCES

Introduction

In chapter 3, we saw that both the occult and science fiction challenge science and suggest their own "scientific" concepts. Science fiction even has a name for this: "speculative science." *Omni,* the most successful science fiction journal of the last decade, is almost entirely devoted to so-called scientific speculations. The challenge to science must be viewed within the more general context of change, flexibility, and stability in the field. The major thrust of this chapter is to illustrate and analyze "deviant sciences." I suggest that what is (and what is not) considered "deviant science" (that is, the demarcation problem in science) is a relative decision and that the concept and phenomenon of deviant sciences are an important way (however, not the only one) to interpret and understand change and stability in the boundaries of science. Furthermore, some so-called deviant sciences are intimately linked with the occult revival.

A deviant science is a science that by virtue of its hypotheses or methodology, is regarded by the relevant scientific establishment as deviant. Deviant sciences usually have a statement to make about the "true" nature of the world. Thus, they challenge orthodox science regarding the very nature of the scientific endeavor. In principle, such claims can shatter conventional theory or methodology or both, so we can expect the relevant scientific community to take such attempts seriously and fight them. This resistance can assume many forms, from deviantization of "deviant" researchers to public denouncement of a whole approach. In order to understand and to illustrate these ideas and processes in detail, we have to understand first the nature of science itself and second the nature of change in science.

Science: A Brief Overview

To attempt a brief characterization of science is truly presumptuous, and I do not pretend to exhaust the subject, neither substantively or historically (for a short review on the sociology of science, see Collins 1983). It must suffice to outline the main points relevant to our discussion.

Truzzi (1979) pointed out that how science is to be defined has been the focal point of many controversies. Truzzi himself distinguished between the social institution called "science" and the basic method of science. By accepting this distinction, scientific knowledge becomes defined not so much by its content as by its form. Dolby suggested that "the most reliable immediate indication of what is scientific is provided by the mature judgment of the relevant expert scientists. . . . Orthodox science is that which commands the approval of all the leading scientific experts of the time" (1979, pp. 10–11). In other words, what is (and what is not) science is determined by the scientific elite. A definition of something as scientific always involves a social evaluation. Zuckerman (1977) chose to focus her definition on the normative structure in science. She distinguished between two classes of analytically separable norms: the cognitive (technical) norms and methodologies, which specify what should be studied, and the moral norms, which specify what the attitudes and behavior of scientists should be in relations to one another.

Science appeared and developed in Europe from about the fifteenth century and became an accepted profession there in the late nineteenth century. There are many sciences: pure and abstract, experimental, applied, and industrial, and scientists work sometimes alone and sometimes in groups on large or small projects. Because it is heterogeneous, it is difficult to define science precisely. The debate is aggravated when comparisons are made between sciences such as biology, mathematics, physics, sociology, history, and literature. Are all these "scientific" in the same sense? It has therefore become easier to discuss the goals of science than its nature. Indeed Merton provides us with a definition that seems to be acceptable to almost all scholars (1968, p. 606). He states that "the institutional goal of science is the extension of certified knowledge" about the natural world. Science aims to discover something true and valid about the world. This means that two important processes take place in science: first, there is a social process that "certifies" knowledge; second, there is a cognitive process that aims to discover, or create, new knowledge. There can be a contradiction between these two processes. Producing new knowledge can counteract the social process of certification; it can especially challenge old certified knowledge. Thus, innovations in science can be perceived as deviant.

Science and Puzzles

In science, the problem of change and its converse, stability, is a major issue for both sociologists and philosophers of science. Although this book cannot do the subject full justice, a brief exposition is in order. Scientific explanations, be they historical, descriptive, or functional, share a common psychological characteristic. They reduce, solve, or eliminate what was previously regarded as a riddle or puzzle. However, questions still remain: What is acceptable as a scientific explanation? What makes one explanation better than another? The philosophy of science has dealt extensively with these types of questions and has suggested numerous formulas.

For our discussion, it is important to note two things. First, not all phenomena evoke puzzlement, but if one does turn one's attention to the "obvious," one can make some very important discoveries. For example, in order to understand basic cosmological problems, one must ask the obvious question of why the sky is dark at night (known as "Olbers' paradox"). The response is not that the sun is shining on the other side of the earth. The reason that the night sky is dark could be due either to the fact that there is not enough energy in the universe to light up the night sky or to the fact that because the universe expands, light from distant galaxies is redshifted and thus its contribution to the night sky brightness is diminished (Harrison 1980, Silk 1981). Basically, it appears that the modern solution to Olber's paradox lies in the big bang cosmology. The simple observation that the night sky is dark, which for most people does not cause any perplexity, can lead to important and insightful ideas about the nature of the universe. Thus, the type of questions we ask ourselves about our social and physical environment and the type of events that cause wonder and curiosity are anchored in our social definitions of reality.

Second, explanations that demystify something will, or will not, be accepted depending on the world view of the individual within the specific cultural matrix that developed and supported that worldview. For example, in the late Middle Ages and the Renaissance, a sense of wonder and awe was created by the sun, stars, and moon, and their movements were explained by the theory that the earth was the center of the universe. Witchcraft, astrology, and alchemy were also accepted as valid explanations for a variety of phenomena. Kuhn offers the following rule of thumb for acceptance or rejection of explanations: "When reading the works of an important thinker, look first for the apparent absurdities in the text and ask yourself how a sensible person could have written them" (1972, p. xii).

What makes something more or less of an absurdity is, of course, determined by general world views. For most scientists, the theories of "ancient astronauts" fostered by Däniken constitute an "apparent absurdity." The same is true concerning areas such as astrology, Velikovsky's theories, ESP, and pyramidology. During the nineteenth century in Germany, Rechenback publicized the phenomenon of Od (after the deity Odin). Od was supposedly present in either positive or negative forms, and there were people believed to be sensitive to it who could see it flow from the fingertips. In the 1950s in the United States, Reich suggested that living cells were made of "bions," pulsating units of "orgone" energy (Goran 1979; Gardner 1957). Likewise, do current constructs such as black holes, quarks, and tachyons make "sense"?[1]

Change in Science

The way that the development of science has been portrayed leaves the strong impression that there is some objective truth "out there" and that science's major effort is to find, to describe, and to analyze it. Plato's famous allegory of the cave perhaps best exemplifies this conception of knowledge. Liberally paraphrased, Plato describes a cave in which people labor for extended periods. They are born in the cave and they die there. They do not really know what goes on in the outside world, but they can see that the intensity of the light changes. They perceive shadows, they feel variations in temperature, and they hear sounds. From this, they try to construct a model of the "real" world outside the cave. For Plato, the concrete world that we research is nothing but a reflection of another real, unchanging, and eternal reality. Indeed this metaphor seems to fit scientific research and innovations after the mid nineteenth century, and it also seems applicable to Maxwell's development of the theory of electromagnetic fields in the 1860s.

The view that there is something eternally true "out there" that can only be experienced indirectly is an essential ingredient of orthodox positivism. This is reflected not only in the natural sciences but in the social sciences as well. Freud's theories and Durkheim's measurements of

1. A quark is one of several types of hypothetical subatomic particles. A tachyon is a hypothetical particle that always travels at a speed greater than that of light (Feinberg 1978, pp. 278–79).

suicide rates are merely two examples of this view, which is reminiscent of religious or transcendental world views, which also assume that there is an eternal truth. The Mertonian concept that science seeks "certified knowledge" is easy to understand in this framework because it implies implicitly that there is "something" there that can and perhaps should be certified. However, since explanations are embedded within a more general world view, it becomes clear that science itself may become a belief system. Thus, acceptance or rejection of specific hypotheses and data and the existence of scientific controversies are areas that are difficult to research because the meaning of any explanation is doomed to be problematic (Barnes 1977). The description of science as a belief system necessarily brings us to Kuhn.

The Kuhnian Conception of Change

The orthodox view portrays the sciences as developing in a linear and progressive manner, accumulating data in a continuous effort to discover the truth. Kuhn (1962) suggested that while science develops from something, it does not evolve toward anything specific. What he calls "normal science" enjoys widespread acceptance by a particular scientific community that shares a specific theoretical and empirical paradigm. This paradigm provides guidelines for research methodologies and for prioritizing research goals, and it establishes criteria for accepting or rejecting data and hypotheses. According to Kuhn, the history of science can be characterized by the dominance of specific paradigms. A scientific paradigm constitutes, for a longer or shorter period of time, the world view, or the definition of reality, of specific scientific disciplines. While a specific paradigm reigns, it will provide criteria for what is "sensible" and what is "nonsense." Phlogiston theory in chemistry, relativity in physics, Parsonian or ethnomethodological theory in sociology, psychoanalysis in psychology, and the idea that the earth is the center of the universe can all be used as examples of specific paradigms. Ultimately, the existence and persistence of many anomalies will force an entire field into a state of crisis. This crisis situation generates questions relating to the very basic assumptions, validity, and reliability of a specific paradigm. Kuhn stated that a crisis situation is solved by what he calls a scientific revolution, which creates a new paradigm that will dominate the field until the next revolution occurs.

The Kuhnian conception provides a very different view from the one fostered by orthodox science. As historical analyses indicate, however, the Kuhnian view is not always valid. Furthermore, his account takes very little (if any) note of the social processes involved in a scientific revolution (Mulkay 1972).[2] The important points for our discussion include, not only Kuhn's view of change in science, but the implication of his work that science is conservative and resistant to change.

I illustrate this point with two examples of mechanisms in science that maintain stability. The first example is the classical statistical hypothesis testing, which gives most probability to existing knowledge. For example, when alpha is set for .05 or .01, it means that 95 or 99 percent respectively are being given to H_0, i.e., to existing knowledge. The risk being taken for the introduction of a new element of knowledge is minimal and is set at 5 or 1 percent. Implicitly, this is a statistical admission that science is 95 or 99 percent conservative. The second example is the process through which papers and books (or grant applications) are accepted for publication by what are considered to be prestigious and reliable journals and publishers. In such cases, manuscripts usually have to be read by three (and sometimes more) reviewers. This procedure can be thought of as, not only a good safeguard against the publication of nonsense, but also as an excellent mechanism for maintaining stability. In this case, obviously, it becomes very important who the reviewers are, and thus, editors have much power in helping (or preventing) a specific report from being published, simply by deciding who the referees will be.[3]

In addition, the concept of professional technical competence (i.e., the recognition that a certain individual's work is reinforced by years of accumulated experience in the field) creates sets of vested interests and controversies over the nature of a phenomenon under study. For example, Barbara McClintock, recipient of the Nobel prize in medicine in 1983 for her work on genetics, made very clear in interviews that in the 1950s her colleagues called her crazy, that she could not find a job and was ridiculed.[4] Her work on the so-called jumping genes ("transposition," see Keller 1983, chap. 8) was certainly considered deviant (Lewin 1983; Judson 1979, pp. 460–61). It took the scientific community about thirty years to acknowledge that McClintock was not, after all, crazy. Brush

2. Since Kuhn's publication of his thesis in 1962, it has been subjected to rigorous and intensive examinations. Some critics point out that his description and analysis of science's development is inaccurate and misleading. For the most interesting criticism, consult Ben-David (1964), Alexander (1979), and Gutting (1980). See Harvey (1982) for a clarification on the use and abuse of Kuhn's ideas, and Barnes (1983) for a sympathetic view.

3. Cole, Cole, and Simon (1981) have indicated that when grant applications submitted to the National Science Foundation were later reviewed by different referees the initial decisions were reversed in about 25 percent of the cases.

4. See, e.g., *Newsday*, October 11, 1983, and interviews on the major TV networks in the New York City area.

succinctly summarizes this point, quoting Max Planck's bitter remark that new theories "rarely get accepted by rational persuasion" and that "one simply has to wait until the opponents die out" (1974, p. 1107). Gould relates that as the New Darwinian orthodoxy swept through Europe, its most brilliant opponent, Karl Ernst von Baer (an embryologist), remarked "with bitter irony that every triumphant [theory] passes through the following three stages: first it is dismissed as untrue; then it is rejected as contrary to religion; finally it is accepted as dogma and each scientist claims that he had long appreciated its truth" (1977, p. 160). Thus, resistance to change and innovation in science has a number of sources. The disciplinary paradigm is a major one. Peer review is a second source since referees—in many cases—see themselves as the gatekeepers of the relevant scientific discipline (Schlussel 1983).

Barber distinguishes between two forms of resistance to change in science. The first is passive resistance in which new ideas are simply ignored. The second is active resistance, where scientists try to debunk new innovations. Cole (1970) uses a third term, "delayed recognition," which includes both forms of Barber's resistance to change. The reaction to deviant sciences can assume all three forms of resistance: passive, active, and certainly delayed recognition. This explains why it is so difficult and risky to introduce new facts or new interpetations. While a well-established scientist can afford to take risks, others who do not enjoy that status can be expected to exhibit more restrained behavior. Young scientists in particular are faced with a problem. Especially for those seeking academic careers, taking risks can be quite dangerous if they do not have a prestigious scientist to back them up. On the other hand, a successful risk can boost a career tremendously.

It is important to understand the basic mechanisms of change within science and to note the language employed to describe the phenomenon. For example, terms such as "scientific conservatism," "resistance to change," "stagnation vs. innovation," "revolution," "change," and "modification" are all emotionally laden and reflect the user's attitude toward his subject matter. For our purposes, and in accordance with this book's theme, I have chosen "stability" and "change."

Change and Deviant Science

Scientific theories cannot explain all the physical, psychological, and social aspects of the world in which we live. For example, science finds it extremely difficult to cope with those aspects of reality that can neither be controlled nor created at will under specific laboratory conditions. Science is only one way of experiencing and perceiving the world. The rationality it represents is only one among various forms of rationality. Deviant sciences challenge the rationality through which orthodox science experiences, describes, and explains the world. They try to break the scientific monopoly on definitions of the nature of the world. Therefore, an essential element in almost all scientific debates and controversies is an explicit, or implicit, argument about the nature of reality. Do UFOs exist? Does the Loch-Ness monster exist? Is it appropriate to associate quantum mechanics with the psychological concept of free will?

The field of quantum mechanics, in particular, has become one of the oddest areas of research, at least for outsiders who are not directly involved in active research. Some of the conclusions and theorems can indeed seem bizarre to the layman (e.g., application of Bell's theorem to quantum mechanics). In a recent analysis, Harvey (1981) showed how various knowledge claims were evaluated in experimental tests of quantum mechanics. In each case, an agreed upon evaluation became possible only due to the shared culture of the physicists involved, making certain evaluations plausible and others not. Furthermore, Brush (1980), who researched the philosophy of quantum mechanics from a historical perspective, showed how difficult and full of objections the path of quantum mechanics was until it became established, accepted and legitimized.

Research in parapsychology was faced with a similar problem, for one of its major hurdles has always been to establish, preferably in controlled experiments, the reality of parapsychological effects. The difficulties in accomplishing this task have been documented (e.g., Mauskopf and McVaugh 1974), giving rise to heated arguments as to whether parapsychology is science, pseudoscience, or perhaps, protoscience.[5] Pinch (1979) demonstrated, among other things, how a hypothesis of fraud (i.e., the assumption that something must be wrong in an area of research) was applied to parapsychology, causing the rejection of plausible explanations of parapsychological effects. The fraud hypothesis denies the very reality of parapsychological effects.[6]

The negation of specific aspects of reality in the natural sciences need not be confined to esoteric and marginal activities such as parapsychological research. The debate between creationists and evolutionists provides another vivid example. Negotiations and arguments about the nature of reality have obviously not been confined to the natural sciences only.

5. See Gordon's (1982) discussion of parapsychology as a "deviant science" and how it has attempted to escape that label.
6. See the debate in *Social Studies of Science*, 11 (1981): 249–57.

Theoretical approaches in sociology, such as ethnomethodology (Garfinkel 1967) and the sociology of the absurd (Lyman and Scott 1970), exemplify this. Furthermore, the dramaturgic approach to the analysis and interpretation of social interactions, as fostered by Goffman and by symbolic interaction as well, demonstrates that reality not only can be negotiated but also that the claim about "something out there" is problematic at best. Phenomenological research in deviance, which holds the definition of deviant acts to be problematic and not immediately obvious, as exemplified by Douglas's 1967 work on suicide and Blum's 1970 work on mental illness, illustrates this claim. Even the more eclectic interpretations in sociology and psychology, such as those of Marx and Freud (not to mention works in "speculative history," such as those by Toynbee), also focused on particular reality constructions as well, hinting perhaps at "ultimate truths."

All this brings us back full circle to basic questions posed earlier that focused on the nature of a particular explanation and on reasons why certain explanations are rejected while others are accepted. Scientific explanations must make some assumptions about the very nature of reality. Hoyle's revised version of his original steady state cosmology is based on very different assumptions regarding the nature of reality than those held by proporents of the big bang and expanding universe cosmologies. Parsons's assumptions, which hold social reality to be stable, obvious, and noncontroversial to the trained observer, differ greatly from those held by ethnomethodologists. Every scientific discipline, therefore, constitutes a belief system. Within this belief system, part of which makes claims about the general nature of reality and part of which makes more specific disciplinary claims, puzzles are raised, anomalies are recognized or denied, and the plausibility of various explanations is weighed. The acceptance of new ideas and the rejection of others, as well as the problem of "resistance to innovation" in science, are all directly linked both to this larger belief system and to the fact that every scientist operates on the basis of an extensive and complex matrix of existing beliefs. This includes the prevailing disciplinary paradigm and the scientist's criteria for evaluating knowlege claims. "Plausibility" and "explanations" are therefore defined within this matrix of existing beliefs (Barnes 1977, p. 279).

It was pointed out that defining science is a difficult task. Likewise, defining "deviant science," demarcating "science" and "nonscience," is not a simple issue (Nowotny and Rose 1979; Gieryn 1983). Generally we can claim that deviant sciences challenge regular scientific disciplines and, in particular, the paradigms (in the Kuhnian terminology) of normal science. The term thus refers to "strange" observations, to anomalies that are not recognized as such by normal science, and to bizarre interpretations about the nature of reality. A deviant science's claims always seem to threaten paradigms of normal science, which partially explains why deviant sciences are so fiercely rejected and stigmatized by the science establishment. The reaction to deviant science, and especially to its supporters, is similar to reactions to regular deviance: rejection, isolation, stigmatization, ridicule, and expulsion from jobs. The case of Velikovsky serves as a very good example for this, as do some other cases that I shall present later.

During the past few years, a number of scholars have written about deviant sciences. The first formulation was made by Langmuir (1953), who coined the phrase "pathological science." Pathological science is not quite deviant science since the term Langmuir suggested referred primarily to "that which cannot be," that is, to reports about observations that were never made or, if you like, to fraud. Deviant sciences, in most cases, are not like this. Two more formulations appeared almost simultaneously in 1979. The first was a book edited by Roy Wallis and entitled *On the Margins of Science: The Social Construction of Rejected Knowledge.* The first article, written by Dolby, deals extensively with deviant sciences. The other chapters deal with subjects such as the normalizaton of deviance in science, astrology, mesmerism, acupuncture, phrenology, creationism, spiritualism, paranormal claims and parapsychology, sea serpents, and ufology.

Dolby's chapter is obviously of special interest to us. He suggests that "orthodox science is that which commands the approval of all the leading scientific experts of the time." In contradistinction, deviant science "is that which is rejected by the orthodox scientific experts, and which they may label 'pseudo science'" (1979, pp. 10, 11). Thus, what constitutes scientific and nonscientific becomes, to a large extent, a matter of social evaluation and recognition. Wynne's 1979 analysis of the J-phenomenon supports this claim, showing how deviance in physics is normalized and pointing out that there are no absolute boundaries between scientific controversies and encounters between orthodox and deviant sciences. Likewise, Frankel (1976) demonstrates how the adoption of the wave theory of light over the corpuscular system of the early nineteenth century profoundly altered the field of optics and posed the first serious difficulty for the action-at-a-distance worldview that had dominated European physical science from the time of Newton. While Frankel vividly describes the conceptual breakthrough of idea of "light as waves," he also demonstrates how difficult it was to initiate this change and how orthodox science rejected the concept. Only after optical physicists lost some of their best colleagues to the wave theory did they stop ignoring it, and change was gradually introduced.

The social position of those who follow various deviant sciences, especially within the scientific community, is of crucial importance if we wish to understand how a "deviant" suggestion is legitimated or rejected. To a large extent, power plays a crucial role here. Lofland defines deviance as "the name of the conflict game in which individuals or loosely organized small groups with little power are strongly feared by a well-organized, sizeable minority or majority who have a large amount of power" (1969, p. 14). Horowitz and Liebowitz reinforce this definition "Deviance is a conflict between at least two parties: superordinates who make and enforce rules, and subordinates whose behavior violates those rules" (1968, p. 181).

Deviant sciences generally fit these definitions. In most cases, we have an individual or a very small group of scholars who are feared by a sizeable group of fellow scholars. Indeed, the reality and specific scientific claims made by the minorities can potentially challenge the agreed-upon paradigms of the dominant science. As I suggested, the Velikovsky affair illustrates this point. In brief, Velikovsky suggested that various religious myths had solid basis in reality. He claimed that there were physical upheavals of global proportions in historical times and that these upheavals were caused by extraterrestrial reasons (mostly, changes in the structure of the solar system). Mcaulay points out that when Velikovsky presented his ideas to Shapley (an eminent astronomer) in 1946, Shapely responded angrily by writing letters to his colleagues stating that "if Dr. Velikovsky is right, the rest of us are crazy" (1978, p. 317). Later, a campaign against Velikovsky was organized in which Macmillan publishing company was threatened by Shapley and asked not to publish any of Velikovsky's books. In 1952, The American Philosophical Society gave his opponents an opportunity to attack Velikovsky but did not allow him to publish a rebuttal. These are only two examples of the fierce resistance Velikovsky encountered. Mcaulay suggests that organized "opposition to Velikovsky among segments of the scientific community was partially mobilized along informal lines by mail, direct contact and, apparently, the personal authority of Harlow Shapely" (ibid., p. 331).

When a deviant scientific idea is brought forth, a controversy is usually generated. During this debate, the status of the scholars or scientists who suggest or support the deviant ideas greatly determines whether they will be accepted or rejected. The frequent flare-up of such an argument arouses debate on the integrity, past achievements and scientific solidity of the supporters and rejectors as well. Becker's 1967 concept of a hierarchy of credibility is useful on this issue. According to Becker, there is a hierarchy of credibility in society whereby some people are considered to be more credible and reliable than others. The more secure and prestigious a scholar's position in the scientific community is, the more credibility he enjoys.[7] Thus, most of Dolby's 1979 paper is devoted to an analysis of belief systems that are in conflict with orthodox science. Processes of change in science do not resemble a democratic procedure. Deviant sciences must inevitably face scientific and political opposition for recognition and legitimization by the scientific community. These struggles are usually fierce because deviant sciences frequently propose, not only a competing world view to the paradigms of normal science, but a different form of rationality as well.

In an example I present later, it will be shown how UFO claims have been discredited and stigmatized throughout this century by both orthodox science and official government bodies (at least in the United States). One of the results of such discreditation (especially if adherents of the deviant science are committed to it) is the creation of institutes and organizations that promote and support the sciences in question outside established and recognized research frameworks. Proponents of unorthodox subjects of UFOs, spiritualism, ESP, ancient astronauts hypothesis (Dänikenism), Velikovsky's ideas and Fortean events have been successful in establishing organizations whose ranks are filled with enthusiasts. In some cases, the extraacademic activity may indicate a high level of popularization (e.g., Däniken and the ancient astronaut society); in other cases it can create the impression of a quasi-academic activity (e.g., UFO research groups or supporters of Velikovskian ideas).[8] This process can also give rise to cults. This was evident in the UFO case (Story 1980a, pp. 305–8, 506) and in the internationally famous transcendental meditation movement and Scientology, or the British and Israeli EMIN.

Some of the deviant sciences can be referred to as modern myths (Goran 1970) and are part of the occult revival we discussed in chapter 3. These myths include Däniken's theories about ancient astronauts, theories about "lost continents," the Bermuda Triangle mystery, pyramid power, ufology, the Loch Ness monster (and other monsters, e.g., Bigfoot), to mention only a few. They attract hundreds of thousands—possibly even millions—of believers. Like to Greeley (1970a, b), I find myself many times facing advanced undergraduate and

7. However, this does not mean easier access to publishing (Cole 1970).
8. See Mcaulay (1978), and the journal *Kronos* (preceded by *Pensée*).

graduate students who find it difficult to accept that Däniken, for example, lacks even one, irrefutable fact to support his claims. The very students who spend hours trying to refute Parsonian theory would not consider spending even one percent of that effort in an attempt to critically examine Däniken's theories. Indeed, Singer and Benassi (1981) state that inadequate science education is to be blamed for this phenomenon. Carroll suggests an analysis of modern myths through Lévi-Straussian structuralism because "like those living in primitive cultures [modern believers are] concerned with the resolution of certain universal oppositions. . . . The popularity of the modern Atlantis myth and the myth of the ancient astronauts derives from their ability to effectively resolve these oppositions" (1977, p. 548). Another Lévi-Straussian analysis is suggested by Ashworth (1980); however, it is considerably different from that of Carroll. Ashworth points out that religion and science "no longer resolve certain structural contradictions which they once did with ease" (p. 374), while modern myths do seem to solve these structural contradictions. Thus, we have here one strong connection between some deviant sciences and the occult revival.

Deviant sciences do not necessarily change normal science, and they can remain deviant. Dolby (1979) specified three ways for deviant science to become normalized: first, ideas similar to those of the deviant science can be developed by orthodox scientists (e.g., continental drift theory); second, orthodox science can take ideas from deviant science and develop them (e.g., as happened in the case of parapsychology, which is one variant of paranormal claims in general); and third, the deviant science itself can become orthodoxy (e.g., as was the case with optics and the wave theory of light or with meteorites).

Above we mentioned Wallis's book on deviant science. A second volume, edited by Mauskopf (1978), is the result of a symposium sponsored by the American Academy for the Advancement of Science on the topic of the reception of unconventional science.[9] The book provides detailed analyses of four cases of what were once considered "unconventional" sciences, but which later received acceptance: acausal quantum mechanics, Wegener's continental drift theory, acupuncture, and parapsychological research. It concludes with a chapter by Truzzi suggesting that a deviant science (or pseudoscience) is one that is methodologically flawed. Truzzi suggested the terms "proto-science" to describe "scientific" claims that assume the existence of an extraordinary variable (e.g.,

9. Somehow the academy felt that the word "unconventional" was better than "deviant."

UFOs, unicorns) and "para-science" to describe claims that assume the existence of extraordinary relationships between ordinary variables (e.g., astrology).

The abundance of scholarly works in both the philosophy and the history of science reveals that the development of science is a much more discontinuous process than what is usually perceived (Truzzi 1979, p. 128). The examples brought forward in this work are reinforced by Kearney's 1971 study of the scientific revolution in the sixteenth and seventeenth centuries, which Kearney demonstrates was not a slow and gradual process of change but a very complex interaction among three different paradigms. The scientific process is so removed from the usual portrayal of it (i.e., gradual and accumulative) that Brush titled a 1974 paper in *Science* "Should the History of Science be Rated X?"

The conclusion is clear. The questions of what is accepted and what is rejected, and where and when, require very complex responses. Much evidence exists that indicates that change in science is neither gradual nor easy, even according to the more orthodox view. Polanyi (1967), for example, suggests that there are cases when experimental data should be dismissed, when the data violate current scientific convictions. He argues further that if the data relate to something real, the results will probably be produced again. If this occurs consistently over time, only then should change be considered. Polanyi states that "deviant" experimental data usually occurs as a result of errors, and the effort required to detect the errors, or fraud, can be of such magnitude that it is preferable to simply ignore the results than to waste time in finding the error.

It is very difficult to evaluate the validity of Polanyi's argument since we do not have systematic data sets on the suppression of innovative ideas in science (Zuckerman 1977, p. 119). Ben-David, however, did a study in which he reviewed discoveries that had at first been dismissed in the nineteenth century but were later rediscovered and found to be significant. He states that the surprising factor was, not the prevalence of various attempts to suppress the ideas, but rather "the fact that they so rarely succeeded and that at no point was there any doubt among those with different prejudices that the contest of views could be resolved by accepted scientific procedures" (1977, p. 289). The only flaw in this argument is that there exists the possibility that many valid scientific conceptions and ideas were buried and never rediscovered.

Both Polanyi's philosophical conviction and Ben-David's empirical work cannot, by their very nature, account for either the number of cases of lost work that has never been recovered or their significance. For example, when in 1964 Penzias and Wilson (and the Princeton team headed by Dicke) discovered the most significant remnant of the primal big bang, no one even remembered the pioneering work done years earlier by Gamow and his group. Because Gamow and some of his original team were still living at the time, a controversy arose as to who should be credited with the idea. It is quite possible that many good ideas have simply been forgotten because they were developed "before their time," that is, before the established scientific paradigm was ripe enough to deal with them. This is often at a very high personal cost to the original developers of the idea, who feel that they have made a true discovery. It is in total accordance with Truzzi's observation that, "like any form of deviance witin a social group, unconventional ideas in science are seldom positively greeted by those benefitting from conformity" (1929, p. 131).

While it appears that junor scholars aspiring to a secure academic position should be careful with new ideas, this is not the situation with established or marginal scholars. Ben-David (1960) illustrated how, in the fields of bacteriology and psychoanalysis, scholars who held marginal positions succeeded in introducing significant innovations. Cases we shall analyze later (such as Wegener's geological theory and Reber's contribution to radio astronomy) demonstrate this point. In the field of sociology, innovations such as ethnomethodology and the sociology of the absurd did not originate from mainstream figures. Both Heirich (1976) and Nowotny and Rose (1979) demonstrated how "counterculture" movements develop within science, creating the potential for both cultural and scientific and conceptual breakthroughs.

Thus, in many disciplines, there has developed in recent years an attack on the demarcation of science and nonscience (Gieryn 1983). Recent analyses of the influence of politics on the development of science, and the ways through which science has given support to various political ideologies, have helped those opposing the division. This attack, admittedly, can become destructive to the point of negating the very value of science. Indeed, one of the results of this situation is that we are constantly being flooded with books and papers assailing us with all sorts of strange phenomena that Western positivist science is at a loss to explain. The academic community does not remain silent and a counterattack takes place. Journals such as the *Skeptical Inquirer* (and, to a much lesser degree, *Zetetic Scholar*) evaluate various fantastic claims and attempt to reveal them as either valid or hoaxes. There have been numerous books published that discredit various deviant sciences such as ufology, ESP, parapsychology, Velikovskian claims, astrology, and rhythm of life (see, for example, Gardner 1957, 1981; Frazier 1981; Hanen, Osler, and Weyant 1980; Abell and Singer 1981; Nowotny and

Rose 1979). Thus, the challenges of deviant sciences encounter contradictory claims and debunking efforts from orthodox science.

This debate undoubtedly helps each side to redefine and sharpen its own boundaries. Gieryn (1983) points out that while demarcation is routinely accomplished in practical, everyday settings, the "actual" boundaries are very ambiguous. He also notes that "boundary work" occurs (a) when the goal is expansion of authority or expertise into domains claimed by other professions or occupations (in this case, boundary work contrasts rivals); (b) when the goal is monopolization of professional authority and resources (in this case, boundary work excludes rivals, labeling them as "outsiders," "pseudoscientists," "deviant," or "amateurs"); (c) when the goal is protection of autonomy over professional activity (in this case, boundary work exempts members from responsibility for the consequences of their work by putting the blame on outside scapegoats). The debate has obviously had repercusssions within the scientific community. Much as Polanyi (1967) advises the rejection of data that do not make sense, Agassi (1975) suggests that there may be times when we should ignore evidence in favor of a hypothesis.

The controversial work of Feyeraband (1975) supports the rights of deviant sciences. He argues that science does not progress according to a rational method but rather by breaking away from rules. According to Feyeraband, no scientific discipline had a monopoly on truth, and extra-scientific activities such as acupuncture, astrology, and witchcraft should have equal rights to make claims about the nature of truth. He maintains that scientific work is so saturated with power and prestige games that decisions regarding what constitutes truth have little to do with actual scientific arguments and that creativity in science seems to have always had a deviant nature. Furthermore, his work implies that small-scale cheating is essential to the advancement of science (Broad 1981, p. 139). According to Feyeraband, the history of science indicates that "everything goes."[10]

Mulkay (1972b), points out that there are five means by which innovations can be introduced into science: information gained through normal science; ideas developed in the course of gradual redefinitions; notions occurring as a result of mobility of researchers between existing areas of research; developments arising from the investigation of obscure areas;

---

10. Obviously, this claim is highly exaggerated. Not "everything goes" in science. Polanyi succinctly sums up the point, "Journals are bombarded with contributions offering fundamental discoveries in physics, chemistry, biology or medicine, most of which are nonsensical. Science cannot survive unless it can keep out such contributions and safeguard the basic soundness of its publications" (1969, p. 54–55).

and conceptions introduced in the course of revolutionary upheaval. While these five categories cover a very broad spectrum, they include neither the possibility of introducing change into science via "deviant sciences" in general nor the more specific admission that in many cases innovative ideas were defined as deviant and were even ridiculed when first presented. In the final analysis, therefore, the question of scientific innovation and change, and the labeling of ideas as deviant or pseudoscientific have much to do with the cultural matrix (paradigm) or scientific belief system that prevail in a specific scientific discipline at any given time (see Brannigan 1981; Latour and Woolgar 1979).

While the social basis of scientific progress is significant, it is only one factor. Other important factors involve processes in which proper scientific considerations are marginal. Introducing innovations into science always involves power struggles and sometimes bitter arguments about the nature of reality and about what constitutes evidence (or fact). Science does not operate in a vacuum. It is influenced by prevailing sociopolitical ideas (via funding) and in turn can support those ideas (e.g., in rehabilitation of deviants). Thus to a limited degree, and in different disciplines, facts, and truth can be shaped socially. Certified knowledge can be geared to specific goals both within and without science.

If sociopolitical ideas play a part in scientific activity, then the next questions must be which part (evidence, interpretation, or methodology) of the scientific work is most influenced. While these questions remain largely unanswered, what constitutes a fact in science has also become a problematic issue. In many cases, scientific paradigms once accepted as valid and reliable were later rejected. Scientists who tried to conduct research along the previous paradigm's lines would be ostracized and lose their jobs. It is difficult to visualize contemporary chemists or physicists doing phlogiston research or astronomers working according to the Ptolemaic view of the universe. However, one need not go back that far in time. In the late 1960s and the 1970s a few physicists nurtured theories about the existence of "gravitational waves" (or "gravitational radiation"). Some intensive research was carried out in which gravitational "antennae" were built to detect, record, and analyze gravitational waves. As Collins's analysis shows (1981, pp. 46–48), the credibility of claims that there exist high levels of gravitational radiation has dropped sharply. Detection of gravitational waves has become "not science," "self-delusion," "pathological science," "science of things that aren't so." Another case is that of the infamous "J-phenomenon" in physics. The J-phenomenon constituted a complicated array of experimental claims and theoretical formulations by the British scientist Barkla. It proved later to be an error, the gravity of which was mitigated since it did not occur within the mainstream of physics (Wynne 1979). Yet it did succeed in generating a large volume of about fifty "scientific" papers.

Detecting cases of scientific innovations that were originally rejected and later accepted as valid brings us to the core of the problem, that is, the ways and means through which innovation can be introduced and institutionalized in science. Some famous examples include the initial resistance to Darwin, Einstein, Pasteur, and to Freud in the early phases of their work. In the 1840s, the Hungarian physician Dr. Semmelweis discovered antisepsis and used it in his clinic. He succeeded in reducing mortality rates in his clinic significantly. About two decades later, Lister discovered the same principle. Both men were originally ignored. Semmelweis was rejected and ridiculed. Ohm's work on electrical resistance and Mendel's work on genetics were also ignored by the relevant scientific communities (Broad and Wade 1982, pp. 136–38). However, rather than elaborate on older, well-documented cases, I shall present a few more recent examples of innovations that were initially condemned by the scientific community as "nonsense," "illogical," "impossible," and deviant. The proponents had to face ridicule and to fight long and hard for acceptance and recognition, which did not always follow. The examples illustrate how cognitive deviance in science contributes to flexibility, and redefinition of the scientific boundaries. They are clustered within four broad categories: (1) scientific ideas that were initally rejected and later accepted; (2) scientific ideas that were initially accepted and later rejected; (3) scientific speculation; (4) anomalies.

Scientific Ideas That Were Initially Rejected and Later Accepted

Surveying and analyzing the field of potentially valid ideas is a fascinating pursuit. After all, what scientist who has ever had a paper rejected by a journal has not harbored the fantasy that he is among those scholars who will later be recognized and respected? Barber (1961) examines the manner in which a number of scientific theories that were accepted as valid by 1960 had been initially resisted by scientists. His examples include Pasteur's and Lister's theories of germs, Mendel's theory of inheritance, and Planck's development of the quantum theory. In another work, Ben-David (1977, p. 259) reviewed various discoveries that had at first been dismissed in the nineteenth century, only to be rediscovered and given validity and credibility later.

Before examining our own examples, it must be pointed out that these cases are not described in an exhaustive manner.

Case 1: Continental Drift Theory

In 1915, Alfred Wegener proposed the first extensive theory of continental drift (see Frenkel 1979; Gould 1977; Eisen 1980). His theory states that the continents are in essence blocks of light sialic material floating upon the heavier basaltic material of the ocean floor. He posited that they undergo horizontal displacement by ploughing through this denser material. He felt that originally all the continents were one mass, forming a supercontinent that he called Pangea. Later Pangea began to break up, forming the various continents, which started to drift away.

His theory encountered fierce resistance, and his work was criticized and ridiculed. Wegener had been trained in astronomy, and most of his previous studies were in this field. He was also acknowledged to be an able meteorologist and he visited Greenland three times on extended research trips. But by 1929, it was plainly clear that virtually the entire scientific establishment was against his theory of continental drift and few, if any, dared to defend it. In that year Wegener, set out on his third scientific expedition to Greenland, from which he never returned. At his wife's request, he was buried under the icecap. Every year, his well-preserved body sinks deeper into the ice until one day it might drift with a glacier into the sea. His tragic death gave him a stature that he had never achieved while alive. The scientific community, however, mourned the loss of an excellent meteorologist, an interesting teacher, and a researcher of the Arctic zone. His contribution to geodynamics was never even mentioned.

His dynamic theory was in sharp contrast to that which prevailed in the field of geology in the 1930s. As late as 1944, Baily Willis argued that drift theory should be buried because it was "an obstruction to knowledge" (Frenkel 1979, p. 69). In the 1960s, however, evidence began to accumulate that strongly supported Wegener's approach. Yet the geological community still overwhelmingly rejected the idea of continental drift. By the end of 1966, however, as a result of the research done by Walter Pitman on profiles from the Pacific-Atlantic Ridge, even the most skeptical were convinced. While Wegener's original theory contained many inaccuracies, he is credited with the revolutionary theory of continental dirft, accepted today by the geological community as a valid explanation for dynamic geological movements.

Case 2: Radio Astronomy in the United States

The field of astronomy provides us with numerous examples for our thesis, such as the Copernican revolution of the seventeenth century and the Galilean "heresy." The major goal of astronomy is to understand our universe, a goal that virtually guarantees political troubles. After all, the nature, the structure, and the origin of the cosmos are issues that politics and religion address as well. The fact that astronomy in general, and modern astrophysical theories in particular, can provide fascinating answers to fundamental questions is obvious from the simple observation that discussions of quite complex modern theories and controversies find their way into the mass media. For example, the March 12, 1979, issue of the international edition of *Newsweek* was devoted to "Mysteries of the Universe." Furthermore, the high cost of equipment in astonomy, such as optical and radio telescopes and satellites, attracts public opinion to its development. Astronomy has one other characteristic that distinguishes it from other scientific disciplines, that is the fact that parallel to professional, academic investigations there have always existed very active, organized groups of amateurs whose contribution to its "certified knowledge" has been considerable (Lankford 1981).

Throughout a long and distinguished history, astronomy has undergone quite a few revolutions and conceptual changes. One was the development of radio astronomy. One should remember that until the 1930s, astronomical research methods and discoveries relied almost exclusively on optical means, that is astronomy was an optical science.[11] This imposed a severe limitation on astronomy because the visible part of the spectrum is very small indeed. However, until then no serious, systematic attempt was made to "see" the universe through wavelengths other than visible light. The first real breakthrough came when in 1930–1931 Karl Jansky, a radio engineer employed by the Bell Telephone Company at their research laboratories in New Jersey, was assigned to uncover the causes of static noises interfering with long distance phone calls (mostly radio-telephone conversations over transatlantic short-wave links of the Bell system).[12] In an open field, Jansky built the first directional radio-telescope. It resembled the thirty-meter wing frame of an early biplane, and it rotated on a circular track on four rubber tires from a Model-T Ford. It did not take Jansky more than a few months to establish that the noise in question could be classified into the following three categories: noise from lightning in nearby thunderstorms; noise from distant thunderstorms; and an unexplained, thin, persistent hiss, which

11. As early as the end of the nineteenth century, a few sporadic attempts had been made to receive radio-wave emissions from the sun. They all failed, mostly because of the low sensitivity of the equipment used (Sullivan 1982).

12. The following account is based upon Kraus (1966, 1981, 1982), Ferris (1977), Edge and Mulkay (1976), Hey (1973), Struve (1962), Sullivan (1982, 1984), and personal communications with Reber and Sullivan.

did not vary with changes in the weather and appeared to be synchronized with the stars (and not with the sun, as he first thought). By 1933, after checking maps of the stars, Jansky had demonstrated that the source of the hiss was a band coincident with the Milky Way. Being somewhat hesitant about his own conclusions, he suggested the construction of a new antenna, specifically designed to find out what was going on in the center of the Milky Way.

Jansky published his findings in 1932 in the *Proceedings of the Institute of Radio Engineers*, presented them in 1933 to the International Scientific Radio Union, and received wide publicity through Bell Telephone's various press releases and radio programs. It is imperative to emphasize that at that time the very idea of radio waves coming from celestial bodies was totally alien to most astronomers' thinking. While Jansky was well aware of the significance of his discovery, the great majority of astronomers were totally impervious to the revolutionary aspect of his work. Kraus (1966) reports that at a convention held on July 3, 1935, scarcely two dozen people came to listen to Jansky. While Bell Telephone was partly interested in some of the sensational aspects of his work, the problem originally assigned to him was solved and he was not provided with further funds to continue his research.[13]

The next step in radio astronomy was taken by Grote Reber, and here, I feel, is one of the most fascinating stories of modern astronomy. Reber, a young radio engineer from Wheaton, Illinois, graduated from the Illinois Institute of Technology in 1933. He was not only a radio engineer but also an avid ham-radio operator. Having read and appreciated Jansky's papers, he decided to pursue Jansky's findings at his own expense and in his spare time. First he had to build a radio telescope. He assembled it piece by piece and completed the entire project in four months, from June to September 1937, at a cost of $1,300. He built it in the side yard of his home in Wheaton, and then he began his observations. He would observe the sky from midnight until six o'clock in the morning and then commute thirty miles to Chicago to his work in designing radio receivers. He would return home, sleep after supper until midnight, and start his observations again. The structure of Reber's radio telescope prefigured modern-day instruments. It was dish-shaped and capable of rotating around its horizontal axis but fixed in azimuth (to coincide with the meridian of Reber's home). While continually improving his equip-

13. As an example of intense public interest, *New York Times* of May 5, 1933, carried a front page report headlined "New Radio Waves Traced to Center of Milky Way" (Hey 1973, p. 7). On Monday, May 15, 1933, the National Broadcasting Company Blue Network announced "Tonight we will let you hear radio impulses picked up from somewhere among the stars" (Kraus 1981, p. 11).

ment, to the amazement and wonder of his puzzled neighbors and various curious tourists,[14] Reber made the first systematic survey and produced the first radio maps of the sky. There is no question that he produced the first extensive quantitative measurements of radio radiation from the sky. Kraus notes that these maps are "remarkably good even compared to present-day maps" (1966, p. 10).

Reber's work began in 1938. He began the first systematic survey of the radio sky in 1941, was interrupted when he went to work for the U.S. Navy, and resumed his work in 1943. Having completed his investigations, he took his maps and charts to Yerkes Observatory, trying to persuade the astronomers there that he had something of value, but to no avail. They either could not or would not realize the significance of his findings. Reber notes that contemporary astronomers viewed "electronic apparatus . . . as black magic" (1983, p. 5). When in 1940, he tried to publish some of his work and submitted a paper to the prestigious *Astrophysical Journal*, the referees of the journal rejected it as unbelievable (Ferris 1977, p. 88). Dr. Struve, the editor, found himself torn between his deep conviction in the validity and importance of Reber's work and his professional obligations, for the referees' reactions made him cautious, and he did not want to publish an article that might later prove to be incorrect or inaccurate. Dr. Struve got responses from astronomers who complained that they could not understand the radio terminology, totally ignoring the significance of the discovery. When he sent the paper to *Radio Engineering* referees, they had no problem with the terminology, but they could not comment on the astronomical implications. Thus Dr. Struve found himself in the position of not having one reviewer who was willing to recommend or defend the paper.

The last avenue Dr. Struve pursued was to establish Reber's credentials. First he noted that Reber was a member of the Institute of Radio Engineers, and in desperation he wrote to the institute's headquarters to find out if it could supply any information on Reber's qualifications and reputation. He received a prompt reply stating that Reber was a member of the institute in good standing who paid his dues regularly. Second, it seems that Dr. Struve decided to travel himself to Wheaton where he inspected the telescope and talked at length with Reber.[15] At this point, he had a real problem. Although he had all the reasons he needed to reject Reber's contribution, he decided to take the risk and publish the

14. Some apparently thought it was a weather-controlling device (Kraus 1982, p. 14).

15. Personal communication, Reber, Jan. 8, 1984. See also Edge and Mulkay (1976, p. 84). A delegation of optical astronomers from Chicago also visited Reber. This whole episode is quite obscure in the relevant literature of the history of astronomy. Reber never wrote much about it and Struve himself also never elaborated.

paper. Years later, he explained that he had felt that a good paper rejected would have been a greater evil than a poor paper accepted.

Reber's paper appeared the *Astrophysical Journal* in 1940. It is important to note that while Jansky had made no real attempt to seek out optical astronomers and share his discovery with them, Reber, in contrast, tried to establish such contacts. He had taken a course in astrophysics at the University of Chicago and took his initial results to Yerkes Observatory. Edge and Mulkay state the obvious when they write: "It is, perhaps, not surprising that the scientific community would not immediately notice the work of a largely self-taught amateur, working under such conditions. . . . Reber's result seemed *theoretically* implausible. . . . The optical astronomers . . . were, of course, . . . rather doubtful about the reliability of the information presented by this unknown amateur" (1976, p. 84, 263).

There is no doubt that Reber's pioneering work is the basis for modern radio astronomy. Radio astronomy itself totally transformed classical optical astronomy, leading to new discoveries and bold new theories both in astronomy and cosmology. Reber's paper appeared during World War II and caught the attention of a few Dutch astronomers (under Nazi occupation) who immediately grasped its meaning and tremendous importance (Kraus 1966; Edge and Mulkay 1976). The Dutch were not the only ones to realize the importance of the work, and groups of scientists in Britain, Australia, and Canada all started to work on radio astronomy simultaneously. Thus, significant postwar developments in the field took place in those places, with the United States lagging behind. Discoveries during the war years, especially in radar technology (mostly in Britain), also gave a great boost to radio astronomy.

The problem of how the relevant scientific community accepted Jansky's and Reber's work is complicated by the question of who that community was? It seems that three types of professionals could be interested in this work. The first and most obvious group were radio engineers. They were not only likely to discover extraterrestrial radio waves but could also comprehend the nature of the discovery without objections. It fit well into the type of work they were doing and the instruments they developed and worked with. It was this group that gave solid support to both Jansky and Reber by letting them discuss their work in their meetings and publish their work in their professional journals. However, the theoretical and practical meaning of the discovery for this group was minimal. It did not affect in any significant way the way radio engineers worked.

The second group of potential supporters were physicists. The discovery of extraterrestrial radio waves should not have surprised this group, but it could change, in a most significant way, some of their formulations. However, they showed very little, if any, interest. Reber recalls a typical reaction

> During 1936 I tried to discuss the subject with Walter Bartky, Dean of the Department of Physical Sciences. He was absolutely sure Jansky had made a mistake for a reason very plausible to him. The celestial radio waves could not get down to earth through the ionosphere. H. G. Gale was head of the Physics Department. He had no ideas and did not want to hear about the subject." (Personal communication, Jan. 8, 1984)

It appears that only Whipple and Greenstein, an instructor and graduate student at Harvard College Observatory, both astrophysicists who were also avid ham radio operators, showed some interest in Jansky's work in 1936. They tried to explain Jansky's findings, but failed. Reber cynically notes that "astrophysicists could not dream up any rational way by which the radio waves could be generated, and since they didn't know of a process, the whole affair was at best a mistake and at worst a hoax" (1983, p. 5). The third group of professionals, optical astronomers, should have been extremely interested in Jansky's and Reber's work. However, this group, for whom the discovery of extraterrestrial radiowaves meant the most, was the least interested.

Jansky's and Reber's work presented a new, unconventional scientific specialty. This specialty had no identity, no structure, and no support or recognition by optical astronomers. While Jansky and Reber worked in a very orthodox way in radio, their "orthodoxy" was alien to astronomers, who simply could not understand it. The problem for optical astronomers was how to incorporate a radically different way of "seeing" the universe and how to cope with an unknown new methodology. The early work in the field leaves very little room to doubt that it constituted a deviant science for contemporary optical astronomers. Optical astronomy was a normal science, dominated by a specific paradigm. Within this paradigm, there was no place for radio waves or radio telescopes. However, it would not be correct to suggest that puzzles or anomalies within this paradigm brought about the development of radioastronomy. Reber and Jansky were totally outside optical astronomy, and their work did not solve any puzzle raised within orthodox circles. They had to convince optical astronomers of the validity of a whole new way of observing and interpreting the universe. Thus, Jansky was virtually ignored. It took an amateur to grasp the true meaning of his work and, with an admirable personal effort, to obtain for it long overdue acceptance.

Optical astronomy could easily descard the early innovations in radio astronomy as "deviant" because of at least two factors. First, both Jansky and Reber were true "outsiders." They had no formal education or training in astronomy and were therefore totally outside the closed circle of optical astronomers. Second, their methods were certainly considered deviant and unintelligible by optical astronomers. While radio astronomy actually revolutionized optical astronomy in many important aspects, it did not change its central paradigm. What radio astronomy suggested—and what contemporary astronomers failed to grasp—was that the energy generated in the universe does not find expression only in the visible part of the spectrum.

Case 3: Astronomical Follies

As we have seen, the field, of astronomy provides us with many examples of ideas initially rejected, only to be accepted later. Here I shall mention a few further examples.

The Ptolemaic world view in astronomy reigned supreme for a long period of time, and it was only in the sixteenth century that it was seriously challenged by the views developed and supported by Giordano Bruno, Kepler, and Galileo. Their unorthodox theories were later accepted, but Galileo's investigations resulted in his excommunication and Bruno's cost him his life.

One need not reach so far back in time, for the modern era provides us with many similar cases, for example, the "big bang" theory, suggested originally by George Gamow.[16] Gamow published an article in the April 1948 issue of *Physical Review*, arguing that the universe started with a massive explosion. Two collaborators working with Gamow at that time, Ralph Alpher and Robert Herman, refined his arguments and indicated that if the big bang theory is correct, that is, if the universe was once very hot and has been in a gradual cooling process, it ought now to be cold, as is really the case, but not absolutely cold. (Ferris 1977, p. 81). The energy of the original bang should still prevail, although greatly diminished in intensity. Alpher and Herman pointed out that the current temperature of the universe should be about five degrees above absolute zero and that

16. The central thesis of the big bang theory is that about 15 or 20 billion years ago, the now observable universe was very dense, in fact, the density of matter was infinite. Then there was a gigantic explosion (the "big bang"), and the universe as we know it was born (Silk 1980, Weinberg 1977).

the residual energy from the big band should take the form of a low-level background radiation from all directions at equal strength.

Although the researchers themselves hypothesized ways to verify the theory, (Weinberg 1977, pp. 118–23) the team broke up in 1956 when Gamow left George Washington University for the University of Colorado. In 1977, Allan Sandage, a well-known astronomer, commented that although nothing came of Gamow's theories, "for a while there, Gamow had the creation of the universe right in the palm of his hand" (Ferris 1977, p. 82). Weinberg (1977) also wondered why Alpher and Herman's predictions were left hanging and attributed this partially to the lack of sensitive instruments in 1948. Furthermore, the very idea of looking for the traces of the big bang itself was so sensational in 1948 that it was not considered by the scientific community as fit for respectable theoretical and experimental effort. As a matter of fact, Sandage himself recalled that when, in the late 1940s, someone from Gamow's team walked into his office at the Mount Palomar–Mount Wilson Observatories headquarters in Pasadena and told him that they were going to look for direct evidence of the big bang, Sandage thought he "was crazy" (Sullivan 1979, p. 136).

In the early 1960s, Bell Telephone hired Arno Penzias and Robert Wilson to develop and operate a microwave antenna so that communications with the first Telstar satellite could be reestablished and improved. Penzias and Wilson solved the problem rather quickly, but they also observed a strange low and steady noise being received by their horn-shaped antenna. It showed up on the chart recorders day and night, regardless of where in the sky the antenna was directed. They dismantled the antenna, tried to eliminate the noise, checked and rechecked every connection, discounted every human-made noise, all to no avail. The level of the unexplained noise was equal to the radio energy of extremely short wavelengths (microwaves) that would be emitted by a totally black object heated to about three degrees above absolute zero. While in itself an insignificant quantity, when one realizes that it fills the entire universe, it represents a tremendous sum (Sullivan 1979, p. 175).

Although Gamow and his team's original work was long forgotten, and Penzias and Wilson were "stuck" with their noisy radiotelescope, in 1964 there was another team in Princeton working independently, in effect, redeveloping Gamow's formulations (Weinberg 1977; Sullivan 1979; Ferris 1977). Penzias and Wilson were puzzled, but they kept the news of their noisy telescope quiet. They were unsure about the nature of the noise and did not want to become subjects of ridicule. By chance, they made contact with the team of physicists working in Princeton (Peebles,

Dicke, Roll, and Wilkinson), who were trying to develop the conceptualization and instruments that would enable them to hear the echo of the big bang. When Dicke, who headed the Princeton team, met with Wilson and Penzias, it became immediately clear that what they had heard was the background radiation believed to be the residual noise from the big bang, which had been predicted earlier by Gamow and his team. This stunning discovery was made during 1964 and 1965 and was labeled by Weinberg, himself a Nobel prize winner, "one of the most important scientific discoveries of the 20th century" (Sullivan 1979, p. 136). In 1978, Penzias and Wilson shared a Nobel prize for their discovery.

When the news broke, the scientists' paper did not mention Gamow, who was then in his sixties, old, tired, and an alcoholic. He reacted to the discovery half in anger (Ferris 1977 reports that Gamow wrote "You see . . . the world did not start with almighty Dicke") and half in jest (when he chaired a session at a conference on microwave background radiation, he said, "If I lost a nickel, and someone finds a nickel, I can't prove it's my nickel. Still, I lost a nickel just where they found one" [ibid., p. 99]). Alpher and Herman's reactions were more extreme. Both dropped out of the field of cosmology. Herman went to work for General Motors and Alpher went to work for General Electric. They both became very bitter about the whole affair and disillusioned with science. Alpher, who gave up science entirely in 1971 for an administrative position with General Electric, said "I left science in part because I was kind of disillusioned by the poor scholarship of so many scientists," and Herman added, "The astronomical community back at that time didn't show much interest in what we had been doing" (ibid., p. 100).

Another representative case case involves the development of the concept of "black holes."[17] Early in this century, Einstein developed the theory of relativity, which lends credence to the idea of black holes. However, the history of the development of this idea is one of resistance to its acceptance. The idea can be traced back to theories of stellar evolution. In 1930, Subrahmanyan Chandrasekhar (cowinner of the 1983 Nobel Prize in physics) suggested the existence of black holes in an analysis submitted to the *Astrophysical Journal*. Chandrasekhar, however, was very careful and did not use the actual name "black hole." He wrote that if a star was large enough, it could not just collapse and pass

17. A collapsed stellar body from which no light, matter, or any kind of signal can escape. Theoretically, black holes are created when the gravitational field has become so strong that "escape velocity" from it approaches the speed of light (Silk 1980). I rely on Sullivan (1979) in the following discussion.

into a "white dwarf" stage but must become something else and thus "One is left speculating on other possibilities" (Sullivan 1979, p. 54). The *Astrophysical Journal* rejected the paper, and it was published elsewhere. When it appeared, Sir Arthur Eddington and Professor E. A. Milne, the famous mathematician, found the idea to be "preposterous" (Sullivan 1979, p. 54). E. A. Milne wrote Chandrasekhar that matter simply could not behave the way that he described. Sir Arthur felt the idea was absurd and flatly rejected it: "I think that there should be a law of Nature to prevent the star from behaving in this absurd way" (Sullivan 1979, p. 55). The respected Soviet physicist Lev Landau wrote that the very idea of a black hole was "ridiculous" (ibid., p. 85). In later years, Eddington remembered this period and mentioned that most contemporary physicists regarded the idea of a black hole simply as nonsense.

The next major step was taken by the German astronomer Karl Schwarzschild. Schwarzschild volunteered for the German army and contracted a fatal disease on the Russian front. As he lay terminally ill in the winter of 1915–16, he explored the simplest possibility of what could happen when gravity became exceedingly strong, as if emanating from a body that was concentrated into an infinitesimal point. From his mathematical calculations, he described what later became known as the "Schwarzschild radius." His discovery was that as one approached a point of infinite density, the effects of relativity became very visible, that is, light (and other) waves became infinitely long, long before the point itself is reached. Although Einstein himself wrote to Schwarzschild acknowledging his contribution, this development did not have any immediate impact. Lev Landau objected to the idea of black holes, stating that there was probably some stabilizing effect to prevent the infinitesimal collapse of stars. However, the American physicist Robert Oppenheimer, as well as several of his colleagues, were not convinced, and in 1939 Oppenheimer and George M. Volkoff reported in the February 15 issue of the *Physical Review* that a star could indeed continue to contract indefinitely. Still the idea did not catch the attention of physicists and only as late as 1963 was the idea raised again. One of the reasons for the renewal of interest was the discovery of quasars.[18]

The story of the discovery of quasars is itself well worth telling, although we shall not delve into it at length. For quite some time, astronomers had the data on quasars, especially their strongly red-shifted spectrum. However, they could not interpret correctly that the "strange"

18. An object that appears starlike but whose emission spectrum reveals a large shift to the red, which is usually interpreted to mean that it recedes from us at great speeds. Quasars are the most luminous (and unexplained) objects in the universe (Silk 1980).

spectra they were receiving from these stellar objects were regular but very shifted. Eventually this was correctly interpreted. Even today, the energy output of quasars and their red-shifts are a mystery that is far from solution.

The discovery of quasars and then pulsars, as well as the identification of many x-ray sources in the sky, gave a strong impetus to the idea of black holes. It seems that in the late 1960s and the 1970s, the astronomical community finally accepted the idea. We must remember that all this turmoil is about a concept; there is no direct and irrefutable observational support for the existence of black holes. The theoretical importance of the concept, however, is tremendous. Davies (1981a) pointed out that the very basic ideas and theories we currently hold about the nature of the universe, its beginning, evolution, and future, are intimately associated with the concept of black holes (and specifically with gravitational collapse and space-time singularities). He makes it clear that, not only does he view black holes as nature's greatest crisis, but in his view, they mark the end of the physical world, of physics, and of space-time as we know it. A singularity is a region in space-time where the known laws of physics break down, the curvature of space becomes infinite, and the universe as we know it ceases to exist. The idea of black holes, therefore, is not easy to understand or accept.

In summary, we have recorded a few modern cases of scientific innovations that were first rejected and later accepted. In all these cases, the theories as originally suggested were rejected by the scientific community and regarded as "deviant." However, hindsight shows us that deviance in this case was really "creative deviance" (Douglas 1977), which introduced change and created new forms of thought.

Scientific Ideas That Were Initially Accepted and Later Rejected

The history of science is paved with examples of scientific beliefs and worldviews that were once popular and accepted, only later to be rejected as nonsense and as deviant. The examples are numerous and, in most cases, well known.

When modern chemistry began to develop in the eighteenth century, "phlogiston" was assumed (but not proved) to explain the process of burning. In fact, the most influential development of chemistry theory of the eighteenth century was the phlogiston theory. Phlogiston was believed to be nonsupernatural, present in all combustible materials, and thus a valid explanation for combustion. When Joseph Priestly's discovery of oxygen was made public in 1775 (as "dephlogisticated air"), the dominance of the phlogiston theory was at an end. Similar example is provided by the term "caloric," commonly used in the eighteenth century. The theory existed that heat is a fluid called caloric that flows from high to low temperature zones. Both phlogiston and caloric theories are considered "deviant" today.

The field of astronomy also has a few cases of initially popular theories that were later rejected. The most obvious, example is the dominance of Aristotelian cosmology in the later Middle Ages. This cosmology was reconciled with Christian theology in the thirteenth century through Saint Thomas Aquinas's impressive synthesis, which stated, among other things, that the earth was motionless at the center of the universe. Around it were a number of moving spheres that formed an arch over the earth and filled the entire universe. Ptolemy, the Alexandrian astronomer, systematized this construct, which remained virtually unchallenged until the sixteenth century.

We have numerous examples in almost all scientific disciplines of theories that were once accepted as established paradigms, only to be later labeled as deviant. Whether in medical theories or sociological conceptions, the process has recurred again and again. Today one cannot find chemists experimenting with phlogiston, physicists testing the J-phenomenon, or astronomers formulating hypotheses according to Ptolemaic cosmology. If scientists did try to work within these defunct paradigms or concepts (with the exception of historical or sociological research), they would no doubt be labeled deviant and be rejected by the scientific community.

Scientific Speculations

The third category we shall analyze consists of various scientists, some central (including Nobel Prize winners) and some more peripheral, who have proposed theories that have not as yet been accepted by their peers and that are regarded as deviant. The word "speculative," one has to notice, is not as loaded as the word "deviant" and is therefore used more frequently. These theories do not involve fraud or conscious falsification of data, but are simply approaches that seem unorthodox to the scientific community.

Not much has been written on the subject of scientific speculation, and the researcher must collect his examples case by case. Good (1962) attempted to collect various "partly-baked ideas" in order, in his words, "to raise more questions." The book contains articles on subjects such as climate control, the development of languages, the various dimensions of consciousness, remote control dentistry, PSI research (e.g., precognition, telepathy, clairvoyance in rats, ESP), artificial intelligence, robots, multipurpose plants, interstellar communication, natural rejection, the mind-body question, quantum theory, paraffin from fermentation, and Jupiter's satellites. A similar book was edited in 1977 by Duncan and Weston-Smith. It is a fascinating account of concepts and problems that seem to be very strange but are offered by some of the world's most eminent scientists. More than anything else, this book is an attempt to redraw the line between science and nonsense. It covers more than fifty topics ranging from the origins of planets, quasars, galaxies, the universe, space, gravitation, time, and relativity to analyses of sleep, drug addiction, immunology, consciousness, and pain. The goal of the book is to clarify the problematic areas mentioned.

Scientific speculation has always been very attractive to science fiction, and much of the subculture has been devoted to "possibilities." Furthermore, Elsevier started to publish some time ago a scientific journal totally devoted to speculation (entitled *Speculation in Science and Technology*). Below, I describe some modern "mild" and "wild" hypotheses. Although any of the ideas presented here could, perhaps, be validated in the future, at present they are only speculations.

Case 1

Our first example is the concept of synchronicity developed jointly by Jung and by the Nobel laureate physicist and discoverer of the neutrino, Wolfgang Pauli. Synchronicity tries to explain the simultaneous occurrence of various events that are prima facie unrelated. The most famous illustration of this phenomenon was reported by Jung himself. One day in 1909, Jung and Freud met in Freud's study and argued about extrasensory perception. Suddenly, for no apparent reason, there was an explosive sound heard from Freud's bookcase. Jung commented that it was an example of a so-called catalytic phenomenon. Freud expressed his disbelief, to which Jung responded by saying that a second catalytic phenomenon was imminent. He had hardly finished his sentence when another explosive sound came from the bookcase.

The obscure principle of synchronicity is meant to explain what seem to be strange coincidences. While Jung was always interested in paranormal effects, Pauli apparently became involved because he himself had experienced numerous strange coincidences, so much so that his colleagues jokingly called them "the Pauli effect." In essence, Pauli and Jung suggested that while there are simple causal laws in nature (the ones that science studies), there also exists a type of acausal explanation called synchronicity, structured in space as opposed to time. This hypothesis, coupled with new developments in quantum mechanics, has given a very strong impetus to various ESP theories and research (see Wilson 1982; Koestler 1972b).

Case 2

Explaining the existence of various bacterial and viral diseases of the human race is not an easy task. In 1978, Sir Fred Hoyle and N. C. Wickramasinghe argued that life on earth originated from interstellar space. In a 1981 study, the two scholars suggested that the viruses and bacteria responsible for plagues and diseases reach our planet from space too. Their theory maintains that microbial life originated in space and was stored in frozen form in comets, which orbited the solar system and eventually fell to earth. By examining pathogenic material from space and analyzing patterns of plagues and epidemics, including influenza and the common cold, Hoyle and Wickramasinghe came to the amazing conclusion that terrestrial diseases originated in the extraterrestrial void. The response to such an unorthodox view was predictable. In the spring 1981 issue of the *Antioch Review* (vol. 39), Bieri commented, "Had my great idol, Fred Hoyle, finally flipped out? . . . It's pure scientific heresy" (p. 261). Yet toward the end of the review, Bieri became more cautious and allowed for the possibility that maybe the two scholars' thesis could be valid.

Case 3

Various theories predicting a "doomsday" for earth are plentiful, both in the realm of orthodox science and in that of science fiction. One of the more popular scenarios portrayed is the collision of a large meteor with earth. Some evidence exists that in the distant past, earth was indeed hit by mammoth celestial bodies. However, erosion of the earth's surface has eliminated most such evidence. The other planets in the solar system (and the natural planetary satellites) provide testimony of the devastating results of such a bombardment or collision. The possibility that a large meteor will hit earth, therefore, preoccupies many. Two recent science fiction descriptions for such an event are the best seller, *Lucifer's Hammer*, by L. Niven and J. Pournelle, and the movie *Meteor* (released in 1979).

Teske (1982) examines the possibility of a large asteroid colliding with earth. He states that there is evidence suggesting that a large asteroid made impact about 65 million years ago around the time of the transition from the Cretaceous to the Tertiary period. This collision caused the destruction and extinction of large numbers of species, including the dinosaurs.[19] However, the probability of a meteor hitting earth and creating a significant crater (10 kilometers in diameter) is about one every 100,000 years. The solar system's heaviest bombardment occurred early in its history.

All this did not deter Hoyle (1981) from predicting that a catastrophic ice age will commence in as little as ten years, triggered by a worldwide dust cloud created from a giant meteor collision. Hoyle's book created quite a stir. It was reviewed in *Discover* in 1981:

> Fred Hoyle breaks all the rules in his analysis of the causes of the repeated ice ages that have brought winter to the world over the last two and a half billion years. He dismisses with contempt a currently popular astronomical explanation, the Milankovitch effect, which attributes alterations in climate to changes in the tilt of the Earth's axis. Hoyle mixes the most casual speculation with his argument." (Davis 1981, pp. 92–93)

The reviewer, Davis, finds it difficult to reconcile Hoyle's reputation as a serious astronomer with his own dislike of Hoyle's theory as presented in *Ice*. He, therefore, accuses Hoyle of being pretentious in claiming to understand a very complicated issue. Yet he also acknowledges that Hoyle does possess a "bright mind" and that, after all, it is possible that his ideas have some merit. Finally, he ends his critique with the statement that Hoyle might be wrong, but that his book will no doubt force the specialists to clarify their own constructs, even if only to refute Hoyle's.

Case 4

In 1976, Linus Pauling (awarded the Nobel Prize in chemistry in 1954 and the Nobel Peace Prize in 1962) published a book in which he strongly recommended taking large doses of vitamin C in order to create resistance to colds. Generally speaking, it seems that the scientific community has not accepted this idea as valid. However, the debate continues and various scientists (including apparently Pauling himself) look for ways to validate this view.

Case 5

Astrology has always been a controversial issue, and heated arguments about its being a valid "science" or pure hoax can be easily found. Much

19. This specific theory about the disappearance of species (notably the dinosaurs) is often debated. For a different speculation, see Kane (1982). For a succinct summary of recent speculations see the May 1984 issue of *Discover* (vol. 5, no. 5, pp. 21–33).

of the debate, especially the arguments for a so-called scientific astrology, has been carried out by marginal scientists.[20] However, in a 1982 study Eysenck and Nias, after arguing in the first five chapters that traditional astrology should be discarded as nonvalid, devote the last two chapters to a defense of the astrology suggested originally about thirty years ago by Gauquelin. Eysenck himself is an eminent psychologist, and his ideas cannot be easily dismissed as "nonsense." Can we take his and Nias's 1982 book as valid? Not according to Gardner (1982), who in an elegant and pointed criticism first discards their ideas as not valid and nonsensical and, second, exposes Eysenck as a incompetent scientist and statistician. When Paul Kurtz reviewed Eysenck and Nias's book in the spring 1983 issue of *The Skeptical Inquirer* he devoted the first part of his review to pointing out how incompetent and dishonest Eysenck is.

There are numerous other examples of scientific speculations. The theories of Timothy Leary, the "prophet of LSD" in the 1960s and now the prophet of ideas about extraterrestrial intelligence, are a case in point. White and Kripner's work (1977) is another example of the "science" of ESP, paranormality, psychotronics, still orgone energy, and the like. Kline claimed recently (1980) that mathematics, as a discipline, has "lost certainty," a process that began around 1800 with geometry and culminated in this century. He claims that many theories and concepts backed by mathematics are actually fiction: "Nobody knows whether there is such a thing as gravity. We have no physical understanding of it. The theory is mathematical: gravity is a scientific fiction. . . . nobody knows what a radio wave or a TV wave is" (Kendig 1981, p. 124). Are these ideas credible?

Paul Davies, a quantum physicist, has advanced a multiuniverse theory that, in his own words, "not only seems bizarre but downright spooky and surrealistic" (1982b, p. 37). According to Davies's theory and those put forth by other quantum physicists, the world we actually experience and perceive is not the only one. "Our universe is only one among many closely parallel universes—worlds peopled, in many cases, by inhabitants much like ourselves!" (ibid., p. 37). Thus, our own universe is only an infinitesimal piece of a giant, complex stock of cosmic images, a "superspace." Although these alternative universes overlap our perceived universe, Davies's superspace theory is very explicit about the possibility of visitations among parallel realities; it is not possible to reach those parallel realities by traveling through our own space-time matrix.

20. See *Zetetic Scholar* 3–4 (1979): 71–121 on scientific astrology.

Modern physics, especially quantum mechanics, seem to have triggered many speculative ideas. Thus, Bohm (1980) suggests the *implicate order* hypothesis in which he tries to reconcile Eastern and Western mysticism with modern physics. This is not the first attempt to integrate modern physics with Eastern mysticism or consciousness. For similar cases, see Capra 1975 and Zukav 1979, both provocative books. It therefore seems that some "scientific" ideas can be more far-fetched than those of science fiction.[21]

Anomalies

Our fourth category includes so-called anomalous phenomena. Anomalies can be defined as all phenomena that fail to fit contemporary definitions of reality within specific cultural matrixes.[22] Kuhn (1962) pointed out that anomalies play a crucial role if we are to understand the process of growth and change in science, especially the demarcation of "science" and "nonscience." Both the sociology of science and the sociology of knowledge are deeply concerned with issues related to the definition, validation, and theoretical incorporation of anomalies (Westrum and Truzzi 1978). Unfortunately, despite the existence of numerous societies—usually extraneous to institutional science—that regularly publish newsletters and journals about anomalies, no consistent typology of anomalies has been developed.[23] Wescott (1982) suggests a typology that seems somewhat better than the usual formulations. He divides anomalies into six distinct categories: paradoxes, such as light that seems to be both particles and waves; displacements, discoveries that somehow "do not belong" where they are found, for example, live amphibians or reptiles in small rock cavities without visible outlets;[24] improbabilities, discoveries that are not likely, for example, the similarity between the Harappan script of the pre-Aryan Indus Valley and the rongo-rongo script of Eastern Island; deviation, an unexpected artifact or behavior,

21. I should briefly mention here Newton's alchemical experiments, an area of experimentation and involvement that is not a well-known facet of Newton's scientific career. Westfall (1980) has showed that these experiments had a definite influence on Newton's career and ideas.

22. These cultural matrixes can include the sciences, arts, common sense, and religions.

23. There is truly a large number of such journals and newsletters, e.g., *Pursuit: Science in the Pursuit of the Unexplained* and *Fortean Times: The Journal of Strange Phenomena*, to mention just two. One need only skim the advertisement section of *Fortean Times* to realize how many specialized journals, societies, and organizations like this exist.

24. Sometimes the term "ooparts" is used for out-of-place artifacts. Patton (1982) provides a fascinating list of ooparts. There is an argument as to who exactly coined the acronym: historian René Noorbergen or Sanderson.

for example, the fact that water is the only common liquid substance known that expands when it solidifies or the unexplained "crystal skull" (Garvin 1974); unexpected occurrences, the development of a structure (physical or social) that is totally unexpected in a specific cultural matrix; and unexplained phenomena such as natural human combustion, UFOs, the Loch Ness monster, suicidal whales, and extrasensory phenomena.

Orthodox science is faced with the very difficult problem of how to account for anomalies. Obviously, establishing that an anomaly exists at all is not easy, and researching it is even more difficult. Both these steps first involve establishing the reliability and credibility of the observers themselves (e.g., the problems of eye-witness testimony, the nature of the evidence, and the like). Next, the reliability of the instruments of investigation have to be established. The recording of data on instruments that can be checked thus becomes a major issue. If and when a true anomaly is established beyond doubt, then science (or the boundaries of a specific scientific discipline) can be seriously challenged.

When as a graduate student in 1967 Bell-Burnell discovered the first pulsars and until they could be explained as rapidly rotating neutron stars, their existence was certainly considered an anomaly. Westrum (1978) demonstrates how difficult it was for scientists in the eighteenth century to establish the reality of meteorites. Anyone reporting on stones that fell from the sky was certainly resisted and even ridiculed. But if a specific phenomenon can be recorded repeatedly and intelligently, the probability of its being studied and explained increases. Phenomena that are irreproducible, elusive, and hard to detect or record are unlikely to be classified as "reality," and thus the level of challenge to science will be significantly reduced. For our purposes, it is important to reiterate that phenomena that had once been defined as anomalous later became "normalized" and were explained (e.g., meteorites).

What constitutes an anomaly to the layman does not have to be regarded as such by the professional and vice-versa. The discussion that follows therefore focuses on those observations that scholars agree indicate that a certain phenomenon possesses an anomalous nature.

The history of anomalies cannot be fully outlined here, but a brief sketch is in order. The name most frequently connected with the investigation of anomalies is Charles Fort (1874–1932). Fort was a reporter and an amateur naturalist who collected for almost twenty-six years documents about strange and unexplained occurrences, for example, UFO sightings, the discovery of a lunar-size body near the planet Venus between 1645–1767, frogs falling from the sky, and the like. Fort published a number of books, full of strange, apparently anomalous cases.

Unfortunately, he did not get most of his data from reliable sources, but in most cases, from newspaper clippings. While he is credited as one of the first to collect systematically information about anomalies (some of which are consequently called Fortean events), he was not alone. Gould, Sanderson, and Heuvelman also collected such information. Today there are a few individuals and organizations, mostly outside the academic framework, who work hard to find, to interpret, and to distribute information about anomalies (Westrum and Truzzi 1978).[25] An important modern figure in the study of anomalies is the physicist William R. Corliss. Corliss started to collect data about anomalies in the early 1970s and since then has edited a number of volumes about anomalies in such different areas as astronomy, archaeology, biology, psychology and geology (Huyghe 1983, p. 109). Obviously, writing about anomalies has captured the imagination of different authors and one can find many references to them, especially in "popular science" magazines (e.g., Patton 1982).

To know if a phenomenon should be considered a true anomaly, one has to be thoroughly acquainted with existing explanations. For example, to know whether a certain archeological artifact is anomalous, one has to be well-versed in archaeology. Therefore, establishing something as anomalous or not involves, not only the problem of authentication of the phenomenon, but also collecting much background information.

Anomalies can occur within specific scientific disciplines. For example, the discovery of pulsars challenged astronomy, as has the discovery of quasars, posing an enigma that has not yet been satisfactorily resolved. However, the pulsar/quasar puzzles, or anomalies, are meaningless for people who lack knowledge in astronomy. Another example is Pasteur's work to resolve an anomaly discovered by Mitscherlich in 1844 regarding crystal forms and polarization of specific chemicals (Mulkay 1972, pp. 9–10). One should note that the results Pasteur obtained were not immediately accepted, and it took quite an effort until Pasteur's findings were absorbed by the scientific community even with the very active support of Biot.

Concluding Discussion

The concept of "deviant sciences" can be used to interpret various challenges to orthodox science. These challenges can introduce impor-

---

25. Truzzi's Center for Scientific Anomalies Research at Eastern Michigan University is an exception.

tant changes and flexibility into science as they change the boundaries of different scientific paradigms. Furthermore, the reactions of the relevant scientific community to clams made by deviant sciences can also help it to redefine its own boundaries and assumptions and in this manner to reinforce rigidity and stability.

Because science seeks to answer so many questions and solve so many problems, its frontiers are necessarily speculative. In a sense, the very goals of science stimulate contestable, or "deviant," beliefs. Cole's 1983 work illustrates that "in all sciences, knowledge at the research frontier is a loosely woven web, characterized by substantial levels of disagreement and difficulty in determining which contributions will turn out to be significant" (p. 111). As was seen in chapter 3, occultists and the subculture of science fiction use this fact to their advantage. They take speculative and deviant scientific beliefs and develop them into complex structures. Like deviant sciences, science fiction and the occult challenge accepted scientific beliefs. Occultists and science fiction fans usually have a respectable amount of scientific education. These people find themselves frequently exposed to the speculative frontiers of science as they attend science classes in universities, read scientific journals, or visit scientific meetings. They have, not only the ability to comprehend scientific jargon, but also the ability to go wildly beyond it. They are keenly aware of where controversies exist, and they know how to exploit and integrate speculative ideas to their own deviant belief systems (see, for example, Nicholls 1983). They can do this precisely because the outermost boundaries of science are fertile ground for wild guesses. In this sense, science likes to view itself as different, more open to innovations than other social systems. In science, theoretically at least, stability can be justified only if it is instrumental to the advancement of knowledge. In reality, this is not always the case.

This implies that a distinction must be made between "deviant" and "speculative" science. Not every speculation in science becomes "deviant." A deviant science, to follow Dolby's approach, is a claim that is so branded by the leading relevant scientific experts. Supporters of such claims are frequently stigmatized, isolated, ridiculed, and prevented from continuing their work. Analyzing the conditions under which a "deviant science" label will be evoked, maintained, or eliminated is a complex task. If an unorthodox scientific claim is made and generates a controversy, then one possible way to solve the controversy is through experiments. When empirical results are inconclusive, or impossible, a complicated negotiating process starts. The end result of that process can be the declaration of an unorthodox idea as deviant or as a new scientific specialty. The negotiating process is intimately linked to the prevailing scientific paradigm and the perceived threat of the new idea. Schlussel (1983) pointed out that the social position of supporters of deviant sciences (as well as the nature of the suggested innovation) is a crucial variable in the acceptance or rejection of new, deviant, ideas. The reaction of supporters in itself is important in determining the reaction of the relevant scientific community. For example, if a scholar presents an idea and gets very negative reactions, he could either drop it or keep pursuing it.

The amount of success, or failure, of the innovation depends not only on its validity but also on complex political processes. Thus, whether a specific innovation becomes defined as a "deviant" science or not is the result of a lengthy process of negotiation and is not based on just one event. This is very similar to identity negotiation processes in other types of deviance—the identification of mental illness, homosexuality, drug use, for example. In all these cases, the negotiation focuses on attempts to characterize the nature of the reality in question and evaluates it in terms of "deviance" or "nondeviance." As is often the case, the nature of the behavior (or the innovation) in question is not the only factor to be evaluated, but the deviant himself and his past behavior are all interpreted and reinterpreted.

For example, the quality of Margaret Mead's work was questioned recently. The fall 1983 issue of the *Skeptical Inquirer* had an article by Gardner documenting some bizarre beliefs supposedly held by Mead (mostly on UFOs, dowsing, psychic phenomena). The article thus suggested that it was not only Mead's work that was questionable, but her integrity and intelligence. Likewise, when Struve had to cope with Reber's "bizarre' paper, he checked his credentials in the association of radio engineers. Thus, both the validity of an innovation and the credibility and competency of those who try to advance it are questioned. One must also make a distinction between a case in which people external to a scientific discipline define an idea or observation as deviant and one in which people inside the discipline invoke this label. In both cases, it is very important who (in terms of hierarchies of credibility) is making this decision. The concept of "deviant" science therefore is, I feel, very important as one way of interpreting how stability is maintained in science and how change is introduced. As a point of comparison, one should note that when many innovations in the arts (music, painting) were introduced, they were ignored, ridiculed, and branded as deviant. In many respects, the process of defining a specific art form as deviant (or, conversely, granting it recognition) closely resembles the processes we have described in science (see, for example, Becker 1978, 1982).

The demarcation of deviant and orthodox (or normal) science is not always clear. Laudan (1983) even suggests that we ought to drop such terms as "pseudoscience" and "unscientific" from our vocabulary. He claims that these terms are hollow and only serve emotional needs because there are so many cases of sciences that are on the borderline. For example, cryptozoology was considered deviant for a long period of time.[26] In recent years, however, it has become a more legitimate as increasing numbers of established scientists have begun to research sightings of strange animals and as more evidence is accumulated pointing to their possible existence (Mackal 1980; Colligan 1981).

My suggestion for a schematic presentation of the possible relations between flawed, normal, speculative, and deviant science appears below:

	Accepted, clear methodologies	Methodologies not accepted, not clear; problematic reproducibility and control
Hypothesis conforms to prevailing scientific paradigms	Regular, normal science	Flawed science
Hypothesis does not conform to prevailing scientific paradigms	New scientific paradigms in crystallization	Deviant, Speculative science

I have focused on the deviant/speculative sciences as a rewarding way of examining how these sciences introduce changes or induce stability in the boundaries of relevant scientific disciplines. Obviously, this work has not explored other, nondeviant ways of doing the same thing.

In the next section, I illustrate the interaction between orthodox and deviant science, examining two claims about extraterrestrial intelligence. In the first case, SETI, orthodox science responded by creating a legiti-

---

26. The term refers to the search for peculiar animals, such as the Loch Ness monster.

mate and respected branch of its establishment. In the case of UFOs, however, a deviant science emerged.

The Extraterrestrial Question

Introduction

A fascinating but highly speculative question is whether or not the human race is the only intelligent life in the universe. Dick 1982 analyzes the extraterrestrial life debate from Democritus to Kant, showing that the question goes back a long time. The number of theories and pseudotheories that have grown up around this question is truly amazing.[27] Obviously, it has tremendous philosophical, religious, and scientific as well as political implications. If you like, the search for extraterrestrial life is the ultimate adventure.[28] It has resulted in two separate approaches. One has become an orthodox science, SETI, the other a deviant science, ufology. The Extraterrestrial Question is intimately linked to various chemical, ecological, biological, and physical questions and to the problem of the origin of life on our planet. The answers to these questions, particularly about the origin of life and the universality of such a process, are essential to determining whether life exists beyond our world. I shall first show that even these areas have some "deviant" theories. Next I shall examine and compare SETI and ufology.

The Origin of Life

The origin of life has interested many biologists and chemists. A variety of solutions have been suggsted for this problem. For example, Oparin suggested in the 1920s that life on earth originated in ancient oceans, which could be conceptualized as a biological soup. The waters contained various chemicals that, under specific physical conditions (e.g., of temperature, electrical discharges, etc.), produced primitive organic molecules. These molecules developed later into simple, one-celled organisms and the evolutionary process began. Another hypothesis developed after Watson and Crick discovered the molecular structure of

27. See Edelson (1979); Christian (1976); Morrison, Billingham, and Wolfe (1979); Bracewell (1976); Sagan (1973); Sullivan (1964); Sagan and Shklovsky (1960); Papagiannis (1980); Billingham (1981); Hart and Zuckerman (1982); Rood and Trefil (1981); Goldsmith (1980); and Ridpath (1975).

28. A simple indication for the widespread scientific, as well as popular, interest in the extraterrestrial question is the fact that this topic receives regular coverage in the national and international media. For example, the January 31, 1983, and the February 14, 1983, issues of *Newsweek* had salient items on the subject.

DNA and the genetic code in the late 1950s and early 1960s. The genetic hypothesis assumed the existence of primitive DNA-like molecules that developed until life as we know it was created. But these answers leave many unresolved issues. For example, it seems that the probability of life developing on earth was very low, given all known and guessed conditions, yet we are here. How is this to be explained? It also seems that all living things somehow employ the same biochemical language to convey genetic information. How can this uniformity be explained? The theory of evolution itself leaves many questions open.

The temptation is strong, therefore, to drift toward magical or religious explanations. Likewise, there is a strong temptation to suggest that life as we know it originated in an extraterrestrial civilization. Thus, various theories have arisen that attribute the origin of *Homo sapiens*, not to a slow, gradual process of development through natural selection and other evolutionary forces, but to the intervention of extraterrestrial, alien intelligence. Science fiction literature has nourished many such ideas.

Däniken has probably done the most to popularize the extraterrestrial origin of life on earth.[29] According to his formulations, many thousands of years ago ancient astronauts landed on earth and performed some genetic manipulations on the ancient apes, the results of which are the human race. His theories have inspired much debate, and most criticism is leveled against the various facts and proofs that Däniken uses. Most of his data do not stand up under close scrutiny.[30] While his theories therefore remain empirically unproven, they continue to attract adherents. They have generated many books by others (see Greenwell 1979b) suggesting numerous additions and refinements and even claiming that human civilization is still being monitored by the extraterrestrial intelligence that orginally created it. Some of these satellite theories clearly are the result of very poor scholarship (in terms of consistency, citations, etc.); some other works are good. Two examples of reasonably good works are those by Temple and by Blumrich.

Temple (1976, 1981) claims that the Dogon of Mali, a so-called primitive tribe, demonstrate a "stunning, impossible, and unexplained" knowledge of astronomy (e.g., that the star Sirius has an invisible companion, Sirius B) and that with no instruments they possessed this knowl-

---

29. Däniken was not the first to suggest this hypothesis, but he has never acknowledged his predecessors.

30. See, for example, Grim (1982), Frazier (1981), Story (1976, 1980b), Wilson (1978), Palmer (1979).

edge long before Western science discovered some of the same facts. Temple uses this case to build a systematic and elaborate theory, suggesting that intelligent amphibian beings from Sirius were somehow involved in the origin of the human race on earth.[31] Blumrich (1974) convincingly suggested that Ezekiel's "vision" constitutes, in fact, a detailed report about the landing of a spaceship.

Since Däniken and many of the writers in his tradition are not academics, it is relatively easy to attack them. The ancient astronaut hypothesis and many of its satellite theories are usually classified as deviant science beyond a doubt. Typical is Palmer's comment, "Däniken . . . is a caricature of positivism, something that has crawled out from under the damp stones of scientific inquiry. . . . closer to soap opera than to science" (1979, pp. 144, 147).

However, in recent years, three prestigious scholars have also raised the extraterrestrial question in connection with the origin of life. We have already discussed Hoyle and Wickramasinghe's work. In a 1978 book, they suggest that interstellar space is filled with prebiotic molecules carried by comets. Early in the earth's history, the crashing of comets spread water and volatiles over the earth's surface, and later (about 4 billion years ago) life was introduced from a life-bearing comet. Hoyle and Wickramasinghe even suggest that primitive life forms may have evolved extraterrestrially on comets.[32] In a later study (1981), they suggest that the origin of various diseases on earth should be attributed to extraterrestrial sources as well. Hoyle is no amateur. He is an established and esteemed astronomer, yet the theory he helped develop is certainly considered deviant and is not accepted as part of orthodox science.[33]

The second upheaval came in 1981 when Frances Crick published *Life Itself*. According to the elaborate theory developed in the book, intelligent beings from another star, galaxy, or world sent spores by rockets to earth. This process Crick calls "directed panspermia." Crick in no way resembles Däniken. In 1962, he shared the Nobel prize in physiology and medicine with James Watson and Maurice Wilkins for their discovery of

31. Obviously, Temple has been under heavy attacks from anthropologists and astronomers alike. See, for example, Pesch and Pesch (1977), Krupp (1977), and Story (1980b).

32. While very few scholars accept this particular view, there seems to be no reason not to assume that comets could have (or actually had) various influences on the evolution of life on earth. See Ponnamperuma (1981) for different views on this.

33. In 1957, Hoyle published what has come to be considered one of the finest science fiction books ever to be written, *The Black Cloud*. In it, he describes a future invasion of interstellar matter into the solar system (the "cloud"). It is later revealed that an alien intelligence exists in the cloud. It is difficult not to compare Hoyle's beautiful fictional creation with his later thoughts on the extraterrestrial question.

the molecular structure of DNA (and therefore of the genetic code). What gives the idea of "directed panspermia" credibility are Crick's own reputation and his persuasive argument. As Stent puts it, "Crick shows that directed panspermia is a genuine scientific theory" (1981, p. 30). Crick's ideas were anticipated by the Swedish physicist Arrhenius, who proposed in the late nineteenth century that life on earth did not start by itself but had been seeded by microorganisms from space. Arrhenius even suggested the term "panspermia." Crick himself had been consistently defending the theory of directed panspermia since the early 1970s.

In 1971, above the Armenian city of Yerevan, in the Byurakan astronomical observatory, American and Soviet scientists met (under the sponsorship of U.S. and USSR academies of science) to discuss the extraterrestrial question in depth. At this meeting, Crick and Orgel first presented their paper on directed Panspermia.[34] As Stent points out, Crick is regarded by many of his colleagues as the greatest theoretician of biology since Darwin. His directed panspermia theory cannot be easily dismissed. The idea, if ever proven, will certainly explain many gaps that still exist in our knowledge regarding the beginnings of life on earth.

It is interesting to note some of the reactions to this theory. In an interview (Rorvik 1982), Crick himself described his theory as "bold," "creative," and "innovative." However, he also used the interview to attack Hoyle and Wickramasinghe's ideas as "very fanciful." (p. 82). It is clear from the interview that Crick is well aware that orthodox scientists are not going to accept his theory of directed panspermia.

On March 25, 1982, Freeman Dyson of the Institute for Advanced Study in Princeton, New Jersey, gave a public lecture at the Van Leer Institute in Jerusalem. The title of the lecture was "Origin of Life." Professor Dyson surveyed existing theories and suggested his own mathematical model. In his entire lecture, he mentioned neither Hoyle, Crick, nor their theories. I found that to be somewhat odd and at the end of his lecture questioned him about it. Dyson seemed to have no qualms about denouncing Hoyle and his theories as fantasies ("The guy wants us to believe that life actually rained on us!?"). However, Crick's directed panspermia was not as easy to denounce or dismiss. Dyson did not criticize the theory but mentioned that he knew Crick to be "a nice and intelligent fellow" and that he could not understand what brought Crick to write his book.[35]

34. See Stent (1981), Sagan (1973), or Crick and Orgel (1973).

35. I have to admit that I was surprised at his response. First, Dyson attended the 1971 conference in Soviet Armenia and his 1979 book has a chapter on the extraterrestrial question. Crick's ideas were certainly not new to him. Second, Dyson himself has advanced

The intellectual sophistication and plausibility of the ideas of Däniken, Hoyle, and Crick differ as greatly as does their prestige. Could any one of them be right? Each of them is certain that he presents the human race with a new, revolutionary concept that is valid. Will any of these hypotheses be one day institutionalized and become "orthodox science?"

As noted before, the question of the origin of life is only one aspect, albeit a major one, of the extraterrestrial question. What of the question itself? Are there other intelligent beings in the universe? One way to address the question is to philosophize about it, something that has been done extensively. The other route is an empirical one, involving three major types of activities. The first is to transmit optical, radio, or other signals to the universe in the hope that if there is an intelligence out there, there will be a response. With a few exceptions, none of the ideas presented here (whether science fiction or serious) have ever been operational. The wisdom of such attempts has been questioned more than a few times. In 1960, NASA contracted the Brookings Institute to study the impact of extraterrestrial contact with alien intelligences. The document that resulted from this study warned that such a contact (especially with an advanced civilization) could have disastrous consequences for humanity (Sullivan 1964). Sir Martin Ryle, Nobel laureate in physics and one of Britain's leading astronomers, in a letter to the *New York Times* on November 4, 1976, urged radio astronomers of the world to aovid "making known the existence of intelligent life on this planet, lest the Earth be invaded by hostile beings" (Goldsmith 1980, pp. 267–68).

The second activity has been to try to detect, through optical and radio technologies, signs of intelligence on nearby planets (e.g., the observation by Percival Lowell of the famous "canals" on the planet Mars and its

---

in the past some highly speculative and controversial ideas. In a paper that appeared originally in 1960 in *Science*, he suggested that an advanced, highly technological civilization with large energy demands would probably choose to capture the entire radiation output of its parent star. This, Dyson argued, could be done by encapsulating the parent sun with a sphere made from the materials of a disassembled star (what later became known as a "Dyson sphere"). Originally, he felt that this could direct the search for extraterrestrial civilizations because the encapsulated star would provide a center of infrared radiation. The idea caused an uproar and has continued to be very controversial. In reply to different questions about the feasibility and stability of such a huge hollow sphere, Dyson himself later agreed that a solid shell around a star was impossible. Science fiction writer Larry Niven, however, put the idea to beautiful use in his Hugo Award–winning novel *Ringworld*, published in 1970, and in its sequel in 1980. Finally, Dyson himself suggested (1979, p. 236) that comets, not planets, were the most likely potential habitat for life in space. Dyson's criticism of Crick thus seems truly peculiar.

supposedly dying culture),[36] or in distant stars and galaxies. The third activity has been to try to find out if there is any evidence that the earth (or the solar system) was ever visited, or is still being visited, by extraterrestrial aliens. Below I compare some of the activities undertaken in these last two categories, particularly SETI and ufology.

SETI

The acronym SETI stands for Search for Extraterrestrial Intelligence. The term generally denotes all the philosophical and empirical efforts made to discover extraterrestrial intelligence. The speculative and empirical work here is multifaceted. First, one must address the nature and origin of life and question whether life forms everywhere in the universe would resemble our life forms (i.e., carbon based). Can there be life based on, say, silicon? Will other life forms resemble life as we know it, or will they be totally alien, perhaps even unintelligible to us? It becomes immediately apparent that one must set very specific objectives. In other words, one has to posit the specific chemical and biochemical conditions in which life can develop. Therefore, some specific chemical and biochemical assumptions must be made. Second, certain ecological assumptions must also be made. What type of planets are capable of sustaining life? Third, the question of contact has to be addressed. What type of contact, under what conditions, and which type of perceptual modality will be used for such a contact?

Almost all scholars agree that interstellar distances are so vast that they render an actual physical search and contact quite impossible. At the speeds attainable by our present technology, a modest trip to the closest star to the sun (not to mention galaxy) would take many years. Even if the trip is made at close to relativistic speeds (which have not yet been attained), it would take several years.[37] The emphasis here is on the limit of speed as we know it, that is, the speed of light. If this limit cannot be surpassed, the explorable universe is not very large. If, as a few science fiction writers would like us to believe, it will one day be possible to travel faster than light (or if there are extraterrestrial intelligences who control

36. Not to mention numerous hoaxes, one of the earliest being the so-called moon hoax of 1835. At that time, the *New York Sun* published a series of reports, supposedly from Herschel, describing in great detail observations made of living aliens on the moon.

37. The speed of light is approximately 300,000 kilometers per second in a vacuum. At such speeds, it is predicted that there are significant differences between the passage of time as experienced by the traveller and by a stationary observer. The observer would age more quickly than the traveller.

such a technological breakthrough), then physical contact becomes possible. Most discussion in this area, however, leaves one with very little doubt regarding its improbabilty. Rather than rush (or expect that someone else would send) "tons of metal" across the vast interstellar void, it is easier (and more economical) to either transmit or receive information in the form of radio waves (Edelson 1979). Electromagnetic waves of some frequency seem to be, not only the best possible way of searching beyond our world, but given our present technology, the only way.

Most important for SETI research to be carried out, one must assume that extraterrestrial intelligence exists. Furthermore, one must also assume that the technological development of such intelligence is such that meaningful communication is possible. Thus, one of the very first preliminary questions to be asked is whether the human race is unique in the universe or not. If we consider the tremendous size and complexity of the universe, it is probable that other intelligences do exist, but the question of where they are remains. Enrico Fermi is reputed to have asked, "If there are intelligent beings elsewhere in the galaxy, where are they?" and "Why are they not here?"[38] The positive response to the speculation was no doubt the major factor in stimulating SETI research in the early 1960s.

One of the earliest documents in SETI research was published in *Nature* in 1959. There, Cocconi and Morrison suggested the commencement of a SETI program that would listen for possible radio transmissions from alien intelligences. Throughout the 1960s and the 1970s, the United States and, to an even greater extent, the USSR were involved in SETI research. Since much more is known about SETI research in the United States, in the following passages we briefly sketch its history.

In the 1960s, a young astronomer named Frank Drake persuaded Professor Struve, director of the Radio Astronomy Observatory in Green Bank, West Virginia, to start a modest SETI project.[39] The project consisted of using the Green Bank radio telescope for listening to possible alien radio transmissions from two relatively near stars: Tau Ceti and Epsilon Eridani. "Project OZMA" (from the *Wizard of Oz*) began in April 1960 and was terminated three months later. No transmissions were

38. Crick (1981, pp. 13–16). Supposedly, Fermi asked this question (called the "Fermi paradox") when he was at the University of Chicago during World War II. It is rumored that his close friend, the Hungarian scientist Lee Szilard, who apparently possessed an excellent sense of humor, answered Fermi that the aliens were already among us "but they called themselves Hungarians" (Crick 1981, p. 14).

39. Struve was the same astronomer who, years earlier, approved the publication of Reber's innovative paper on radio astronomy.

detected (Drake 1961). Nevertheless, the project has become the prototype for any subsequent listening strategy (Edelson 1979). Following this pioneering work, a small SETI meeting of about a dozen select scientists was assembled in 1961 at Green Bank and SETI research began to gain momentum.

In 1971 two significant events took place. The first, and most famous, was the SETI convention held in Byurakan in Soviet Armenia. The conference attracted many respectable and important scholars from both the Soviet Union and America and constituted a turning point in SETI research. Ideas about research strategies were crystallized, and the field acquired more momentum, credibility, and prestige. Historically, it is clear that the 1971 Byurakan convention was the single most important event in the history of SETI research, giving it scientific legitimation.

In the same year, a design-study meeting took place at NASA's Ames Research Center. The meeting was attended by both communication engineers and astronomers, and the result was the publication of a now famous report known as Project Cyclops. The project suggested the construction in a large area (about twenty kilometers square) of a thousand one hundred-meter radio-telescope dishes, all computer controlled and feeding into one single data-processing system (Oliver and Billingham 1971). The meeting was also a precedent for a series of NASA-sponsored scientific conferences and workshops as part of determining various strategies for SETI research. More scientific reports followed (e.g., Morrison et al. 1979).

Throughout the 1970s, various listening projects using radio telescopes were carried out in different locations. The Soviet Union has encouraged some of its scientists to engage in such research since at least the mid 1960s. As we have seen, in the United States, Project OZMA, launched April 1960, marked the first real attempt at listening. More attempts followed both in the United States and Canada. Between 1960 and 1981, there were at least thirty-three different SETI projects (Murray, Gulkis, and Edelson 1978; Tarter 1982). In recent years, a number of sophisticated attempts have been carried out, using new technologies, for example, a new multichannel spectrum analysis and new optical searches for possible alien space probes. (For a review and up-to-date works see Tarter 1982; Valdes and Freitas 1983; Bowyer et al. 1983). These refined technologies are an obvious sign of the vitality and the further institutionalization of SETI as science. Yet none of these efforts have yielded positive results. No alien radio transmissions have been detected.

The other strategy employed by SETI scientists was not merely to listen but to transmit. One such "transmission" was the plaque carried by the Pioneer 10 and 11 spacecrafts (launched in 1972 and 1973) (Sagan 1973). A second attempt was made on November 10, 1974, when a complicated, mathematical, three-minute message was sent into the interstellar void from the giant Arecibo radio telescope located in Puerto Rico (National Astronomy and Ionosphere Center, 1975). The third attempt used the Voyager 1 and 2 space probes sent in 1977 to explore the outer planetary stars. The two Voyagers each carry a long-playing phonograph record with messages describing human civilization (Sagan 1979).

While some of its theoretical foundations were laid out as early as the late 1950s, only since 1971 has SETI research developed as an accepted scientific activity. Hypothesizing about alien intelligence (an essential part of SETI) has become a respectable scientific activity in many fields. As we have seen, speculating about the nature and origin of life on earth and about possible life forms on other planets has become a major issue.[40] Professional journals have numerous papers by astronomers trying to develop techniques to detect whether distant stars have earthlike planets, capable of supporting life as we know it. SETI research activities have thus been reported consistently in various scientific journals and at respected scientific meetings. SETI has developed its own hypotheses, research methods, and respectability.[41] All these activities, and NASA's involvement, have helped legitimize and create a specific scientific discipline.

The growth of SETI as science depends on an affirmative answer to a very elusive question. Obviously, challenging this answer can, in theory, take away the very basis upon which SETI research is founded. Such a challenge has been formulated in recent years by a group of scientists who claim that it is likely that humankind is the only intelligent species in the universe (e.g., see Oberg 1980; Hart and Zuckerman 1982). In November 1979, some of these scientists met in College Park, at the University of Maryland, and held their own conference. The proceedings of that symposium were published in 1982 in a book edited by Hart and Zuckerman entitled *Extraterrestrials: Where Are They?* Among other things, the study concludes that "there are no intelligent beings from outer space on

---

40. The study of life forms outside the earth, in fact, became another speculative science. Joshua Lederberg, Nobel prize winner in biology, coined the term "exobiology" to describe such study. At the moment, the field of exobiology is badly in need of substantial subject matter.

41. SETI even had its own phase of hoaxes. For a brief review of some of them, see Stonely and Lawton (1976, pp. 42–48); Ridpath (1975, pp. 156–64); Edelson (1979, pp. 129–33). Most of the hoaxes revolved around claims that signals were received either from alien intelligences directly or from interstellar probes sent by them.

Earth now," that "an extensive search for radio messages from other civilizations is probably a waste of time and money, and [that] in the long run, cultures descended directly from ours will probably occupy most of the habitable planets in our galaxy" (pp. 1, 8). There can hardly be a doubt that the 1979 Maryland conference and its summary in Hart and Zuckerman's book provides the most sophisticated and serious challenge for SETI research, undermining its most basic assumption. In 1981, Rood and Trefil also published a book challenging the notion of alien intelligence. They concluded, somewhat hesitantly, that "we are alone" and that the probability for the existence of extraterrestrial intelligences is either zero or very close to it. However, because of what the authors felt could be a "possible beneficial payoff of a positive search result," they recommended that SETI be continued.

While skeptics had earlier raised their voices individually, 1979 marked the first time that they organized their ranks. It is possible that, in the long run, the Maryland conference will prove to have the same impact as the Byurakan symposium, but in the opposite direction. Nevertheless, today SETI researchers have established themselves as legitimate scientists. When Professor Frank Tipler from Tulane University wrote a paper in 1981 challenging the basic SETI assumption, they were effective in preventing its publication in both *Science* and *Icarus* (Rondinone 1982).[42]

However, the field has recently encountered serious obstacles. In late 1981, Democratic Senator William Proxmire of Wisconsin demanded that SETI funding by NASA be terminated. While SETI research cost NASA only $1 to $2 million a year, Proxmire felt it was a waste of the public's already-strained budget. He awarded SETI research his infamous Golden Fleece Award and was fairly successful in killing the project and eliminating NASA as a central funding agent for SETI research.[43] SETI was not totally eliminated since some private and other funds remained available to it on a very small scale. Scientists (especially those involved in SETI research) responded angrily, and dramatic, full-page advertisements appeared in the April 1982 issue of *Astronomy* urging people to donate money to SETI research.

The public debate about the basic validity of the assumption of the existence of alien intelligence was waged openly in the March 1983 issue of *Discover*, which had a large section entitled "Life in Space," totally devoted to the extraterrestrial question. Out of five papers written by eminent scholars, four were very favorable to SETI and only one, by

42. Tipler succeeded in publishing his papers in other journals.
43. See reports in *Discover* 2 (Nov. 1981): 64, and in *OMNI* 4 (Jan. 1982): 37.

Tipler (1983), clearly stated that "we are alone." Typically Sagan's opening paper warmly endorsed the view that "we are nothing special" and added a dramatic call to action, "we urge the organization of a coordinated, worldwide, and systematic search for [Extraterrestrial Intelligences.]" More of these arguments were published in 1983 in the journal *Science* (see, for example, Tipler 1983a).

A few facts facilitated Proxmire's success. First is the consistent failure of SETI research to pick up any alien transmission so far. Second, the SETI community has remained rather small, with a tendency to inbreed. The same names appear again and again on different committees and panels (Edelson 1979, pp. 125–26). Third, the federal budget for research was severely cut in the early 1980s. In a situation where one's gains in research funding mean someone else's loss, the competition becomes very stiff.

Proxmire's campaign against SETI, however, was somewhat counterbalanced when, after almost two years of study, the National Academy of Science's Astronomy Survey Committee published its report on astronomy and astrophysics for the 1980s. The report recommended that a specialized working group should conduct SETI research. It was generally recommended that an astronomical search for extraterrestrial intelligence be continued at a modest level, undertaken as a long-term effort rather than a short-term project (Waldorf 1982). Furthermore, Sagan was able to talk with Proxmire and was effective in changing his position. SETI has been reinstated in NASA's budget at about the five million dollar level. Whether it will continue to develop as a science is an entirely different question. The scientific basis of SETI and its hard-won legitimization indicate perhaps that we can answer it affirmatively.

UFOs

The amount of literature that has been published on UFOs is truly overwhelming. There are numerous periodicals, journals, research centers, interest groups, and regular annual conventions.[44] The acronym UFO stands for unidentified flying object. The term generally encompasses all the theoretical and empirical efforts to explain strange and puzzling phenomena, usually aerial. Throughout the years, its exact meaning has become problematic (Martin 1982). While SETI has established itself as a legitimate scientific activity both in content and methodology, ufology has developed into a true deviant science.

44. It is virtually impossible to mention here even a significant part of this vast body of literature. For condensed reviews of the field, see Story (1980a, 1980b), Hynek (1972, 1977), Jacobs (1975), Sachs (1980), and Story and Greenwell (1981), to mention only a few.

Although it is difficult to determine the exact nature of a UFO, a brief description is nonetheless in order. A UFO can refer to a variety of aerial phenomena—fire balls, strange lights, and flying objects in various forms (e.g., discs, "airships," pulsating-light objects, and the like). Most of the credible literature on UFOs is very clear about the fact that most of these phenomena are explained and become IFOs (identified flying objects). Misidentification of objects such as meteors, airplanes, meteorological balloons, strange formations of clouds, lightning, experimental flying vehicles, and satellites can often result in an unjustified UFO report. Although these objects might be perceived as UFOs by the untrained observer, close investigation usually reveals their identity.

Hoaxes—reports on observations that were never made and fabricated photographs and artifacts—have done much to damage the field's credibility. The number of hoaxes perpetrated in the name of ufology is much too high. This is not surprising because reports of actual contacts with UFO occupants, or of dramatic abductions by UFO occupants, usually make the media headlines, with obvious rewards for the hoaxer. However, especially during the last years, reporting techniques have been refined and a few criteria have been defined to distinguish UFOs from hoaxes. The most famous typology is that of Hynek (1972), which is based on three types of encounters. Close encounters are sightings of brilliantly-lit objects in close proximity to the observers, usually less than 500 feet away. A close encounter of the first kind is that "in which no interaction of the UFO with the environment or the observers is reported" (p. 100). A close encounter of the second kind takes place when "the reported UFO, generally a bright illuminated 'craft,' leaves a visible record of its visit, or encounters with human observers" (p. 126). Close encounters of the third kind constitute the most bizarre and incredible aspect of UFOs, that is "those in which the presence of animated creatures is reported" (p. 158).

While the experience accumulated over the years enables us to discard most UFO sightings as misidentification and others as hoaxes, there still remains a rather small, but intriguing number of cases that cannot be explained. These include reports of UFOs by highly reliable observers (in many cases, trained professionals such as astronomers and airline pilots), as well as reports that utilize external criteria and not just human observation, for example, radar contacts, photographs, and traces on the ground. The most reliable category is that in which a UFO sighting is, not only reported by a few independent, reliable observers, but also corroborated simultaneously by radar contact or photographs. Such reports, and there are a few of them, cannot be easily explained or dismissed. Furthermore, although most reports on close encounters of the third kind are strange, vague, fantastic, and often unbelievable, there are some that seem reliable and hard to refute. In a few cases, lie-detecting machines, hypnosis, and other techniques were used, sometimes reinforcing the reliability of the reports.

A UFO's presence is usually associated with a variety of unusual observations: severe disturbances in the functioning of electrical appliances, disturbances in magnetic fields, car engines supposedly stall and refuse to start, batteries go dead. UFOs are often described as flying at tremendous speeds, sometimes making a humming or buzzing sound, performing all sorts of impossible aerial maneuvers, and flashing dazzling lights. The phenomenon of sightings is worldwide. In many cases, the UFO was observed by more than one person and sometimes by whole towns. The various reports seem to suggest a coherent set of observations, despite obvious national and cultural differences (e.g., Story 1980, 1980b, 1981; Sachs 1980).

Whether there is solid evidence that UFOs exist has never been satisfactorily resolved.[45] Thus there is a debate whether UFOs constitute a legitimate anomaly. This is closely linked with the question of what we are willing to accept as evidence, that is, with the complicated social process of defining what is acceptable evidence. What cannot be debated, however, is the profound and documented personal and social effect evoked by a close encounter of the third kind (and, to a much lesser degree, close encounters of the first and second kind).

Thousands of people in the United States in the last century have claimed that they have seen and heard airships (see Jacobs 1975). However, the witnessing of unexplained aerial objects is not exclusively contemporary. Vallee (1965) gives a fascinating account of such episodes in biblical times and in the days of the Roman Empire. He claims to have evidence of more than three hundred UFO sightings prior to the twentieth century, out of which there are about sixty cases that clearly refer to heavy, self-motivated and guided bodies observed in the skies over various parts of Europe and the British Isles prior to the nineteenth century. There can be little doubt that the nineteenth century witnessed an intensification of these phenomena in the United States, Europe, and in South America. There are numerous UFO reports from that century, some of which even appeared in the scientific journals of the time.

The twentieth century has also witnessed numerous and varied reports

---

45. For a recent debate, see papers by Guerin (1979), Greenwell (1979c), and the reactions in *Zetetic Scholar* 7 (1980): 57–113; 8 (1981): 47–124, and 9 (1982): 96–97.

about UFOs. A close examination of the more reliable and accurate ones reveals that the objects observed in the first half of the century are similar to the ones described later (ibid.) It seems that the first modern sightings occurred during World War II when Allied bomber pilots reported that strange balls of light and disc-shaped objects followed them in flight (both in the European and the Far East arenas). American pilots called these objects "foo-fighters" (Jacobs 1975, p. 30). While initially these objects were considered some form of a secret weapon, they never attacked the planes, but just followed them, sometimes in a most frivolous way. In the second sightings, between the years 1946 and 1948, observers in Sweden and Finland reported many unidentified cigar-shaped objects flying in the sky.

The third occasion of a UFO sighting in the modern era occurred on June 24, 1947, in the United States. This is the famous case of Kenneth Arnold, considered by many to be the father of UFO sightings in the modern era. Arnold, a thirty-two-year-old civilian pilot, was flying over the Cascade Mountains in Western Washington at about 3 P.M. when he reported nine shiny objects in a chain-like formation to his left, aligned from north to south, flying at a very high speed (Arnold estimated their velocity at about 1,600 mph). The duration of the sighting was two to three minutes. Arnold was a well-trained and experienced pilot; he knew the territory very well and was considered a very reliable person. He later described the motion of the objects, "They flew like a saucer would if you skipped it across the water" (Story 1980a, p. 25). Thus the famous term "flying saucer" was born. Arnold's sighting was a most significant event in the history of UFOs because his credibility and the accuracy of his observations caused many people in the United States to come forward and report unexplained experiences and strange objects in the sky without fear of being ridiculed.

Following this incident, the media, the police, and the United States Air Force began to receive many reports. Concerned citizens in other countries started to make similar reports as well. The major center for recording and investigating UFOs, at least since the late 1940s, has been the United States, whose air force felt compelled to respond to the UFO "menace" and expended much effort in this area. It had defined its response by the end of 1947, after having received 156 reports (some of them quite disturbing) amid growing fears about a new Soviet weapon.[46]

46. On January 7, 1948, a UFO was sighted over Goodman Air Force Base, Fort Knox, Kentucky. Godman control tower asked a flight of four National Guard F-51s, commanded by Captain Thomas F. Mantell, to investigate the UFO. Captain Mantell started

A major reason for the air force's involvement in UFOs was the fact that reports were becoming frequent and more varied, including puzzling stories of abductions and contacts between UFO occupants and humans. There were waves of UFO reporting both in the United States and abroad: in 1954 in Spain, France, and Italy; in 1967 in Brazil; and in 1947, 1952, 1957, 1965–67, and 1973 in the United States. A recent worldwide wave occurred in 1979.

In 1948, the United States Air Force created a special team (Project Sign/Saucer) to investigate UFOs. In that year, the Project Sign team submitted a report to the army chief of staff, General Hoyt S. Vandenberg, suggesting that the available evidence indicated that the UFOs were of extraterrestrial origin. General Vandenberg returned the report stating that it lacked proof. In 1949, Project Sign was changed by the air force to Project Grudge, and the team was ordered to maintain a minimal level of activity, trying to keep the UFO issue at a low profile (Ruppelt 1950; Smith 1980). Captain Ruppelt took charge of Project Grudge in 1951. He initiated a complete reorganization, creating a very efficient system of reporting UFOs.

The wave of UFO reports in the mid 1960s once again brought the whole issue to the fore. The result was that in October 1966, the United States Air Force contracted the University of Colorado to conduct a two-year independent study of UFOs. The project began that year under the direction of Dr. Edward U. Condon from the Department of Physics and Astrophysics. It was called Project Blue Book. After it submitted its report in November 1968, the Project Blue Book team was disbanded. The report was reviewed and fully endorsed by a special panel of the National Academy of Science. While it left many cases unexplained, its major conclusion was clear-cut: UFO phenomena were not worthy of further scientific study. There can be little question that this report freed the air force from the burden of studying UFOs. It effectively delegitimized and buried the issue for the scientific community. Jacob's analysis (1975) illustrates how the air force systematically discredited UFO claims and how the Condon report justified its tactics. This case constitutes yet

---

chasing the UFO with his F-51 and, at 3:15 P.M., transmitted his last radio message. Later in the day, his body was found in the wreckage of his plane near Fort Knox. The official version was that Mantell blacked out at 20,000 feet from lack of oxygen, lost control of the plane, and crashed. It is also probably true that Mantell was chasing a weather balloon. The incident, however, caused much turmoil in the USAF and drew much public attention. A more disturbing (and frightening) case was the unexplained wave of UFOs, mostly in the form of lights, over Washington, D.C. in 1952 (for a short description see Jacobs 1975, chap. 3).

another example of how science reinforced the political motives of the United States Air Force in its attempts to discredit UFO claims.

There was one exception to the trend exemplified by the Condon report. In 1968, the astronomer Carl Page, then chairman of the astronomy section of the American Association for the Advancement of Science (AAAS), proposed an AAAS-sponsored symposium on UFOs. After much scientific and political debate, a two-day, four-session seminar did in fact take place on December 26 and 27, 1969, the same year that Condon's report was released. The symposium did not resolve any problems and was ambiguous about the nature and reality of UFOs (Sagan and Page 1972).

The UFO subject has evidently refused to die for a number of reasons. The first is that the Condon report itself was fiercely attacked by scientists and laymen alike. The research project had been beset by scandals, principal investigators had left the project, and it seemed that Condon was determined to prove that UFOs did not exist. The project lost the support of various local UFO research groups and networks, and when its report was finally released, there were some serious questions regarding its reliability and credibility. The report was inconsistent and left many UFO cases unexplained. When taking into consideration the cases that the Colorado team ignored, its conclusions seemed unfounded (Greenwell 1979). Many people who had been investigating UFOs (not to mention the thousands who claimed to have encountered them) were unconvinced by Condon's conclusions. The fact remains that even after the Condon report was released, thousands of reports of UFO sightings in the United States and abroad continued to be recorded. It is exceedingly difficult to persuade people who saw and experienced very strange and incredible sights or contacts that they had actually not experienced anything.

While academic interest in the study of UFOs, never very strong, dwindled even more after Condon's report, citizen groups in the United States, Italy, France, England, Australia, and other countries flourished outside the academic framework, devoting much time and effort to voluntarily investigating UFOs.[47] These groups maintain national and international communication networks, publish journals, and organize annual conferences. Various commercial publications and newspapers have continued to publicize reports on UFOs, thus maintaining the feeling that the problem really exists. All these factors combined have

47. For a partial listing of such UFO organizations consult Story (1980a), pp. 420–22) and Sachs (1980, pp. 393–400).

kept the UFO enigma from fading and have contributed to the creation of a conspiracy theory, that is, that the government is deceiving the public and covering up the truth about UFOs (See Story 1980a, pp. 87–89 and Fawcett and Greenwood 1984).[48]

While one can find from time to time articles about UFOs in scientific journals and books (see Blake 1979; Westrum 1977), there are no academic disciplines that recognize ufology as a legitimate field of study. The scientific community at large is tolerant of occasional papers about UFOs, but direct involvement in the study of UFOs is discouraged and even ridiculed, especially when claims are made that UFOs constitute an integral part of reality. The major burden, therefore, of developing research paradigms and investigating techniques has fallen on voluntary organizations.

Some of these organizations have attracted a few good and reliable scholars who have helped develop the science of ufology outside of the university framework. In the last forty years or so, much experience and techniques have been accumulated and analyzed. Today we even have a few of what can be legitimately called methodological books of how to investigate cases of UFOs (e.g., Hendry 1979). In summary, ufology has become a focus of interest for thousands of people from various countries and backgrounds. Although it developed outside recognized research centers, it has its own methodologies, hypotheses, journals, communication networks, and body of knowledge.

In attempts to describe precisely the nature of UFOs, numerous theories have been advanced. Some of them claim that UFOs are elaborate hoaxes, mere hallucinations, or misidentifications of common aerial phenomena such as ball lightning or swamp gas. These theories usually deny the existence of UFOs as a specific anomaly. Those who actually believe that they constitute a legitimate anomaly usually adhere to one of the following theories:[49] UFOs are secret weapons of one or more armies on earth; earth is a hollow sphere and UFOs belong to secret civilizations living inside its cavity; there are secret, underwater civilizations that operate UFOs; UFOs are unique animals that live either within or without our biosphere; UFOs are time-machines from other eras, mostly from the future, that transport time-travelers to earth; UFOs are vehicles from parallel universes and travel freely between different universes; or UFOs actually constitute a psychic phenomenon, perhaps generated by

48. Naturally, conspiracy theories on UFOs are very popular with the public. One is that UFOs have crashed on earth and bodies of aliens have been secretly recovered (Berlitz and Moore 1980).

49. Based on Story (1980a, pp. 360–64).

what Jung called the collective unconscious, and they merely represent psychic projections.

The most popular and widespread hypothesis, however, is the one that attributes the origin of UFOs to extraterrestrial intelligence. This hypothesis is the most elaborate, and compared with the more esoteric and bizarre theories, it somehow seems to make the most sense to many ufologists. As a popular and appealing explanation of UFOs, and like its counterhypotheses in SETI research, it is based on a few assumptions about chemistry, biology, evolution, and technology. Thus, it goes one step beyond the SETI ideology in claiming that the earth has in fact already been visited by alien intelligences. Obviously, the major obstacle to this theory is the elusive nature of UFOs themselves and the limitations of our technology. Opponents of ufology point out that within technology and physics as we know and understand them, the cost of interstellar travel would be so expensive and out-of-reach as to to be hardly conceivable. Furthermore, knowing what we know about the efforts of building and launching a spaceship and about the possible number of extraterrestrial intelligences, there could not possibly be as many extraterrestrial UFOs as have been reported.[50]

SETI and UFOs

Both SETI and ufology are directly involved in the same problem, that is, the extraterrestrial question. Both fields lack scientifically acceptable evidence that would convince skeptics that aliens or UFOs actually exist. However, the differences between the two are salient. The clearest and most obvious is the fact that SETI has become a legitimate and orthodox science, but ufology has not. While Blake (1979) suggests that ufology is a science in development, an intellectual product of social groupings, not of the intellectual elite, there can hardly be a doubt that it is a deviant science. In addition, there seem to be at least twelve other major differences between SETI and ufology.[51] First, SETI research is done in universities and research institutes (mostly within the well-established field of radio astonomy). It is funded by NASA in the United States and by the government in the USSR; it enjoys widespread popularity and respect among scientists. Ufology is not funded by any official body, nor is it pursued in recognized research centers. Since UFO research (at least

50. Counterarguments emphasize that the problem is not a technological one but rather an economic one. Furthermore, it could be pointed out that it is possible for just one spaceship to come to the solar system. That ship could launch scores of subprobes (which might, perhaps, explain some of the UFO sightings).
51. I am grateful to Swift's work (1981), which inspired part of this analysis.

since 1969) has not been significantly funded and has even been ridiculed, scientists have been reluctant to enter the field. Thus, it is more a subject for researchers of popular culture than for orthodox science. Not only do SETI scientists rarely interest themselves in UFOs (Friedman 1973), a few view UFO research with scorn and sometimes even hostility. Thus, a second difference between SETI and ufology is that the former involves many world-famous professionals, scholars, and scientists (mostly physicists and radio astronomers) and its results are published in prestigious scientific journals. UFO research, on the other hand, does not involve first-rate scientists (with a few exceptions such as Professor Allan Hynek). Most UFO researchers and voluntary associations consist of nonscientists or marginal scientists. They usually do not publish in refereed scientific journals but in the nonacademic UFO journals put out by their different study groups.

A third contrast between the two is that, while UFO cases and studies usually make headlines and create a stir in the media, SETI keeps a very low profile. Meetings are usually restricted to invited scientists only, and advances or setbacks in research rarely find their way into the headlines. Fourth, and a most important point, is that SETI research utilizes the accepted methodologies of radio astronomy, methodologies that are active, clear, controlled, reputable, and replicable. Ufology follows no such methodology.[52] It has ways and means to evaluate and validate data, but they are not active, clear, controlled, or replicable.

Fifth, while neither SETI nor ufology have proven their cases, the type of evidence they each present is very different. Most of the ufologists' evidence consists of eyewitness testimonies and, to a much smaller extent, material evidence (e.g., photographs, radio interference, artifacts, and other traces of UFOs). No one knows where or when to anticipate a UFO encounter, and UFOs certainly cannot be reproduced under laboratory conditions. The SETI work consists mostly of passive listening through advanced electronics. However, while the UFO phenomenon does not lend itself to controlled and systematic study, SETI researchers do not have any evidence at all for the existence of an alien intelligence. Typical of modern practice in the natural sciences, SETI scientists build a model and then employ proven methodologies to test its validity. It is worth our while to examine Tipler's criticism in this context. Tipler

---

52. In the few cases where UFO researchers have tried to employ "orthodox" methodology (i.e., systematic observation with cameras, tape-recorders, and the like), they have come up with intriguing results, usually supporting the existence of UFOs (e.g., Rutledge 1981). However, such works are often controversial.

(1983b) pointed out that SETI can positively conclude that extraterrestrial intelligence exists in the universe once radio signals produced by that intelligence are received on earth. However, he also pointed out that SETI cannot conclusively rule out the existence (or nonexistence) of aliens if no signals are received (that is, SETI assumptions are not falsifiable). "SETI will become science only when its proponents tell us exactly what will convince them that it is reasonable to assume we are alone" (p. 60). While both areas have suffered from hoaxes, there can be little question that ufology has been discredited to a much larger extent than SETI.

Our sixth point refers to differences in the basic assumptions and interpretations of the two fields. Ufology is based on the fact that a large number of reports on peculiar aerial phenomena exist. Some of these reports suggest that earth has been visited by aliens using very advanced means of transportation. In many cases, they suggest that earth is still being visited by extraterrestrial intelligence. Much of ufology research is thus geared to validating these reports and the extraterrestrial hypothesis. SETI research assumes that alien intelligences exist, probably on very distant planets, which, given present technology and knowledge, makes the probability of an actual visit very slight. Logically, therefore, the SETI assumption is that the best way to initiate research to make contact with galactic civilizations is via radio.

SETI and ufology also vary a great deal in the way data is collected. SETI data are collected by professional scientists using accepted and established methods. Ufology data are collected by amateurs, according to methods and criteria established by ufologists themselves.[53]

The eighth contrast is in the area of communications and methods of information dissemination. SETI uses regular scientific channels such as journals, conventions, papers, books, and articles. Ufologists hardly, if ever, publish in professional journals. They have their own network of communication, conventions, and journals.[54] They have generated an impressive quantity of written reports on UFOs, including analyses, investiations, debates, theories, and hypotheses, and they have even helped establish an international service of newspaper clippings on UFOs.

53. The parallel here to astronomy is striking. In a recent paper, Lankford (1981) documented the major (albeit usually neglected) advances that amateurs have made in astronomy and astrophysics. It was the amateurs who were willing to take risks in the early days of the discipline. One cannot help speculating whether the amateur activity in ufology will not prove to have played a similar role.

54. For example, *Flying Saucer Review*, *Journal of UFO Studies*, and *MUFON Journal*.

Ninth, and as Swift (1981) and others have noted, SETI research does not pose any threat to science. Indeed, in contrast to ufology, it is possible to train for a professional career in SETI research in recognized institutions of higher education.[55] Even if alien radio transmissions were picked up and contact established, no shift in scientific paradigms would be required. However, if the reality of UFOs were to be established, or if any of the hypotheses regarding the origins of UFOs were to be validated, science would be severely challenged and would probably require the revision of basic paradigms (Story and Greenwell 1981).

Another striking difference between ufology and SETI is the fact that while SETI has not given rise to any type of cult or sect, the number of cults, sects, and religious activities centering on UFOs is amazing (see, e.g., Balch and Taylor 1977; Story 1980a).

The eleventh difference I shall mention is the reaction to Ufology and SETI. SETI research started very hesitantly and had to cope with suspicion and disbelief. However, the support of eminent scientists, coupled with its use of accepted methodologies and the fact that it posed no threat to orthodox science, helped reduce resistance to SETI to a very low level. In contrast, ufology has always been under severe and discrediting attacks from scientists, the media, and even from "sympathetic debunkers" (see Oberg 1982; Sheaffer 1981). In fact, when Rutledge (1981) published his pioneering observational study on UFOs, Sheaffer's review in the spring 1982 issue of *The Skeptical Inquirer* stated that the study is "from start to end a massive exercise in self delusion" (p. 69).

The last difference is the involvement of governmental agencies in SETI and UFO research. While SETI was very effective in securing governmental support, ufology was not. The only official agency that invested any resources to speak of into UFO research was the United States Air Force. But even the air force seems to have been relieved with the results of the Condon report, and since the late 1960s, virtually no governmental agency has been seriously involved in researching UFOs. Obviously, this situation helped to discredit ufology and helped SETI gain respectability.

Thus, while SETI and ufology have strikingly similar hypotheses, in other ways they differ greatly. In this analysis, we have seen the process by which and the reasons why ufology became a deviant science and SETI did not. This process had to do with establishing the reality of UFOs and aliens; with the type of scientists who supported each field and the vested

55. However, it is possible to conduct research on various aspects of UFOs, such as their relationship to religion or cults, the social characteristics of ufologists and their psychological needs.

interests of governmental agencies (and in the UFO case, the apparent motivation of the United States Air Force to rid itself of the problem); with different methodologies and the perceived "threat" of each field to orthodox scientific paradigms. All these created the conditions that made SETI a legitimate scientific specialty and discredited ufology. Furthermore, SETI scientists generally reject ufologists, in part because of basic and valid divergences of opinion, but mostly because of a justified fear of being ridiculed and losing prestige and credibility.

5

DEVIANT SCIENTISTS

Introduction

In the last chapter, we examined deviant sciences as a way of changing the boundaries of orthodox science. This chapter examines deviant scientists. Quite simply, deviant scientists are those who cheat, report nonexistent observations, falsify data, or "do not let the facts interfere with their theories." The exposure of deviant scientists is usually employed by the scientific community to enhance stability, solidarity, and rigidity. Indicating how, where, and when different scientists have falsified data and how such practices can be prevented is of major concern to the scientific community. By dealing with such cases, it indicates to its own members, and to the public, that it has safety controls and mechanisms to detect and punish deviants, that it is a cohesive community with clear-cut boundaries, and that it knows its moral-ethical limits and obligations. Therefore it is a vested interest of the scientific community to detect deviants—but not too many of them. Science is supposed to seek the truth. Too many liars and cheats, and its very legitimacy will crumble. Nothing could be more dangerous for the scientific community than the discovery that a large number of its members are engaged in fraudulent practices. This is certainly not meant to imply that the scientific community covers up deviants. The sad truth is that it is not easy to detect deviant scientists.

Unfortunately, while the field is a most fascinating subject for scientific inquiry, it is also one that has been poorly researched to date. The lack of theoretical and empirical knowledge reflects both the reluctance of scientists to discuss this issue openly and the difficulties of investigating it. Only in the last few years have scientists hesitantly begun to probe this mysterious terrain, and they have had intriguing results. One must also note the strange fact that a community dedicated to the systematic recording of data has virtually no systematic data on deviant scientists.

Science, as we saw in chapter 4, is dedicated to the accumulation of "certified knowledge." The next question is thus, Under what conditions should the pursuit of "certified knowledge" be carried out? Merton (1973, pp. 12–14) outlines the following four norms as central to science: universalism, that is, the validity and truth of scientific statements must be totally separated from the personal characteristics of the person who makes them; communality, that is, scientific findings should be freely shared with others (secret or classified research is antithetical to the spirit of science); disinterestedness, that is, the scientist's research must be guided, not by personal motives (e.g., profit), but by the wish to extend knowledge; and organized skepticism, that is, scientists must be encouraged to openly, honestly, and publicly examine each other's work.[1]

These four norms are "energized" (Storer 1977) by the need of scientists for professional recognition and by organized knowledge, in other words, the scientific effort is made within a cultural matrix of interactions among scientists. Conforming to the four Mertonian norms should prevent deviance in science and guarantee that the scientific effort is oriented toward accumulating certified knowledge. This issue obviously leads to the problem of social control in science and to an examination of those factors and forces within science that enhance conformity to the rules and those that create pressures toward rule-breaking and deviance.

Social Control in Science

Sociological constructions of deviance and criminological theories developed in the last decade provide a few general formulations of control that share some common elements. Deviance, according to these theories, is not caused but is made possible because societal agencies can no longer prevent its occurrence. All the theories, in one way or another, follow a very basic Durkheimian approach, which states that deviance will happen whenever the hold of societies and groups on individual members is neutralized, broken, or weakened (Frazier 1976). Stated this way, the problem then becomes how to map the various control mechanisms, how they function, and how they are rendered ineffective.

Theories of control focus on two main mechanisms, which can function either separately or together. The first is an inner mechanism that assumes many names or forms but is essentially created through the internalization of norms and various other socialization processes. This

1. To this list, Barber adds individualism, rationality, and emotional neutrality (Zuckerman 1977, p. 89).

mechanism can be labeled "superego," "conscience," or "morality."
Second, we have so-called external mechanisms in the forms of family,
community, and control agents (e.g., policemen, judges, psychiatrists,
teachers). In principle, every control theory plays with these two mechanisms.

Social control in science is no exception. Most researchers would agree
that through the long process of training and creating a scientist, the
norms of the scientific inquiry and method are internalized. The scientist
is taught what types of questions to ask, what types of methodologies to
use, and above all, scientists are taught that their only guide should be the
search for scientific truth. Cheating, fraud, and the like then become the
most serious crimes conceivable. The scientist is primarily committed to
his profession and its ethic. Zuckerman specifically states that "social
control in science depends partly on scientists' internalizing moral and
cognitive norms in the course of their professional socialization and partly
on social mechanisms for the detection of deviant behavior and the
exercise of sanctions when it is detected" (1977, p. 90). What, then, are
the external forms of control in science? As Weinstein rightly points out,
"In science, as in polity, policing requires suspicion that a 'crime' has
been committed, collection of evidence, and finally punishment of the
offender" (1979, p. 647).

Since a police or a crime-detecting unit does not exist in science, the
first, most obvious, mechanism to prevent scientific fraud is the norm of
"communality" mentioned by Merton. Adherence to this norm means
that scientists' actions, experiments, and their results are visible. Most
forms of deviance become possible because they are not done in public.
Concealing deviance in science therefore must be so sophisticated that
even when findings are presented publicly the probability of detecting the
fraud is minimal. The second mechanism is the norm of "organized
skepticism." This implies that scientists are a suspicious breed, trained to
criticize each other and to search actively for defects, improbable statements, and bad methodologies.

The first and second mechanisms receive direct expression in the way
in which scientists present their work, whether at conventions and meetings or in published articles and papers. The work is submitted for an
open and thorough peer review and its scientific merit is judged. Reputable professional journals do not publish works that have not passed a
satisfactory peer review. Most journals solicit the judgments of two to
four anonymous referees.

The third, and probably most important, external control mechanism
is replication. This stems directly from Merton's norm of universalism

and is grounded in the theory that if experiment x yielded result y in one specific time and place, the same experiment should yield the same result in a different time and place.

In the following section, we shall see that social control in science is much weaker than what is usually accepted and that there are a number of structural, as well as personal, incentives in science to commit fraud.

Forces Conducive to Creation of Deviant Scientists

The Mertonian Norms Re-examined

Despite the controls just described, deviance does occur in science. There are ample structural elements in the methods of scientific inquiry and in the scientific community that are conducive to the creation and maintenance of deviance. First, we must examine the four Mertonian norms once again.

The first of these is universalism, meaning that the truth of a scientific statement is separate from the personal characteristics of the individual scientist. However, this may not always be true. The very process of discovery, of invention, of innovation is clearly dependent on the personal, and especially on the psychic, make-up of the scientist involved. Philosophical theories and conceptualizations of social orders and changes are often linked to the world views of particular scientists. A Marxist sociologist and a Parsonian sociologist would not explain the Russian revolution similarly.

The second norm, communality, is also easy to attack. According to this norm, scientists should share their findings with each other freely. However, for a variety of reasons, this norm is violated very frequently. The simplest example is so-called secret or classified research. In other cases, because of fierce competition, scientists fear that others will steal their ideas, and they may become very protective of their theories and findings. In fact, accessibility to original data is extremely difficult. Weinstein (1979) and Rensberger (1977), for example, report on an Iowa State researcher who requested the raw data from thirty-seven authors whose works were recently published in psychology journals. He received replies from only thirty-two of them, of whom twenty-one claimed that their data were lost or accidentally destroyed. Only nine researchers (about 24%) sent copies of their data.

Sharing ideas can be expensive. The time lag between submission of a paper and its actual publication can be as long as two years. Therefore, conferences, congresses, and informal meetings have become a major channel for exchanging new ideas (especially the so-called invisible college, [Crane 1972] which constitutes a network for the informal exchange of information). To participate in this international network means expensive trips abroad, which in most cases, young scientists can hardly afford. Their ability to be part of meaningful scientific networks is thus severely limited, and sharing theories, data, and findings outside of journals becomes an activity of very specific groups of scientists.

The third Mertonian norm is organized skepticism, institutionalized encouragement of scientists to criticize each other. Skepticism, however, is not a simple matter. An older, well-established, and secure scientist would feel much more comfortable about criticizing a junior faculty member than the other way around. A junior faculty member in a department of statistics told me that a few times he was present in lectures given by a senior colleague who made some obvious mistakes. However, neither the young statistics instructor nor any of the other junior faculty present commented on it, since none of them wanted to antagonize their senior, fearing that when time for their tenure reviews came, the older professor would vote against them. In 1980, a new book on witchcraft was sent to me for a review by a sociological journal. I did not like the book, and my review was negative overall. After the review was published, a senior sociologist in my department commented that I should not have been so critical. He said that since I was not tenured yet, it could be dangerous, and useless, to antagonize other scholars. His advice was, of course, well intended and from real concern for my future. However, it does reflect the fact that skepticism is a complex problem. The question of who criticizes whom, and how and when, is crucial.

However, in another area, the norm of organized skepticism is perhaps the only one that is followed down the line. While, in theory, it is an invitation for constructive criticism, in reality it frequently inspires and covers up blatant aggression. A Scientist who sends a paper to a journal usually gets it back with the anonymous referee's comments (in many cases, the referee received the paper without the name of the author as well). This in itself could be taken to indicate scientists' fear of confronting each other openly, and it legitimizes hostility and aggression. It provides orthodox, and new, scientists with an excellent opportunity to kill or promote new ideas. Since editors give much weight to referees' opinions, the scientist who submits a paper is virtually at the referee's mercy, as in most cases it is virtually impossible to respond to the referee's comments. Furthermore, referees can be so chosen that the editor can increase or decrease the probability of a favorable or unfavorable review. (The same logic, by the way, is valid for the review of research proposals.) Most scientists who have had to cope with referees' comments know how agonizing this process can be. In some cases, the comments are helpful and constructive, but in others, they are pointless, useless, opinionated, and aggressive.[2]

Examples abound. A social scientist told me about his research on analyzing power interactions between therapists and patients and about a paper he sent on that topic to a specific journal. The journal did not accept the paper because one of the referees wrote, among other things, that psychoanalysts were not involved in power interactions: "We psychoanalysts invite our patients to cooperate with us, but they need not believe word we say." In another case, a scholar sent a paper to the prestigious *American Sociological Review* (published by the American Sociological Association). The paper was rejected because it did not use what the referees called "advanced statistical methods." However, the scholar had constructed her argument without the need for techniques such as regression analysis or correlation matrixes. Later, the very same paper was sent to an equally prestigious journal published by the American Psychological Association, received very favorable reviews, and was published. When in the late 1930s, Grote Reber submitted his paper on radio astronomy to the *Astrophysical Journal* (the first time a paper reporting on radio emission from the sky was submitted to an astronomical journal), the referees flatly rejected it because the reported findings were "unbelievable."

This state of affairs, especially in the social sciences, may encourage contributors to overstate their cases. Authors can repress or manipulate data in a way that is hard, if not impossible, to detect so that referees will allow them to pass. Such practices are not exactly fraud, but neither are they scientific truth. The anonymous editor-mediated interaction between author and referee is certainly not conducive to a free and open exchange of views. In such an interaction, power flows in one direction only. Under these conditions, one can expect a certain degree of distortion and bias.

The fourth Mertonian norm is disinterestedness, meaning that a scientist's research should not be guided by expectations of personal profit and reward. In reality, this norm cannot be maintained. A scientist derives two rewards from his work: psychological and economic. In some cases, the two are interconnected. The psychological rewards are mostly in the form of prestige and recognition. A scientist's self-esteem is usually very

2. Cole, Cole, and Simon's work (1981) supports this view. It illustrates that random factors have a very strong influence on the decision whether a specific research proposal will be funded or not. Furthermore, Peters and Ceci's work (1980) demonstrates that a high degree of unreliability exists in editorial practices.

high and many bask in the honors an international reputation brings. This is certainly a far cry from disinterestedness. Especially today, scientists are often consulted by high government officials and participate in top-level policy discussions on national, international, social, medical, and political issues. Many scientists appear on radio and television and enjoy popular admiration. There can be little doubt that Carl Sagan, through his 1981 television series, "Cosmos," earned himself a worldwide reputation (not to mention income). The scientist is perceived as a wiseman who reveals the ultimate truth and unravels the secrets of our physical and social universe. The highest award any scientist can attain, the Nobel prize, is very personalized. It is awarded to an individual scientist and not, for example, to an idea or invention.

The other element of reward is economic. Well-established scientists usually enjoy financial security and a moderate to luxurious life style. Many travel throughout the world very comfortably. They have access to research grants that further bolster their already considerable salaries. Thus we find that scientists are attracted to fields where research is heavily funded, such as cancer, energy, law enforcement, gerontology, drugs and alcohol, and mental health. The list of fields changes with time and priorities. Receiving money from research grants also means building up small "empires" of equipment, institutions, laboratories, manpower, and jobs. In other words, individual scientists can become very powerful by virtue of their ability to provide jobs, salaries, and career opportunities. From the very nature of science, scientists have profound interest in the success of their ideas. Their interest may be propelled by a personal quest for fame and recognition or by economic considerations. In short, disinterestedness does not appear to be a realistic norm.

Replication and Refereeing

Two important control mechanisms against fraud and deviance in science are replication and refereeing. Of the two, replication is probably the single most important safeguard. It is the essence of the scientific spirit. Irreplicable research is very suspect and in some disciplines is simply considered nonscientific. Unfortunately, replication itself is problematic.

First, it is not considered very prestigious or interesting work for scientists who have been trained to innovate. Very few would like to be identified as "replicators" (Weinstein 1979). Furthermore, full replication is not always possible because, in many cases, not enough information is available about the original work. When sharing information becomes difficult, so does replication. For example, Wolins (1962), Craig and Reese (1973) found that a significant portion of published papers in psychology could not be replicated or verified because the original data were conveniently "lost" or "unavailable." This situation is aggravated by the fact that in many disciplines no institutionalized mechanism exists for cataloging original data. In many cases, it is the scientist who is vested with the responsibility of keeping the data. In addition, granting institutes (as well as scientists) are reluctant to provide funds (or time and effort) for replication alone, unless the replication itself is significant in some important way. Even when one suspects fraud, if checking the original data would take a long time, it is quite possible that no one will want to do it. If the suspicion of fraud is not validated, then the examiner-replicator has wasted time retesting something unnecessarily, and no publications would result from this effort, (not to mention the embarrassment). In a recent case of suspected fraud (Colin 1984b), a commission found "no compelling evidence" substantiating the charge. Lack of full replication was certainly one of the major reasons for this conclusion, and the commission "urged" the experimenters to repeat their experiments.

Second, in some disciplines, not only are replications considered of secondary importance, but they are perceived as problematic in themselves. The idea of replication is most applicable to experimental disciplines. They are not possible for ideas and theories. In addition, methodologies and techniques like surveys, participant observations, and ethnographic analysis virtually guarantee that their results cannot be replicated. Such sciences as sociology, history, and anthropology focus on interpretations. The observations of, for example, an anthropologist who studies a remote tribe, are unique and not replicable. In many such cases, when two observations are made, with different results, the scientist can have a very good and legitimate explanation for the discrepancy. This happens often in surveys and anthropological field work where the nature of the observed phenomenon itself can (and does) change. For those who cynically want to utilize this fact for deviance, this could be a gold mine. Thus, they could choose areas of research that are considered interesting but where the chances for replication are either remote or impossible (e.g., field work on some remote tribe). Committing fraud or deviance, then, becomes easy because the chances of detecting it are virtually nil.

Replication, therefore, can only be considered a good safeguard against fraud in a few specific disciplines and fields. I learned from a famous survey researcher that if someone is well-acquainted with survey analysis techniques, he can forge data so that the fraud will not be detected. Since replication of survey data is very problematic anyway, this type of deviance would probably not be exposed.

Survey techniques, in this case, include all types of questionnaires. In 1976, when I worked as a therapist in a methadone maintenance program in Chicago, a few psychology students from Northwestern University asked to test some patients on the MMPI, which is a long, complicated personality test.[3] Some of the patients agreed to fill in the full version of the test. Weeks later it was reported to us that most of the patients who were tested showed schizophrenic traits. This had us all puzzled. On the one hand, Laing, among others, has maintained that drug addiction usually camouflages hidden schizophrenia, and the test results strongly supported this theory (with very specific clinical implications). On the other hand, most of the therapists who knew the patients and who had previous clinical experience with schizophrenia could not concur with the findings. We checked with the patients, and it turned out that many of them had tired of the long test and had smoked marijuana, filling in parts of the test when they were feeling high. The testers should have detected this, but had failed to do so. This illustrates that when data are manipulated at the most basic level, it can be extremely difficult to detect the bias or forgery.

Anthropologists who spend time among so-called "primitive tribes" are sometimes witness to bizarre events and patterns of behavior. If they are not regarded as trustworthy and credible, it is exceedingly difficult to validate many of their observations. The recent case of the Don Juan materials of Carlos Castaneda demonstrate this point (See Hooper 1978; de Mille 1980). There are those who argue that Castaneda reported nonexistent observations, just writing superlative fantasy. De Mille is apparently convinced that Castaneda perpetrated a literary fraud and told Hooper that he "respects Castaneda as being both talented and shrewd, both in hoaxing the UCLA Anthropology Department and the reading public, as well as knowing the signs of the literary times" (Hooper 1978, p. 29). In a similar fashion, Arens (1979) states that there is no good evidence that cannibalism has been practiced regularly by any tribe, and that the custom has probably never existed. This implies that generations of anthropologists have reported on observations that have never been made and that were based on uncorroborated secondary sources.[4]

In interviews I have held with quite a few sociologists and anthropologists, some have admitted openly and freely that as a "career line" they

3. The acronym stands for Minnesota Multiphasic Personality Inventory.
4. Arens's work has been attacked severely, especially on the grounds that he did not take into consideration all cases and that his work is biased. One has to remember, however, that even if biased, the cases cited by Arens are very instructive.

chose areas of specialization that no one could possibly replicate or examine. Under the convenient guise of "originality," they could discard "inconvenient" data, manipulate reports, and get more published.

A mechanism similar to replication is the screening procedure employed by most journals. In theory, journal referees can detect fraud and deviance. In reality, however, virtually no fraudulent methods or data have been detected by this process. In many cases (especially recent ones), the fraud was detected by close associates of the deviant scientists. Referees cannot detect fraud simply because screening a paper is neither a process of replication nor an in-depth examination. If what is written makes sense, with no severe violations of existing knowledge, then the probability of arousing the reader's suspicion is very low. Armstrong (1982) has analyzed what is published in scholarly journals and concludes that the chances of a paper being accepted for publication are tremendously increased if the paper is about an unimportant topic, in agreement with existing beliefs, if it uses convoluted methods and is written in a somewhat unclear way. He states that the probability of papers with "surprising" results being published is very low. Deviant scientists can take advantage of these conditions.

The following case exemplifies the point.[5] A team of three physicians in a well-known medical school received grant money to do a survey on the epidemiology of a rare form of cancer. The team started work, but after collecting data on fifty percent of the cases, two of the physicians left for new jobs. The work stopped for a few months, but then the granting institution started demanding reports. The remaining physician contacted the other two members and together they forged the results. They doubled the number of cases for which they had data in order to "complete" the analysis. However, they got some "funny" results, so they used a table of random numbers to introduce "random errors" into the original data tapes. Then, they checked the literature on the topic, which consisted of about four old papers, all suggesting similar epidemiological dispersions and course of the disease. The results the team had did not fit the literature. They therefore changed the observations (by changing the actual numbers entered into the computer tapes) until they got results consistent with the literature. Their paper was presented at a major scientific meeting and published in a very prestigious medical journal. Obviously, these scientists took all measures necessary to cover their tracks. It is now virtually impossible to detect the fraud, and the whole act of falsifying and fabricating data took them only about ten days. Fur-

---

5. I am grateful to one of the physicians involved for giving me all the details.

thermore, since their results are consistent with the literature, no one will probably want to replicate the work. To summarize, I concur with Broad's conclusion in his 1981 survey of deviant scientists, which states that replication and duplication of results is not a major factor in discovering fraud.

Another problem with replication, or close examination of original data, is that sometimes existing technology cannot detect fraud. The most famous case is probably that of the Piltdown Man forgery by Charles Dawson.

The Piltdown Forgery

Charles Dawson, an amateur archeologist, came in 1912 to Smith Woodward, keeper of geology of the Natural History Museum in London, with some human bones and a skull that Dawson claimed came from Piltdown in Sussex. These, he told Smith, were found while excavating a pathway. After the initial excitement in anthropological circles, Piltdown Man was found to be more and more anomalous. The advent of the x-ray and other technologies made it possible eventually to declare the Piltdown Man a forgery (Weiner 1980; Zuckerman 1977, pp. 100–101.).

However, even modern technology cannot always prove fraud. Zuckerman (1977, pp. 105–6) examines five examples of suspected fraud that are hard to establish as such, even with modern knowledge and technology. Of these five, I shall quote only one. The statistician, R. A. Fisher, claimed in 1936 that Mendel, who is considered by many to be the father of genetics, could not have achieved the results he reported because the agreement with theoretical expectations was far too close. Did Mendel commit a fraud? Not according to Dunn (1965) and Wright (1966) who point out that Mendel's procedures have to be understood in the context of what was known about statistics and probability at the time he conducted his experiments. They argue that although Mendel's results were biased, no fraudulent practice was involved.

Apprehension and Sanctions

This returns us to the problem of the prevention of fraud in science. The probability that any deviant act will take place depends, in principle, on two factors: the chances of the deviant being caught and the severity of the sanction. Only where both factors are high can effective prevention be achieved. The fact that replication is not a major activity, and is problematic in itself, means that the probability of fraud detection is not high. The complicated and elaborate division of labor in science, leading to extremes of specialization, makes the detection of fraud even more

remote. Only in very meaningful research efforts, in so-called breakthrough research, are replications made, and then they are done intensively. Zuckerman points out that "the more consequential the scientific
result, the more immediately efforts are mounted to reproduce it and
thus, the greater the probability that error or deception can be detected"
(1977, p. 95). Alas, most research is not of this nature.

Spector's Fraudulent Experiments

At the annual meeting on tumor viruses at Cold Spring Laboratory in
May 1980, Mark Spector, a twenty-four-year-old graduate student in
biochemistry from Cornell University presented a revolutionary paper.[6]
Spector suggested a new explanation of how viruses work and cause
cancer. Steven O'Neal, a postdoctoral researcher in Cornell's biochemical laboratory, had worked unsuccessfully for more than two years trying
to isolate a specific protein (sodium-potassium ATPase). When Spector
came to Cornell in December 1979, he had been assigned to isolate the
protein. He accomplished the task in less than a month. This discovery
was the first milestone in Spector's development of his innovative theory
about viruses and cancer. The news of his findings spread rapidly in the
scientific community, and in July 1980, some of his work was published in
respected journals such as *Science* and *Cell*.

However, signs of fraud were soon apparent. Raymond Erikson, a
virologist at the University of Colorado Medical Center in Denver, had
found that a sample serum from Spector's experiments contained certain
antibodies that, if the theory were correct, should not and could not be
present. Another warning sign was that a few of the experiments worked
only under Spector's very personal supervision. By late July, some of
Spector's own laboratory colleagues began to be suspicious. During the
rest of the summer, Spector was asked to stay away from the laboratory
while his supervisor, Professor Racker, tried to replicate his results. New
discrepancies appeared. In September, Racker sent letters to both *Science* and *Cell* partly retracting the previous reports, and he also withdrew
papers that were scheduled to appear in two other journals. The university began to investigate Spector's past and discovered that he had never
even received a bachelor's degree. Spector withdrew from Cornell and
denied all the allegations. The puzzling fact is that some of his work does
indeed seem to be valid and replicable.

While Spector foolishly enough (from his perspective) chose to com-

6. For a fuller description, see McKean (1981), Broad and Wade (1982, pp. 63–73), and
Kolata (1981).

mit fraud on a "breakthrough" discovery, not all research is like this. In peripheral, or nonbreakthrough research, there is little incentive to replicate and thus the probability of detecting deviance is very low. Furthermore, while the norms of organized skepticism and communality imply that each scientist is a potential policeman for colleagues' work, in reality this is not so. When a policeman or a detective suspects that a crime has been committed, there is a clear procedure to follow, both in terms of technology and institutions. If a scientist suspects that a colleague's work is fraudulent, how is he to pursue or establish the suspicion? Who should be addressed? What technologies should be used? When one reads the different cases of deceit in science (see, e.g., Broad and Wade 1982), it becomes apparent that the problem of detecting, reporting, and handling a suspicion is a very complicated, painful, fragmented and nonuniform process. To this one has to add that the question of who (or what) exactly is victimized by deviance in science (the one who should "complain") has not been satisfactorily resolved.

Another factor to examine is the punishment for deviant scientists. They do not go through court and are not subject to prison sentences, probation, or fines. Unlike other transgressors, a deviant scientist is not submitted to anything like the criminal justice system. Suspicion of a deviant procedure does not lead to a complaint to a public control organ (such as the police); the accused does not have any formal rights or obligations; he is not investigated other than by peer review nor is he given a public chance to defend himself (or to get a professional defense); a trial usually does not take place. Accusing a scientist of fraud is usually done via informal channels (making such cases hard to document). In many cases, the deviant scientist's act does not become a matter of public knowledge. His superiors are never anxious to disclose the case, for it might damage their own, and the institution's, prestige and credibility. Thus, if the case is not fraud and fabrication on a mass scale, the most that can happen is that the deviant scientist loses his job. While this in itself is quite serious, it hardly compares with the punishments to which other white-collar offenders are subjected.

Both Weinstein (1979) and Zuckerman (1977) admit that punishment is usually not very harsh. The scientific institution in which the deviant act occurred is usually not quick to admit it. For example, even though Professor John Darsee of the Harvard Medical School was stripped of his position after admitting that he falsified data, he nevertheless continued to work at the laboratory, publish papers, and appear at conferences (Broad 1982). Only in February 1983, nearly two years after the infraction, did the National Institute of Health announce that Darsee would be barred from receiving federal funds and contracts for a period of ten years (Wallis 1983). This, one has to notice, was an unusually harsh punishment. Furthermore, Harvard University was asked to return $122,371 to NIH. Darsee himself, however, was then in the first year of a two-year fellowship in critical care medicine at Ellis Hospital in Schenectady, New York.

In another case, described by Broad (1981), Marc Strauss, a researcher from Boston University, was accused in 1978 by his twenty-person staff of submitting falsified reports. Strauss resigned in 1978, insisting that he was the victim of a conspiracy planned and executed by his staff. Strauss re-established himself and applied to the National Cancer Institute (NCI) for a new grant. He was given a $1.32 million. When the NCI board learned of Strauss's past, there was an uproar that initiated a congressional investigation. During the inquiry, it was made clear that the National Institute of Health (NIH) would neither allow the creation of blacklists nor let allegations prevent anyone from receiving support. John Long, who forged data on cancer cells between 1978 and 1980 (Broad and Wade 1982, pp. 89–90), later found a comfortable position. William Summerlin (who was caught putting ink on tissue grafts of mice to "prove" a theory) was offered a long period of medical leave on full salary ($40,000) to enable him to rest and obtain professional care (Culliton 1974, p. 1155).

Thus the combination of a low probability of detection and lenient punishments provides, in theory, a fertile context for deviance. However, there are signs that this is changing. In a few recent cases of fraud, the granting body demanded that the institution where the deviant scientist worked return the research money. In the long run, this could mean that cases of deviance will no longer be dealt with on the individual level and that institutes will find better, more efficient ways to detect and deal with deviant scientists, simply in order to cut down their loss of both research money and prestige.

That there are elements and forces conducive to scientists' committing deviant acts is in itself not enough to explain the behavior. What we need to understand is motivation: Why should scientists commit deviant acts at all?

Motivations Favoring Deviance in Science

To state that deviant scientists have "something wrong" in their psyches or professional upbringing (that is, the "bad apple" theory) cannot explain their deviance. The few cases we have examined indicate that the deviants knew fairly well that they were not supposed to do what they did, and in most cases they did not seem to be psychotic or otherwise disturbed. We must, therefore, look elsewhere for the reasons behind their actions.

The 1960s and the first half of the 1970s witnessed the expansion of scientific establishments such as universities and research institutes, but opportunities diminished during the second half of the 1970s. During this time, it became clear that advancement in most Western scientific establishments depended primarily on published papers, books, and research reports. This state of affairs put heavy pressure on young scientists to publish. The slogan "publish or perish" reflected the community's priorities, and quality of teaching became only a secondary concern. Those who could write fast and had good contacts with editors and publishers flourished; others agonized. When the idea of producing a lot of work quickly is impressed upon a young scientist who very badly wants an academic career, recognition, and security (tenure), the motivation to deviate is created. Broad notes that there has apparently been an increase in cases of fraud in science during the past few years and quotes Professor Robert Ebert, former dean of Harvard Medical School, "The enormous importance that is attached to the number of publications by committees that consider people for promotion, . . . the pressure to produce, the pressure for publication" are probably the reasons for deviance in science (1982, p. 484).

Professor Ebert and Broad both refer to the Darsee affair. John Darsee, at age thirty-three, had nearly one hundred published papers and abstracts to his name. Apparently, this rate of publication was not enough for him, for as we have seen, in May 1981, several young researchers at the Harvard Medical School were amazed to witness that Darsee "flagrantly concocted data for an experiment" (Broad 1982, p. 478). It took the university six months to discover that the original data for many of Darsee's experiments were unaccountably missing. Darsee himself confessed to only one case of fraud and denied any recollection of similar acts (Culliton 1983).

Another young scientist in desperate need of publications was Vijay Soman (Broad 1980b, c; 1982). His case also got much publicity. It was discussed in the November 1, 1981, issue of the *New York Times Magazine*. The Soman case occurred in 1980 at the Yale Medical School. During the course of a scientific audit, Soman admitted to having falsified work in a paper. After an investigation, twelve papers involving Soman as a researcher were retracted (Broad 1982, p. 479). This case, perhaps more than any other, reflects how pressures to publish, with lack of proper control result in plagiarism, fudging, fraud, forgery, and widespread destruction of laboratory data. Weinstein (1978) reports on a 1977 case of a postdoctoral researcher in an institute of biochemistry in West Germany. This scientist spent almost two years measuring under various conditions the level of a certain chemical in neuroblastoma cells. Being under high pressure to produce, he published several papers reporting his results. Only after he left the institute did some of his colleagues try to replicate his work, with virtually no success. He was asked by the institute to replicate his studies under close supervision, but he was unable to obtain the previously published results. Only then did he admit to "having invented the results of all his experiments." Likewise, in December 1982, Dr. Joseph H. Cort was found by a committee of the Mount Sinai School of Medicine to have fabricated data on drugs he claimed to have synthesized. Cort admitted to this fabrication because he was under "a lot of pressure" to produce (Wade 1983, p. 3).

The structural elements conducive to deviance in conjunction with the pressures to publish can turn many scientists, especially young ones, into cynics. Cynicism may be the first milestone on the road to disenchantment and eventually deviance. If one needs to publish, and publish quickly, what could be more tempting than to commit a fraud that is not likely to be detected? This cynicism is probably magnified by other factors: "Since one must publish to get grants, and promotion in many institutions hinges on the size of grants, publications and grants rather than discovery become the goals in the laboratory. . . . Scientists are tending to select research where money is available, such as cancer or energy research" (Weinstein 1978, p. 7).

The pressure from the grant-bestowing research institutes can also create tendencies toward deviance. We have already mentioned the case of John Long, a respected pathologist from Massachusetts General Hospital, who was researching Hodgkin's disease. The research involved establishing several human cell lines with traits characteristic of the disease. These lines are difficult to create and maintain, but they are of tremendous value for studying the disease. Stephen Quay, another researcher and a colleague of Long's, suspected in October 1979 that Long's results were faked. Quay formally expressed his suspicion in a report that he prepared in January 1980 accusing Long of reporting on experiments he never actually performed. Under pressure, Long admitted to having made mistakes and attributed them to "pressure for a grant application.'"[7] He subsequently admitted to the charge that he had forged

7. Wade (1981, p. 1023). In a later testimony (Woolf 1981, p. 11), Long specifically took the blame upon himself and did not accuse the system.

data. He resigned from the hospital on January 31, 1980, and agreed not to engage in research any longer (he works now as a pathologist in a midwestern hospital). A similar case occurred in May 1981, when Dr. Arnold Rincover, from the Department of Psychology, University of North Carolina, was found by a faculty committee to be guilty of plagiarizing a student's thesis, almost word for word, in order to obtain a $723,000 grant (Wade 1983, p. 4).

Thus granting institutes, especially those that demand relatively "quick results," are a prime factor in the motivation to deviate. Fabricating or distorting data in order to show 'success' can gain a specific scientist, institution, or laboratory considerable economical gains. In the Darsee case, it was stated that "the tremendous pressures to 'publish or perish' may be a factor.. . . These pressures have been exacerbated by the intense competition for limited federal research funds" (Wallis 1983 p. 41). As Albert Hastorf, Stanford's provost, argues, "Science is more expensive these days. You need a big grant or you are out of business" (ibid.). Furthermore, institutions that deal with research grants or are under strong pressure 'to produce' are good suspects for deviance. Thus, one should really not be surprised to find deviance in biomedical, biochemical, or pharmaceutical research (see Silberner 1982). In fact, Pontell, Jesilow, and Geis (1982) pointed out that in a specific medical health-delivery system, the organization of the program itself invited fraud. McCaghy (1976, pp. 118–19) also notes that there are many forms of fraud in medicine (e.g., fraudulent devices, bogus healing, and the like).

During interviews, I have also learned of scientists who go to scientific conferences, contact fund executives to learn what the most recent "hot" area for research is, and make a quick switch to it. In many cases, this appears to be simple economic entrepreneurship, which can keep someone's big laboratory (or research team) alive, a far cry from Merton's standard of disinterestedness.

The structure of the scientific community is also problematic. It is characterized by a large number of relatively young scholars in the lower ranks (junior faculty) and much smaller numbers at the top (senior faculty). All young faculty members obviously desire upward mobility, but in particular, there are relatively young scientists who are in intermediary positions. They are very close to becoming seniors but need a further push in terms of publications to be granted that coveted status. One of the results of such situations, depending on the structure and pressures within a specific department, is that the middle-level scholar has his name printed first on research reports and papers that he never wrote or with which he had very little to do. Although Zuckerman (1968) studied patterns of name-ordering among authors of scientific papers, researching the elusive problem of "who did what study and under whose name it appeared" is exceedingly difficult. Whatever the circumstances may be, if one's name appears as the first (or only) author on a scientific work one did not conduct, one is getting the credit for something one did not do. This is a fraudulent, deviant act that contradicts the expressed ethos of science.

Trying to research this problem is virtually impossible, for who is going to admit such an act? I have managed to uncover four such cases, in addition to more publicized ones.[8]

A young pediatrician worked for a long period during 1980–81 on a paper analyzing a specific disease. The work was done in a well-known, prestigious university medical school. When the paper was completed, she was instructed by the head of the department to put someone else's name as the first author of the paper. The individual in question was due to be promoted and needed the publication. He had had absolutely nothing to do with the study. It is ironic that before he could report the results and analysis of the work at a professional convention, he had to spend a great deal of time with the pediatrician in order to acquaint himself with the study. The second case is similar. A young researcher was forced to appear second on the list of contributors of a study he had completed in order to promote a colleague. This case took place in a clinical setting at a different medical school in the late 1970s.

The third case involves a certain university's department of political science. A paper appeared in a prestigious journal, bearing the name of a member of the department who had had nothing to do with its preparation. That person was also due for promotion. In this case, the original researcher's name appeared only in the acknowledgments. The fourth case concerns a now senior faculty member of a psychology department of a large university. The professor showed me a book that was written in the late 1960s and bore the name of a certain author. The first name to be acknowledged was the professor's, and by his own account, he was the one who actually wrote the book. But the other person's name appeared because he too was due to be promoted. The professor specifically told me he would never forget the case and regrets very much having participated in the deception.

When I spoke about these cases to two former chairmen and one current chairwoman of different departments in a medical school, their

8. All four cases were reported to me personally. Anonymity was guaranteed to all informants.

responses were almost identical. One told me, "Why, this is a very common practice to help faculty." For a community that places such a heavy emphasis on accreditation and personal competition, such a "common" practice does indeed seem bizarre.

The fifth category includes a few examples involving Nobel prizes. A Nobel prize, obviously, is a focal point for many scientists. The prestige and amount of the prize are such that it is sometimes hard for scientists to maintain even the appearance of disinterestedness. For example, the 1923 Nobel prize in physiology was given to Macleod and Banting for discovering how to isolate insulin. In a recent book, Michael Bliss (1982) showed how Macleod (and others) twisted the truth about who should have gotten the Prize.

A more publicized example is reported by Zuckerman (1977), Metz (1977), and Wade (1975) and involves the discovery of a peculiar type of star, a pulsar. Jocelyn Bell-Burnell, a graduate student at Cambridge University, discovered in September 1967 a strange celestial radio source that pulsated regularly. This was considered impossible at the time. Bell-Burnell, however, pursued the matter and found three other such objects in different parts of the sky. The 1974 Nobel prize in physics was awarded for this extraordinary discovery. The prestigious award, however, was not given to Bell-Burnell, but to Anthony Hewish, himself a radio astronomer and Bell-Burnell's graduate advisor. Although Bell-Burnell herself maintained that she got enough recognition (her name, for example, appeared on the paper announcing the discovery), others did not agree. Fred Hoyle publicly accused Hewish of deliberately understating Bell-Burnell's contribution. Motivated by the same feeling, the organizers of the Texas Symposium on Relativistic Astrophysics in 1976 invited Bell-Burnell to be the after-dinner speaker at their banquet. On that occasion, Tom Gould of Cornell University credited her with "perhaps the greatest single discovery in astronomy in this century" (Metz 1977, p. 277). Reed's 1983 analysis indicates how problematic this affair has become to astronomers.

A similar case is reported by Fletcher (1982), who complains that when he was a graduate student, he suggested the idea of using oil drops instead of water drops in Millikan's famous experiment. Furthermore, Fletcher claims that he wrote most of the 1910 paper that helped Millikan win a Nobel prize. However, Millikan took all the credit for himself. Finally, Sayre (1975) reveals that Rosalind Franklin was dishonestly and systematically deprived of her rightful recognition in the discovery of the structure of the DNA, for which Watson, Crick, and Wilkins were awarded the Nobel prize in 1962.

Getting credit for someone else's work reminds one of the old "tradition," still practiced in some places, where a senior scholar has one, or many, graduate students working for him for very long periods of time. These students hardly—if ever—get proper credit and recognition for their work. The published work always carries the senior faculty name on it. There are a number of sociologists who have gained a reputation for taking credit where it is not due. In some instances, published papers based on a graduate student's M.A. or Ph.D. work carry the name of the faculty member who supervised that work as the first author. This can be done despite the fact that in most cases such research is done independently by the student. I remember vividly that both at Hebrew University and the University of Chicago, where I was a student, students always warned each other not get into X's or Y's project because it could be an "intellectually castrating experience." One was advised to work with them only if one really had no choice.

Taking official credit for someone else's work brings us to the related problem of plagiarism. Zuckerman (1977) points out the ways plagiarism violates scientific norms, and Ben-David indicates why it is so easy: "Scientific results, because they are specific and are independent of writing style, are easy to steal. Moreover, because of the frequency of genuinely independent simultaneous discovery, it is difficult to detect plagiarism or, in the case of genuine multiple discovery, to assign property rights" (1977, p. 250). The fact that hundreds of journals exist in different languages and are not accessible to all scholars makes the theft of ideas, and even whole papers, both possible and probable. The following case exemplifies the point.

Pirated Papers

In 1977, a Jordanian student named Elias A. I. Alsabti came to the United States on a fellowship, apparently to study medicine. Alsabti gave the impression that he was working hard on his Ph.D. degree. In 1979 alone, he published more than sixty papers. While some of the papers were published in "junk" journals, others appeared in quite respectable publications. As it turned out, some of Alsabti's papers were proven to be pirated, word for word, from papers published elsewhere by others. Indeed, there is reason to believe that all of his papers were stolen from other scholars. Broad (1980a) argues that Alsabti, apparently a wealthy and intelligent person, was motivated by a desire to become famous quickly. His thorough knowledge of the academic system and his fraudulent methods of gaining entry into various schools and laboratories enabled him to pursue his deviant career. He was shrewd enough to build his papers in a conventional way (adding a few fictional authors) and to be careful about the titles he chose for his papers so as to make the detection of plagiarism more difficult. Alsabti, however, was not careful enough. Other scholars, especially those who worked with him, discovered some of his tricks, and the case was exposed.

Pressure to publish is not the only factor contributing to deviance. Another equally important fact is that one of the hallmarks of science is competition. Competition for discoveries, positions, grant money, and recognition can cause deviant behavior or something very close to it. Plagiarism is an obvious case. "Stealing" ideas is another. For example, a researcher told me that her team was preparing a proposal for a large grant. She met in a conference with a very famous sociologist and discussed the proposal with him. Later on, her proposal was submitted and rejected. She was amazed to realize that the sociologist had submitted a similar proposal, improving many of her suggestions, for a lower cost and had won the grant. Throughout their conversation, he had never mentioned that he intended to submit a proposal to the same foundation on the same topic using the information she gave him.

Another similar case was reported to me. An Israeli biochemist, a Ph.D. student, was in a scientific conference in Europe where he met a senior scientist. He was impressed with her work and spent almost a year in her laboratory in the United States. After this, he took all his notes, the skills and methods he had learned, including some of the synthesized materials, and returned to Israel. This was done without the senior scientist's permission or knowledge. The work he did was in a very promising area of cancer research, and he was accepted back to an Israeli university. Apparently, no one there knew the details of his U.S. adventure. Shortly after arrival, he used the materials he had taken and published quite a few papers. The papers had as a first author the name of the Israeli laboratory chief and his own name next to it. The laboratory chief claims to have not known that the results were "stolen" from somewhere else. A year later, a conference on cancer research took place in Israel and the Ph.D. student opened it with a discussion of "his" work. Unfortunately, the American scientist was present there (she was actually supposed to be the second speaker) and was shocked to realize what had happened. However, after many discussions she decided to keep the whole thing quiet. The only result was that until 1983 (when I stopped following the case) the former Ph.D. student did not get tenure despite many publications.

More recently, Stanford University investigated suspicions that Professor Kenneth Melmon, chairman of the Department of Medicine at Stanford, "incorporated large chunks of copyrighted material from a book he helped edit into a chapter he wrote for another textbook. The material was used without attribution and apparently without permission" (Colin 1984a, p. 35). It is clear that taking credit for someone else's work can have a boomerang effect. In 1975, Robert J. Gullis published a lengthy work in biochemistry, which summarized his Ph.D. work done at Birmingham University in England. The name of Gullis's supervisor, Charles E. Rowe, appeared on the paper, and it was considered an important analysis. In 1977, it was discovered by scientists at the Max Planck Institute for Biochemistry in Germany that Gullis had been fabricating data since his arrival there as a postdoctoral student. There, too, he had produced a few papers with names of colleagues on them. Failure to replicate the important work eventually led to Gullis's admission that he fabricated data (Broad and Wade 1982, pp. 151–52).

Pirated work, plagiarism, and taking unjustified credit are all close to the problem of "hired hand research." Hired hand researchers are people who actually write scientific papers but whose names do not appear on the final, published version of the work. Roth (1966) suggests that when these people realize that they have been hired to do somebody else's work and that they will receive no credit for it and that their suggestions will be ignored, they become disillusioned and careless. Thus, accuracy can become secondary in importance, corners may be cut, and some fabrication of data is also likely.

A Matter of Belief

While older, well-established scholars seem to be less prone to deviance, there are some aspects of their position conducive either to actively committing or implicitly supporting deviant acts. Senior scholars sometimes have young scholars working under them. An effective way to help a young scholar is to let his name appear as the first author of a paper. Zuckerman reports that it "has been found for samples of American scientists that thoroughly established scientists, and in particular Nobel laureates, often exercise noblesse oblige by ceding prime authorship to juniors whose careers are less secure" (1977, p. 170). While Zuckerman uses the positive label "noblesse oblige," she nevertheless states that this is a deviant procedure.

Older scientists in charge of junior scholars are often vested with two major responsibilities. The first is to be a gatekeeper of science, to monitor and closely examine various innovations.[9] Many of them believe in the accepted and established scientific paradigms and spend much of their lives proving them or working them out. They can be expected to have a natural inclination to suspect new ideas and to support ideas, experiments, and findings that support the paradigms they believe in, and thus to reject, at least initially, new or contradictory information. Furthermore, Shapin's (and others') recent work on the history and sociology of science illustrates that the field is not free from cultural and political influences.[10] This becomes clear in the following nine cases.

Case 1

We have already discussed the case of Mark Spector in another context. Spector is the graduate student at Cornell University who "discovered" a revolutionary explanation for cancer that turned out to be a fraud. McKean states that the fraud was possible because "scientists were eager to accept a theory that seemed to show a chemical chain leading to cancer" (1981, p. 19). Professor Togasaki, a former instructor of Spector's, mentioned in an interview his concern that scientists may become overly suspicious of each other's work because "the whole (scientific) system is based to a very high degree on trust" (ibid., p. 23). Spector's supervisor and others were entrapped by their desire to believe in the type of theory that his work developed.

Case 2

In the "painted mice affair," (Weinstein 1979, pp. 1–2; Zuckerman 1977) William Summerlin, a scientist at the Sloan-Kettering Institute, painted the skin of a mouse with simple ink and claimed that he had successfully completed skin grafts between genetically different animals. The discovery of this fraud was rapid but uncomfortable. Peter Medewar, who was well aware of what was going on, found himself, by his own confession, "Lacking in moral courage . . . to say at the time that . . . we were the victims of a hoax or confidence trick" (Zuckerman, 1977, p. 96). Although a scientific investigation into this case found Summerlin guilty, he was convicted of misrepresentation and not of fraud (Culliton 1974),

9. In fact, the NIH report on the Darsee case specifically criticized Kloner and Braunwald for not paying close enough attention to Darsee's activities and thus enabling him to perform his fraudulent acts (Wallis 1983).

10. Shapin's public lecture at the Van Leer Institute, Jerusalem, March 3, 1982. See also Shapin (1982). Gould (1981) shows how some scientists have actually distorted or invented data in order to uphold their political theories and prove that certain types of people were inferior.

Summerlin himself admitted he had inked the back of a mouse, making this a clear case of intentional fraudulent practice, because he was determined to prove that skin grafts between genetically different animals was possible.

Case 3

Asimov (1979) describes the case of a French chemist, Ferdinand Frederick Moissan, who took it upon himself in 1893 to show that he could create artificial diamonds. Today we know in detail the conditions under which graphite will change into carbon and how diamonds can be created. However, this was not known in 1893, and Moissan, with the technology available to him, could not possibly have created diamonds. The only problem is that his experiments did result in the creation of diamonds. Small, impure, and colorless, but diamonds nevertheless. Historians of science generally assume that one or more of Moissan's assistants wanted to help him, or perhaps to play a joke, and introduced the diamonds into the experimental set. Moissan fell for it and the assistant could not back out.

Case 4

The fourth case concerns n-rays (Nye 1980; Asimov 1979; Zuckerman 1977, p. 193; Gardner 1952 p. 745). The reputable French physicist from the University of Nancy, Prosper Blondlot, claimed in 1903 that he had detected n-rays. This claim was made about eight years after the German physicist, Willhelm Konrad Roentgen, had discovered x-rays (for which he received the first Nobel prize in physics in 1901). The period witnessed all sorts of discoveries of various rays, and Blondot had apparently pressured himself to discover some new form of ray. This "discovery" was well-received in France and the French Academy even awarded Blondlot a prize, but an American physicist, Robert Wood, was much more skeptical. He visited Blondlot in his French laboratory and while "Blondlot was observing and describing an n-ray spectrum, Wood slyly removed an essential prism from the apparatus. This had no effect on what poor Blondlot fancied he was seeing" (Gardner 1952, p. 345). As Asimov states, Blondlot was probably not a conscious faker but "wanted to believe in something desperately—and he did" (1979, p. 137).

Case 5

This concerns the famous Lysenko case. "Seldom in the history of modern science has a crackpot achieved the eminence, adulation, and power achieved by Troffim D. Lysenko, the Soviet Union's leading authority on evolution and heredity. Not only [were] his opinions . . . pronounced dogma by the Kremlin, but his Russian opponents (whose views [were] held everywhere but in the USSR) [were] systematically eliminated from their posts" (Gardner 1952, p. 140). Lysenko, a former peasant and plant-breeder, publicly defended and endorsed the Lamarckian view that the mechanism by which evolution works is the inheritance of traits various organisms acquire when responding to their environment—inheritance of acquired characteristics. Lysenko's views accorded fully with the political views of the Soviet Communist party at that time. The year 1948 marked a decisive victory for Lysenko and the agonizing end of his opponents' careers.

This is a good example of how a deviant scientist can introduce a "science" into a general cultural matrix that wants to believe that this idea is valid and true. The Lysenko case is not unique. A fierce argument recently arose in the United States between "creationists" and "evolutionists." The former, mostly religiously inspired, want to demonstrate that creation as described in the Bible is the only way to conceptualize the development of various species on earth.

Case 6

This case is very similar to the painted mice affair and involves Kammerer's "midwife toad" (see Zuckerman 1977; Koestler 1972a; Asimov 1979). Paul Kammerer was an Austrian biologist who strongly believed in the Lamarckian view that acquired characteristics are inherited. From 1918, he worked with toads and salamanders in an attempt to validate the theory. Specifically, in some species of toads, the males possess dark-colored thumb pads. The midwife toad, however, does not have this characteristic. Kammerer manipulated environmental conditions in a fashion that he hoped would create a dark-thumbed midwife toad. Since this did not occur, he painted the thumb pads of his toads with India ink. Kammerer was very secretive about his experiments, and detection of fabrication was not easy. However, it was finally discovered and he was discredited. After the exposure, Kammerer committed suicide.

Case 7

Cyril Lodowic Burt (1883–1971) taught at both Oxford and Cambridge Universities and became chair of psychology at University College, London, from 1932 to 1954. He studied the occupational status of parents and compared it with the IQs of their children. He found a correlation between IQ scores and occupations. The higher the parent ranked in the social stratification system, the higher the IQ of the child. However, professor Burt died before his studies were investigated.

Suspicion about his work was aroused as early as 1972 when Leon Kamin, a social psychologist, read Burt's studies and immediately sensed that they were fraudulent. However, it was not until 1978, in the September 29 issue of *Science*, that D. D. Dorfman proved beyond any reasonable doubt that Burt had fabricated data (Weinstein 1978; Asimov 1979; Hearnshaw 1979; Broad and Wade 1982). Asimov noted that in this case, as in case 6, Burt probably falsified data so that they would fit his theories. "Kamin's interpretation was that Burt's data remained unchallenged because they confirmed what everyone wanted to believe" (Wade 1976, p. 918).

Case 8

Berkowitz has conducted an intriguing research report (1971) that bears directly on our discussion. In his study, Berkowitz found that of seventeen social psychology textbooks he checked, very few had given an accurate report of a particular experiment. Most of the textbooks reported only portions of the conclusions, thus distorting the experiment's original meaning. It appears that the authors simply selected those aspects of the experiment that supported and fitted the textbook's general theme, disregarding such details as accuracy, validity, and reliability.

Case 9

Jay Levy was a research assistant of J. B. Rhine, a famous and respected ESP researcher. Levy was found tampering with the equipment that recorded the movements of experimental rats in order to make it appear that the rats had modified the operation of a random number generator, proving the experimental hypothesis. Apparently, Levy wanted Rhine's work in ESP to succeed at all costs (Zuckerman 1977, p. 116).

In all nine cases above there was a clear intention to commit fraud. Obviously, scientists can make honest mistakes. The area, however, between intentional fraud and simple mistakes is a grey one and includes cases that are difficult to classify. For example, in 1974, John Gribbin, an astrophysicist, and Stephen Flagermann published the book *The Jupiter Effect*. In it, Gribbin put forward the idea that an alignment of the planets in 1982 would lead to increased solar activity and cause great earthquakes on our planet. Los Angeles was expected to be the site of a massive and devastating quake. Gribbin was immediately attacked by various astronomers who condemned the book as "astrology in disguise" and "pure fantasy" (Gardner 1981, p. 345). In the July-August 1979 issue of *Mercury*, the Belgian astronomer Jean Meeus debunked the "Jupiter effect." E. Upton (see also his paper in the Jan. 1982 issue of *Sky and Telescope*) published a paper in January 1975 in the *Griffith Observer* (published by the Griffith Observatory in Los Angeles) entitled "The Great Earthquake Hoax." Eventually, in the June 1980 issue of *Omni*, Gribbin publicly retracted the idea, admitting that the whole basis of the 1982 prediction had been proven wrong.[11] Was all this an intentional hoax or an honest scientific mistake?

Deviant Scientists and Theories of Deviance

We have seen that deviance in science does take place. It occurs for at least two reasons. First, it is possible because social control mechanisms in science are weak. However, one must add that a much tighter social control, even if possible, would probably conflict with the nature of the scientific work itself. Second, science and the scientific community possess a number of structural and motivational factors that permit, if not encourage, acts of deviance. The pressures to deviate have very little to do with the scientist's personality, but are related to the very structure of science, its goals, the way it functions, and the differing positions scientists hold. In discussing possible ways to explain deviance in science, we must examine its forms, scope, apprehension, punishment, and some other factors.

Deviance versus Mistakes

First we must state that by deviance in science we have in mind primarily those acts strictly forbidden by the scientific ethos that are committed deliberately by scientists. One has to distinguish between these intentional acts and simple, honest, mistakes.

If a scientist does his utmost to research a specific problem within existing conditions and methodologies, and makes an innocent mistake, this certainly does not constitute an act of deviance. For example, William Herschel, the discoverer of the planet Uranus, thought that the sun was cold, dark, and habitable under its flaming atmosphere. The American astronomer Percival Lowell was sure he saw canals on Mars. Johannes Kepler was a firm believer in astrology. Many famous scientists believe in spiritualism and a few Nobel prize winners believe in "a hidden

---

11. In February 1982, Vintage published another version of the book. In it Gribbin and Flagemann analyzed how, where, and why their 1974 prophecies failed.

spiritual world" (Gliedman 1982). A cause of mistakes in the social sciences is the so-called demand characteristics, especially in psychological experimental studies. Orne defines 'demand characteristics' as: "the cues . . . which communicate what is expected of (the subject) and what the experimenter hopes to find" (1969, p. 146). A similar problem concerns experimental biases created by the experimenter's expectations of the subject's performance, mostly in psychological, or social psychological, studies. It was found that, in some cases, either visual or auditory cues from experimenters—in most cases unintentional—were received by their subjects and interpreted and understood by them (Rosenthal 1979). It is interesting to examine how scientists who err explain their mistakes.

> Whereas correct belief is portrayed as exclusively a cognitive phe-
> nomenon, as arising unproblematically out of rational assessments
> of experimental evidence, incorrect belief is viewed as involving the
> intrusion of distorting social and psychological factors into the
> cognitive domain. . . . Asymmetrical accounting for error and for
> correct belief is a social device which reinforces the traditional
> conception of scientific rationality and which makes the community
> of scientists appear as the kind of community we, and they, recog-
> nize as scientific (Mulkay and Gilbert 1982, pp. 166, 181).

Zuckerman (1977) distinguishes between what she calls reputable and disreputable errors in science. By reputable errors she means all the unintentional errors made by scientists, despite their attention to strict hypothesis formulation and methodologies. Disreputable errors, on the other hand, are errors committed by not following the right methodologies, omitting important elements of experimental design, and the like. Disreputable errors are, in fact, deviances. When in 1953 Langmuir coined the term "pathological science," he had in mind all those scientific claims due to both neglect of adequate methodologies and self-deception.[12]

The line between an "honest" mistake and an intentional one is not always clear. As we have seen, scientists commit or abet fraud because of pre conceived ideas or because of internal (scientific) or external (cultural) factors. Shapin (1982) describes some of the external (political, cultural) factors contributing to the development of various scientific ideas. Provine (1973) studied the inferences drawn by biologists from

---

12. For a recent discussion of the concept "pathological science," see Hyman (1980). Contemporary examples of this kind of deviance can be found in some ESP research, some UFO research, Dänikenism, astrology, and psychic healing.

their research on the genetics of racial mixture and found that the morals of the scientists changed their beliefs without any actual change in their knowledge. Nettler noted that "frequently scientific hypotheses are accepted or rejected, not just because of the evidence available, but also because of a moral pressure to interpret the evidence in a congenial way" (1972, p. 167). The rise and fall of 'Project Camelot' (Horowitz 1974) is another example. The cultural matrix in which science operates can thus lead to deviant acts—of which the Lysenko case is just one glaring example.

Forms of Deviance

Deviance in science can assume many forms. Babbage (1975) identified three forms of deviance. First is forging (or falsification), which means the recording of observations that were never made (e.g., the Summerlin, Kammerer, and Burt cases). Babbage stated that forging is motivated by the hunger for scientific reputation. Second is trimming, which means that the researcher manipulates data so that the results either support or at least do not contradict his theory. Such cases, naturally, are hard to detect. Third is cooking, which means that the researcher reports selectively (see Berkowitz's 1971 study) and suppresses data. Babbage added hoaxing as a fourth form of deviance. For him, however, hoaxing was more practical joking. Babbage felt that these practical jokes become true deviance only if they are repeated and taken seriously. Unfortunately, hoaxing can become a very serious matter. The whole field of ufology fell into disrepute partly because of the large number of hoaxes perpetrated. The Piltdown hoax, various "inventions," and other similar cases (see e.g., MacDougall 1940) do not lend much support to Babbage's definition. Many hoaxes were definitely not meant to be harmless. For example, between 1976 to 1979, Bonassoli bilked the French government for $150 million for an "oil sniffer" (*Discover*, March 1984, p. 8). Zuckerman (1977) defines three forms of deviance: fabrication, manipulation of data, and data suppression, which are similar to Babbage's. Another is plagiarism: the "stealing" of ideas, taking unjustified credit for a discovery (or work), and using students' work without giving them proper acknowledgment.

Another form of deviance scientists commit can be classified as unethical behavior, for example, experimentation with human subjects without their informed consent. Both Zuckerman (1977) and Toch (1981) have discussed this problem. Toch points out that the field of science is one of intense competition and rivalry: "It is a tamed jungle, with 'ethics' marking the delicate intersection of its veneer and its core. We therefore invoke 'ethics' to keep the mess under control, but invoke it sparingly to assure continuance of the game" (pp. 191–92). Contrary to this view, Zuckerman puts under the "unethical" heading behavior such as not giving proper credit to authors and eponymizing. She feels that ethical deviance in science is a limited phenomenon and not a general problem. Thus, ethical problems in science revolve around a few axes: the relations between science and the public, the relations among scientists, sex discrimination in science, topics for research, rights of subjects, and the like.

Finally, one must note that regardless of the specific form of the deviant act, in the majority of cases, the mechanism of control was not the referees. It was usually the colleagues of the deviant suspecting that "something" was wrong. In a few cases, replication (by the colleagues) helped to substantiate the suspicions.

Prevalence of Deviance

The next issue we have to cope with is the prevalence of deviance in science in general and in specific scientific disciplines. Zuckerman (1977) notes the fact that science, which is devoted to the careful formulation and preservation of detailed records, has not introduced procedures to record and analyze deviant behavior of scientists. Since science lacks a formal code of professional ethics and a body of pertinent law, there is no organ whose job it is to detect, prosecute, and punish. Therefore, the basis for record-keeping of deviant acts is altogether lacking. There is no policing force that chases deviant scientists and scrutinizes their records. In a number of cases, scandals were not reported via the scientific communication network, but became public through the media (Woolf 1981). *Science* and *Discover* are probably the only journals that have tried to report on deviant scientists. However, the few reports that do exist are just that, journalistic reports. There are virtually no systematic scientific studies of deviance in science. Nor is there a systematic study of deviant scientists as a category.[13]

It is not surprising that there is little or no documentation of deviance in science. Any respectable criminology textbook differentiates between visible and hidden levels of crime in a society. Criminological estimates for various types of crimes state that, on the average, only about 10–30 percent of crimes are reported. It is estimated, for example, that there are

13. Two recent books, by Broad and Wade (1982) and by Kilbourne and Kilbourne (1983), analyze the phenomenon of fraud in science. However, these books are the only ones available on the subject and, while important, are still very far from being systematic studies.

about twelve instances of unreported fraud for every reported case.[14] This state of affairs exists even with large law enforcement agencies whose job and interest it is to record deviant and criminal activity. Thus, unrecorded deviance and claims that deviance is much more prevalent than what can be estimated by so-called official reports (the "iceberg theory") are not unique to science.

In science, as in other instances of deviant behavior (e.g., police corruption), there is therefore a bitter argument between those adhering to the "iceberg theory" and those adhering to the "bad apples" theory (Kilbourne and Kilbourne 1983). Our discussion of Mertonian norms, of replication and refereeing, and of the structural and motivational aspects conducive to deviance in science indicates that its prevalence is probably much higher than is generally believed. The amount of known, publicized cases is, indeed, relatively small. However, these cases are biased. Most of these reports are on deviance in areas of science where "hot" issues and "breakthrough" research are debated. There, the chances of replications are increased and one's work is supervised and monitored more closely. Thus, the disclosures of deviance in science, more than anything else, should be taken, not as an indication of the prevalence of deviance in science, but rather, as an indication of what, and when, specific forms of deviance get publicized. Most scientific work is very far from that in which acts of deviance have been discovered. In many cases, it involves one, lonely scientist who is doing his job in very mundane research. If a careful fraud (or deviance) is being committed in one of those areas, the probability of its ever being detected is very slim.

We can expect deviance to be more prevalent in commercial scientific areas, such as pharmaceutical research. However, one must note that some recent works (see Broad and Wade 1982; Higgins 1983, for summaries) strongly suggest that eminent scientists have in the past committed acts of colossal fraud. For example, Laplace is accused of stealing ideas "outrageously, right and left, whenever he could," Leibniz is accused of similar acts. Galileo is said to have "shamelessly" stolen ideas from Kepler and others. Likewise, Newton, Ptolemy, Dalton, Lavoisier, Pascal, Mendel, and Pasteur may have all been involved, and guilty of, some form of deceit in their work. Masson (1984) has recently accused Freud of deliberately and intentionally ignoring some of his findings in order to pacify public opinion and be more popular within the medical establishment. In a somewhat similar argument, Becker (1984) accused Merton of misinterpreting and ignoring sources (to the point of faulty use

14. For summaries of this problem, see Hood and Sparks (1970), Downes and Rock (1982, chap. 2), and Bonn (1984, pp. 49–65).

of evidence), thus calling into question his conclusions regarding the relationship between German pietism and the rise of science over the past four centuries (see also Merton's superb rebuttal [1984]).

The fact that some famous scientists may have committed fraud, as well as the structure of the scientific community and the nature of its work, seems to imply that the "iceberg theory" is closer to the truth than the "bad apple" theory. It also seems safe to assume that while deviance is probably more prevalent in science than what is usually assumed, it is also probably much lower than in other areas, for example commerce, politics, dealerships, consumer fraud, white-collar criminality, con games, and the like.

Deviance in Science and Theories of Deviance

It is difficult to apply different theories of deviance to deviant science. The labeling theory of deviance, for example, would hardly apply, since most deviance in science is committed in secret and it is in the scientists' interest to keep it hidden. If the scientist wishes to be promoted, the best possible strategy is to publish but not to "make waves," especially not to be accused of fraudulent work. Publishing in what are considered to be good, but not top, journals can minimize, or even avoid, the chance suspicion and of replication and the exposure of fraud. Unlike the drug-user who indulges his habit in company or the embezzler who wants to flaunt his money, successful deviants in science will never be detected, enabling them to lead comfortable, interesting, and prestigious lives.

Nor can one apply Sutherland's differential association theory to deviance in science. This theory states explicitly that deviance is a behavior learned through association with other deviants who provide the novice with the ideology and the technology of deviance (e.g., the ideology of thieves and the "know-how" of stealing).[15] Deviant scientists, however, rarely—if ever— associate themselves with other deviant scientists. Scientists, in most cases, do not come from deprived homes or slums, nor are they psychotics suffering from various genetic, brain, or hormonal problems that can cause deviance.

The best way to understand deviant scientists and interpret their acts is

---

15. In a recent anonymous survey among undergraduate students in a U.S. university, 75 percent admitted to "cheating" at least once (in examinations, in plagiarism, by sending another person to take an examination). This could mean that students do in fact learn how to deviate professionally and how to "get away" with it. While this finding could, perhaps, support the differential association theory, it also seems that those who cheat are not the best students, but the weak ones who get through school with these deviancies. (I am grateful to L.H. for giving me the data.) Most known fraud cases, in contrast, were not committed by weak students.

probably from the perspective of social control. The various theories
developed originally to explain deviances such as theft, prostitution,
addiction, and juvenile delinquency do not apply to deviant scientists. Of
the few control theories available (see Frazier 1978 for a short survey),
Matza's (1964, 1969) is perhaps the most appropriate to our subject.
Matza has tried to explain how people become deviant, coping with one
of the most paintful dilemmas of the sociology of deviance, that is,
whether humans are free to choose a deviant career or whether they are
passive subjects whose conduct is determined by forces over which they
have little, if any, control. He emphasizes the process of becoming
deviant, mapping the conditions that facilitate deviance, taking into
consideration human choice as well.

The last few pages of *Delinquency and Drift* (1964) lay the groundwork
for Matza's theory. First, there is his concept of "drift," which is what
occurs when an individual becomes detached from a specific societal
group or from society's more general moral codes. For this situation to
come about, however, two conditions must be met. The first is neutralization. By this Matza is referring to the process through which the individual disassociates himself from the morals of society through different
techniques (e.g., denial of responsibility, denial of injury, denial of
victim, condemnation of the condemners [Sykes and Matza 1957]).[16] The
second condition is what Matza called "subterranean convergence," an
analytical concept that refers to the process through which conventional
morality and culture mixes with and gives support to deviant morality.
Good illustrations of subterranean convergence are the cases we described of scientists who deviated because of belief in a specific theory or
because of cultural and political factors intervening in the scientific
process.

Thus, according to Matza, when subterranean convergence takes
place with neutralization, the probability of drift becomes very high.
However, being in drift does not guarantee that deviance will actually
happen. For that to occur, three more conditions must be met. The most
important of these is the motivating element, which actually propels a
person to deviate. This is what Matza calls "will." Will, however, has to
be created, and its creation depends on the two other conditions: preparation and desperation. Both conditions indicate specific feelings that, as
Frazier (1976) indicates, activate the will. When subterranean convergence couples with neutralization to produce a drift situation, and when

16. For example, Spector, who fabricated data in cancer research, "accused Racker and
Vogt [his superiors in the laboratory] of unethical behavior and said 'they're going to have to
live with themselves'" (McKean 1981, p. 23).

preparation and desperation join together to activate will, deviance will take place. In *Becoming Deviant* (1969), Matza describes the processes of affinity, affiliation, and signification and interprets the process of becoming deviant as an interaction of external, uncontrollable factors and the individual's free will.

Our description of the structural elements in science conducive to and the motivational aspect of deviance in science fits very nicely into this scheme. Thus, scientists are not born prone to deviance, rather, they become deviants. A lonely scholar, hungry for recognition, in stiff competition, and in desperate "need" of tenure can—relatively easily—enter into a situation of drift and hide it quite effectively. Neutralization of guilt is also relatively simple (e.g., fabricating results to support previous research so that the possible damage is thought to be minimal). With the low probability of being caught and the perceived lenience toward those who are caught, deviance can almost become irresistible. The ease and speed with which deviant acts can be committed only reinforces this.

Deviance in Science and Similar Forms of Deviance

While those who promote "deviant sciences" apparently seek some form of "truth," even if by unorthodox means, deviant scientists display cynical contempt toward the truth—whatever it might be. They use their knowledge of science to abuse science and to ruthlessly advance their careers. Deviance in science resembles professional deviance, white-collar criminality, and government corruption. Governments, corporations, and the professions are usually believed to employ serious, honest, and respectable people. These institutions have extensive power and provide centers for morality negotiations, thus shaping the nature of reality—very much like research institutes. At the same time, white-collar criminals, government officials, and professionals are usually model citizens, successful by all economic and social standards, bearers of conventional morality, and recipients of the benefits of being loyal, conforming members of the social system (see Douglas and Waksler 1982; Thio 1983).

Quinney (1964) characterized professional (or occupational) deviation as those forms of behavior that deviate from the norms of a specific profession but are not illegal. This characterization fits nicely many cases of deviant scientists and deviance in science. White-collar crime, on the other hand, can be characterized as professional deviance, but it is also illegal. For example, while fudging and suppressing data could fall into the first category, plagiarism and perhaps fabrication of data could fall into the second category. Indeed, Geis and Meier (1977) have suggested that white-collar criminality should include deviance in the professions. Cases of deviance within police departments are also very similar to those of deviant scientists. McCaghy points out that, as in the scientific community, "tendencies toward corruption are built into the law enforcement system" (1979, p. 191). Governmental forms of deviance, political corruption, illegal police activities, also parallel forms of deviance in science.

There are a number of correspondences between deviance in science and professional, governmental, and white-collar deviance. First is the problem of damage. Professional deviance—pollution, unsafe machines or drugs, chemicals in food, fraudulent research in pharmaceutics, unnecessary surgery—endangers the public. Likewise, fabricated or biased results on I.Q. tests can damage the image of a whole category of people. White-collar deviance also has numerous victims and a particularly heavy economic cost, possibly tens of billions of dollars annually. However, the main threat of all these forms of deviance, and of deviance in science, lies elsewhere. White-collar crime clearly damages important social values and norms like trust and morale. Government corruption breeds contempt for the law, cynicism, and disrespect for the social order. Likewise, deviance in science can lead to distrust of science and shatter its legitimacy. Kilbourne and Kilbourne (1983) argue that in the United States this has led to a depletion of a vital national resource, that is, science itself.

The second correspondence is the problem of evaluating the prevalence of deviance. It is in the interest of each of these groups to show that they can detect and punish internal deviance. However, none of them is interested in finding too much deviance because it could undermine the group's legitimacy. The debate whether deviance in science is a "bad apple" problem or only the tip of an iceberg characterizes the study of white-collar, professional, and government deviance as well. There too, data are not systematically recorded.

Third, it is extremely difficult to detect deviants in the professions, government, and the sciences, not to mention white-collar criminals. With a few exceptions (e.g., Wheeler, Weisburg, and Bode 1982), most criminologists and sociologists of deviance would agree the punishments for deviants in these areas are relatively light. In fact, Thio has suggested that such deviance should be called "profitable deviance" because "the individuals involved can illegally acquire a lot of money, power or influence with a relatively low risk of harmful consequences to themselves" (see his 1978 edition, p. 343).

Fourth, it appears that the essence of professional, governmental, and white-collar deviance is similar to deviance in science. All are focused on violations of, or deviation from, socially defined professional, business, or political roles (Edelhertz 1970; Conklin 1977). Fifth, in all these areas, people who are otherwise considered respectable, with no past criminal record, bearers of conventional morality, commit the deviant acts.

However, there are also at least two marked differences between these forms of deviance and deviance in science. First, white-collar criminals are usually after money or other economic gain. Deviant scientists, more like deviant government officials, are usually after recognition and job mobility. Second, while the results of deviance in the cases discussed here in practical—nonsymbolic—terms are severe, one has to recognize that the amount of damage in some areas, like anthropology, sociology, political science, and literary studies, is probably negligible. Fraudulent work in these areas can result in a wrong interpretation, but with usually no actual injury.

Concluding Discussion:
Reactions to Deviant Scientists—A Question of Boundaries

The way the scientific community regards acts of deviance by its members is very instructive. Obviously, like any other organization, it has a vested interest in minimizing publicity about deviant cases. Too many public disclosures of hoaxes, fabrications, and fraud would severely damage its credibility and prestige. Admitting that public, political, or cultural factors may bias scientific research would have much the same result. However, it is also very important for the scientific community to expose cases of deviance and thus show to the public, as well as to its own members, that it has the ability to detect such cases, to be open about them, and to punish the scientists concerned. It is predictable, then, that the scientific community will try to defend itself. One obvious defense is not to keep records of cases of deviance in science. Another is to deny that there are internal factors that contribute to and facilitate deviance in science. The most common defense, however, is to deny the "iceberg theory."

Although in a recent case of fraud (Broad 1982, p. 482), Robert Ebert, former dean of the Harvard Medical School, supported the "iceberg theory" and was quoted in *Science* as saying that fraudulent cases in science are much more frequent than often acknowledged, the scientific ethos and community usually refute this possibility vigorously. This attitude is best exemplified in Zuckerman's analysis: "Almost all those who have bothered to look conclude that seriously deviant behavior in science is rare" (1977, p. 98). Surprisingly, she goes on to add that "scientists themselves repeatedly note this one fact," although no direct empirical evidence exists to support this claim. She does not stop here and quotes different scholars, reinforcing this view. Noteworthy is Merton's opinion that cases of fraud are virtually nonexistent in the annals of science. However, Zuckerman is careful to point out that this view is impressionistic and not grounded in facts. She mentions the absence of statistics on deviant behavior in science and comments that this situation inevitably arouses speculation. While she recognizes that there are reasons to assume that deviant behavior in science is an "iceberg phenomenon," she also states that cases of fraud in science are rare.[17] Alas, as we have already seen, fraud is only one (and probably a minor) example of deviance in science. Zuckerman examines cases of assumed deviance in science by such distinguished scholars as Ptolemy, Galileo, Newton, Mendel, and Freud, but she immediately contradicts these claims, as if to prove by assertion that scientists do not commit deviant scientific acts.

McKean, in his vivid documentation of one instance of scientific deviance, also notes that "whatever new facts emerge from the Spector case, it remains true that fraud in science is rare" (1981, p. 33). Asimov, in his short and informative paper (1979), also gives the strong impression that deviance in science is unrepresentative and rare. While Woolf notes that "scientists as a group are generally reluctant to acknowledge falsification of data or a pervasive problem and seem unwilling to take formal notice of this serious deviation from prescribed scientific norms" (1981, p. 9), her biased paper certainly leaves the reader with the distinct feeling that deviant scientists are truly a rare breed. She quotes Philip Handler, president of the National Academy of Sciences, who said in testimony on March 31, 1981, that the problem of falsification of research results "has been grossly exaggerated. . . . It is rather a relatively small matter which is generated in and is normally effectively managed by that smaller segment of the larger society which is the scientific community" (ibid., p. 10). These opinions are contradicted by a fascinating study conducted by Ian St. James–Roberts (1976). His evidence was drawn from questionnaires published in the pages of the *New Scientist* and indicated that deviance in science is quite prevalent. Dr. St. James–

17. Actually, the United States Congress has become concerned about the problem of fraud in science. The Committee on Science and Technology formed a subcommittee (chaired by Albert Gore, Jr.) to investigate this problem in 1981 (U.S. Congress 1981).

Roberts was alarmed by the responses received and strongly recommended that science develop "more stringent" controls.[18]

Higgins (1983) cynically notes that scientists are extremely reluctant to admit that deception is common in the history of science and that the "bad apples" theory is simply not valid. He describes vividly what he calls the "science game," noting that most scientists can estimate fairly well the amount of fraud in science while still engaging in the " game." He states that science has "science watchers," that is, those who construct and maintain the images of science and who are responsible for the public relations of science with other human institutions. He documents some of the techniques used by science watchers to "cover" or discount cases of fraud and deceit in order to draw a positive picture of science—a picture in which science progresses gradually through the accumulation of certified knowledge by honest people. An example is Aronson's attempt (1975) to discount Koestler's book on Kammerer (who was accused of blatant fraud in biology). Koestler (1972a) implied that Kammerer was not a pathological deviant, but that he fell victim to professional infighting. Higgins argues that the existence of "science watchers" itself helps to conceal acts of deviance in science and provides a positively reconstructed picture of it.

Denying that deviance or, to use the more neutral term used by St. James–Roberts, intentional bias is a common phenomenon in science is only one defense mechanism. To support this claim, scientists usually come up with a complementary claim, perhaps best expressed by Dr. Togasaki's opinion in regard to the Spector case (he was Spector's former instructor) "The whole (scientific) system is based to a very high degree on trust. It may have backfired . . . but I hope we don't lose sight of the biggest issue" (McKean 1981, p. 23).

Another common defense usually emphasizes the integrity of science and focuses attention on the deviant scientist himself. In this case, the personality, background, world view, or history of the deviant scientist will be highlighted so that most of the blame will fall squarely on his shoulders. A paper by Asimov entitled "Alas, All Human" exemplifies this approach:

> Science itself, in the abstract, is a self-correcting, truth-seeking device. There can be mistakes and misconceptions due to incomplete or erroneous data, but the movement is always from the less

18. Interesting to note that the term used for deviance in St. James-Roberts's study was "intentional bias." There is no question that the sample was biased and that a great deal of intentional bias occurs in industrial research.

true to the more true. Scientists are, however, not Science. However glorious, noble and supernaturally incorruptible Science is, scientists are, alas, all human." (1979, p. 133)

Another example involves Broad and Wade's book (1982), which is probably the first comprehensive study of a large number of cases of deviance in science. The authors argue that competition in science is so intense that a strong inducement to deviate is created, that internal scientific controls are very weak, and that deviance (mostly fraud) in science is widespread. The scientific community reacted angrily to their analysis. The editor of *Science 1983* (published by the AAAS) noted that nine scientists (six Nobel laureates) declined to review the book and that sociologist Robert K. Merton advised against purchasing it (see discussion in *Science and Government Report*, March 1, 1983, pp. 3–5). Zinder's 1983 review criticized the book heavily and reminded the reader that the thirty-four cases of fraud reported by Broad and Wade took place over a period of two thousand years, cleverly using the low amount of detected fraud cases in science as an argument against their conclusions. I myself have, so far, seen only one review that could be considered positive. I must admit that the book often falls short of its overambitious goals—especially in the general interpretations and suggestions; there are also some unfortunate overgeneralizations. However, the book is important in the sense that it does offer a fascinating, comprehensive account of deviance in science by two reporters who knew many of the people involved first hand.

Like deviants in other situations and other periods—whether modern thieves or seventeenth-century witches—the most important function of deviant scientists is obviously in creating and maintaining moral boundaries, in creating rigidity and stability. Aronson illustrates this function in his review of Koestler's book on the Kammerer affair:

> Although [the] notorious [Kammerer] scandal had reached its climax twelve years before with the suicide of the then illustrious Professor, . . . I was familiar with this amazing story, for it was regularly told to biology students as an object lesson. In essence [we were taught that] falsifying evidence is just about the worst sin that a scientist can commit since such actions threaten to destroy the very heart of the scientific system. (1975, p. 115)

Asimov (1979) recounts similar socialization processes.

Exposures of deviant cases in science are sometimes published in the prestigious *Science* and in the widely circulated *Discover* (but usually in no other journals). These revelations in print serve a number of functions. First, the institution of science confesses that intentional bias can and does occur. Second, however, it implies that such biases are infrequent. Third, it demonstrates that the biases are detectable and that science is self-correcting. Thus, more than anything else, the detection of deviant scientists promotes cohesion, integration, and rigidity among the nondeviant scientists.

Finally, to conclude that honest science does not exist and that it is all fraudulent would be a misinterpretation. Somehow when analyzing deviance, it is easy to imply that the whole world has gone wrong. One has to realize that large numbers, if not an overwhelming majority, of the scientific establishment do strive to work according to Merton's norms. A scientific community does in fact exist, there is intensive scientific activity, and this activity functions according to explicit, well-established norms. Certified knowledge is produced and transmitted from generation to generation of scientists.

An analysis of deviance in science necessarily focuses on its unpleasant aspects, which do not add credit to the profession. One should not, however, infer from this that all of the scientific activity (or scientists) are suspect. Our discussion has revealed that the conservative view of science is somewhat misleading. The Mertonian norms must, therefore, be conceptualized as ideal, and not as a reflection of reality in its entirety. Ben-David states that the Mertonian norms "apply only to the evaluation of results to be made public" (1977, p. 265). This, however, evades the real issue, that is, the existence of scientific research that is not conducted according to these norms. This is similar to the distinction that Ichheiser (1970) makes between "appearances and realties," that is, between those images presented for public evaluation and what really goes on. As we have seen, the two need not necessarily overlap.

6
CONCLUDING DISCUSSION

This conclusion has two purposes: first, to summarize the main arguments of the book, and second, to suggest the concept of a motivational accounting system as a possible bridge for the various levels of analysis of deviance and as an explanation of how change is introduced or stability maintained.

Summary and Discussion of Main Arguments

In our analysis, we have applied the concept of deviance in a different way than is usual. When Durkheim suggested that deviance is functional because the reaction to it creates both flexibility and rigidity, he created a double-bind for sociologists. How can deviance trigger these two, apparently contradictory, processes at once? As we saw in the introduction, commitment to any one of the Durkheimian claims leads to very different methodologies, research priorities, and sociologies of deviance. The solution I suggested for the Durkheimian double-bind was to view it within a broader context of societal processes of change and stability. In this way, first, the Durkheimian dilemma is resolved because change and stability themselves, while contradictory, are essential parts of all social systems. Second, deviance is taken out of its marginal status and put within the central context of the sociological tradition.

This book clearly implies that deviance is a relative phenomenon. What is and what is not defined as deviance depend on the cultural matrix in which a particular form of behavior takes place. Thus, the links between deviance, change, and stability are strong and intimate. Our analysis adds two explicit dimensions to the sociology of deviance that were previously only implicit—the Durkheimian connection and the significance of change and stability. The case studies bear this out. The fact that the cases are drawn from different time periods only adds strength to the thesis because the validity of the analysis is not time-bounded. We come to an interesting conclusion from this discussion regarding "radical" (or Marxist) criminology (e.g., Taylor, Walton, and Young 1973). Radical criminology implies that a crimeless society is possible because it is the capitalist social order that is "criminogenic" in itself. Once this social order disappears in favor of a better one, crime will disappear as well. The analysis presented here, however, suggests that this claim may be problematic or even invalid. Changing the social structure would mean changing societal moral boundaries, which in turn means that crime would not disappear but new definitions and new forms of deviance would emerge. If this interpretation is correct, then some revision must be made in radical criminology's idealistic portrayal of a crimeless social system.

As is clear from the four different cases we examined, deviance is an important sociological construct if we wish to understand better the ways societal boundaries change, or remain unchanged. These four cases were analyzed along two main axes. One showed how in each and every case, problems of change and stability could be utilized to explain the specific deviance discussed. Thus we emphasized the problem of societal boundaries in each case. The second analyzed the natural history of each type of deviance discussed. In this manner, each case of deviance was thoroughly described and analyzed, and the main problem of societal boundaries was kept in focus.

We first examined the European witchcraze of the late Middle Ages. The analysis focused on the changing boundaries of all aspects of medieval society in order to explain the invention of a demonological theology, the timing of the craze, why the main victims of the craze were women, and why this fabricated ideology was so readily accepted.

Next we looked at the modern occult and science fiction scene, focusing on the nature of modern, pluralistic, and complex society. We analyzed the nature, timing, meaning, and future of deviant belief systems by utilizing the concept of recentering and searching for the beyond. The concept of recentering one's world illustrates how deviant belief systems can, and do, change the boundaries of modern societies. We also saw that humans *need* mystery, that a full understanding of every phenomenon would place humanity in an unbearable spiritual state. This implies that human nature seeks tension rather than resolution. It is therefore clear that a major part of the occult and of science fiction is religious in the functional sense of the term. However, much in both systems challenges science as well.

The nature of this challenge became clear in our third case, that of deviant science. The concept illustrates how unorthodox scientific beliefs, including the occult and science fiction, challenge the accepted boundaries of various scientific disciplines. Because of the nature of science, its outermost frontiers are necessarily speculative. Thus, the goals of science may stimulate "deviant" beliefs. These deviant beliefs are exploited by science fiction fans, devotees of the occult, and others who hunger for meaning. Thus, deviant sciences force orthodox science to re-examine its boundaries, and have the potential of introducing vital changes into it.

One point made by Durkheim (1938) is that deviant "innovations" become possible when collective morality is in a weakened state. The fifteenth through the seventeenth centuries brought a variety of bold and innovative ideas; so has modern society. In both cases, we have a weakened collective morality. The gradual dissolution of medieval societal boundaries created a witchcraze on the one hand, but on the other hand, it helped create science and introduce new innovations in the arts, religion, and politics. Modern complex societies, characterized by a pluralistic morality, have given rise to many social ills, but they have also encouraged new ideas in science, the arts, religion, policy and new social forms, in marriage and in other areas. Thus, the scientific norms that Merton identified could inhibit risk-taking and creativity if they operated with perfect efficiency. From this point of view, campaigns against science fiction and the occult "sciences" do nothing to advance real scientific innovation. They only help to ossify the boundaries of normal science. Since science fiction and the occult, in many respects, are by-products of science, we cannot have one without the other. Thus, deviance promotes scientific progress not only because they stem from the same source. Opposition to deviant sciences and scientists (and science fiction and the occult) is therefore healthy only as long as that opposition is not absolute. If it were, it would not be possible to introduce any changes and, in the long run, inflexibility (and possible collapse) would result. If there is too much opposition, whatever potential social, religious, or scientific innovations that could have come from the occult and science fiction will be crushed.

We looked last at deviant scientists. Cases of fabrication and falsification of data in science allow the scientific community to redefine its boundaries and to reassert what is methodologically permitted and what is not. The existence of a few cases of deviance enables the scientific community to tell its own members, and the public, that it has effective control mechanisms and knows its boundaries and obligations.

Motivational Accounting Systems

A major problem for sociological analysis is the application of broad theories to specific considerations, that is, the macro versus micro levels of analysis. Simply put, how are metasociological concerns reflected on the personal level and vice versa? Thus, to complete our discussion, we must address the problem of individual actions, motivations, and subjective meaning within the larger context of stability and change. Solving this puzzle can lead us to understand the basic actual mechanism through which deviance operates in processes of change and stability. Bridging the macro- and micro-levels of analysis means that we shall have to break away, to some extent, from the Durkheimian positivistic view emphasized so far. With the exception of the concept of "anomie" and its possible interpretation as a dispersion of the individual's cognitive maps, the Durkheimian typology does not provide the necessary equipment for our task. While a full analysis of this problem is far beyond the scope of this study, let me suggest some ideas of how the gap can be bridged, and possible directions for continuation of the work presented here.

The process of "becoming a marijuana user" provides the novice with a motivation to use marijuana, for it helps him define the effects of the drug as pleasant; it provides him with social acceptability, support, and security against societal stigmatization and police raids; and last, but not least, the process of "becoming" provides the novice user with a vocabulary by which he can justify, and meaningfully interpret, his experience in a way that increases the probability that he will use the drug again (Becker 1953). This process is infused with values and needs from two directions: first, the users' group's needs, values, norms, and definition of social reality are transmitted to the novice; second, the novice's needs, such as social approval, support, acceptability, and pleasure seeking, are being negotiated and met through his joining the group. The end product of this process is that a novice drug user "becomes" a regular user. In other words, the process of "becoming a marijuana user" provides the user with a "motivational accounting system."

The credit for developing this concept must be given to C. Wright Mills. In 1940, he published a paper in which he argued that statements of motivation have a basic social character because they enable people to be integrated into social groups and provide the actors with direction for subsequent actions. These motivations reflect morality, and thus a vocabulary of motives serves as a prime internal source of social control. "Motivations" in this context becomes a sociological (rather than a psychological) concept, and language can be conceptualized as another form of social control. Mills was aware that vocabularies of motives differ from one group of people to another because this vocabulary reflects moral stands, which change themselves from one society to another and within one society.

Motivational accounting systems allow the individual to justify his acts and to influence others.[1] These systems can justify behavior not only after, but before it occurs. The types of motivational accounting systems the individual chooses to use are not arbitrary inventions. They reflect the type of justification acceptable in a specific cultural matrix. Thus, social control mechanisms are tied very closely with motivational accounting systems. Whether internal or external, these mechanisms provide actors with the necessary vocabulary to justify past, present, and future deviancy. Motivational accounts are used in face-to-face encounters, that is, in symbolic interaction, and provide, on the one hand, the bridging mechanism for the macro-micro analysis and, on the other, a way for boundaries to change or stabilize. Macrosociological concerns such as values, morality, and interests infiltrate face-to-face interactions, influencing definitions of situations, participants' roles, and an interaction's outcome. Since language is the most important tool in symbolic interaction and in motivational accounting systems, our analytical "break" from Durkheim is not complete. Durkheim certainly considered morality and values as most important mechanisms in achieving social integration and control. Furthermore, any change or stability in boundaries finds its expression in situations of symbolic interaction where people provide accounts for their actions. Thus, motivational accounts reflect prevailing morality. Any change in morality, or in what would be accepted as a valid account, will be immediately reflected in the accounts. For example, years ago when prisoners wanted an early release for good behavior they had to "work", today, they have to "talk" (mostly to social workers and probation officers). An interesting example of a prisoner who changed accounts several times is Patricia Hearst. When booked at the San Mateo County Jail, she

> defiantly listed her occupation as "urban guerrilla." In the course of the legal proceedings against her involving bank robbery, assault, and kidnapping, Patty Hearst came to accept an alternative psychiatric definition of her behavior as illness induced by traumatic

---

1. For some recent work on this topic see Ditton (1977), Taylor (1972), Cressey (1962), Lyman and Scott (1970, pp. 111–45), Bruce and Wallis (1983), and Wallis and Bruce (1983), Gilbert and Abell (1983). Modern attribution theories provide many insights into vocabularies of motives as does Sykes and Matza's analysis of techniques of neutralization (1957).

episodes of solitary confinement and extreme anxiety. Ultimately, her behavior was defined as criminal in nature and
intent. . . . What makes this . . . particular episode unusual is the
ease and rapidity with which a single actor moved from political to
medical to criminal definition of the same behavior. (Inverarity
1980, p. 204)

As part of my university training, I spent a year doing clinical-
rehabilitative work with chronic schizophrenics. One evening, I was
walking with one of the patients from downtown Jerusalem to the clinic,
and we encountered a traffic light. The light being red, I waited for it to
turn green. My companion, however, did not wait and crossed the street.
When the light changed, I crossed the street and, hoping to make a just
and therapeutic comment, I told him that he should not have crossed the
street against a red light. "But Nachman," he said, "what can they do to
me if they catch me? I am crazy!" and he triumphantly took out a small
card confirming that he was a chronic schizophrenic. Clearly, he was
using a motivational account, provided to him by a macrosystem, to
justify a deviant behavior before and after it took place. Rosenhan has
pointed out that mentally ill patients learn, after a lengthy process of
resistance, to "accept the diagnosis, with all of its surplus meanings and
expectations, and behave accordingly" (1973, p. 254).

On the other hand, new orientations, values, meanings, and moralities, which are being constantly negotiated on the most basic level, can
influence values, meanings, and orientations of a whole social system.
Thus, the content and structure of motivational accounting systems are
basically fluid, negotiated between various societal levels as well as within
each level, resulting either in the reinforcement of stability or in change.
The motivational accounting system themselves, when analyzed over an
extended period of time in one culture or comparatively among cultures,
should reflect the amount of societal change or stability.

By their nature, motivational accounts not only link the macro-micro
levels of analysis but can provide the actual mechanisms through which
boundaries remain stable or are changed. One need not confine the
concept of motivational accounts to the micro level only. It is quite
possible to conceptualize ideologies and values as forms of generalized
motivational accounts. In this way too, institutional justifications can be
thought of as accounts.

The cases analyzed in this book illustrate this well. However, to avoid
an unnecessarily long discussion, I shall elaborate only on the European
witchcraze and deviant sciences.

The ideology of the European witchcraze gave the masses an easy solution for their problems. This solution was popularly accepted and served as a generalized motivational accounting system to explain the misery people were experiencing. Monter notes that "secular judges . . . remodelled popular beliefs in order to make them conform to official 'notions' of how witches ought to behave" (1980, p. 33). The "official" demonology was thus reflected in the witches' confessions. Because of the nature of the crime, it became obvious that a witch would not confess easily. Consequently, a witch had to be tortured into confessing. Under torture, the suspected witches gave almost uniform confessions to uniform questions and usually confirmed the witchcraze ideology. This should not really surprise us. However, some sources (e.g., Parrinder 1958; Hughes 1952) also report on cases where people voluntarily confessed to practicing witchcraft and then were put to the torture to make sure that their confessions were not false. Trevor Roper notes that "For every victim whose story is evidently created or improved by torture, there are two or three who genuinely believe in its truth. . . . Again and again . . . we find witches confessing . . . without an evidence of torture. . . . it was this spontaneity, rather than the confessions themselves, which convinced rational men that the details were true" (1967, pp. 125–26).

Thus, we see that despite the terrible consequences of a confession, people accepted the official demonology and freely admitted to an imaginary crime. The confessions reflected the official ideology regarding witchcraft. This ideology, coupled with the social stress, provided in turn the motivation and the accounts for the confessions, which constituted a "positive feedback loop." Apparently, some of the people who freely confessed had a strange (and for us unintelligible) pleasure from the fear they generated as Satan's powerful servants. Thus, the general stress, the official ideology, and the degradation ceremonies (Garfinkel 1950) that the accused suffered resulted in a cultural and social transformation that produced a new identity—witch—that received the meaning, content, and motivation for its existence from the official demonological theories and in its turn, reinforced them.

The motivational accounts used by orthodox sciences, especially the science keepers and adherents of deviant sciences, also reflect the connections between different sociological levels. Westrum states

> The zoologist interested in the existence of "bigfoot" is lumped together with astrologers and psychics under the label "pseudo-scientist." The UFO researcher . . . is often considered to be a

contemporary flat-earther and ufology is generally ignored by scientists interested in exobiology and interstellar communication. Indeed, the scientific community's general feeling about such "pseudoscience" is something like: "If science is the competent study of what is real, then pseudoscience is the incompetent study of what is not real." Or, more simply: "Pseudoscience is the study of the nonexistent by the incompetent." Some critics have gone even further and suggested that cryptoscientists are delusional. (1982, pp. 89)

We have seen similar reactions throughout our discussion of deviant sciences. For example, Shapely's stating that "if Velikovsky is right, the rest of us are crazy"; Palmer's comment that "Däniken is a caricature of positivism"; Sandage's opinion that Follin "was crazy" to look for the remnants of the big bang. Likewise, negative responses to Reber, Jansky, Wegener, and other innovators illustrate the point. Cheney (1981) documents the opposition to the ideas of the eccentric genius, Nicholas Tesla. Thus, generalized motivational accounts used against deviant sciences on the micro level, clearly reflect the macro level.

On the other hand, we should also look at the reactions of adherents of the deviant sciences. One of the cases we examined was that of Gamow's staff, who originally developed the big bang theory. After their failure, Gamow's two assistants left science altogether, bitter and disillusioned. If their reaction can be considered common, then science pays a high price for rejecting, ridiculing, and stigmatizing deviant sciences that are later proved to be true. There are, however, many cases of scientists who propose theories and persist in their attempt to establish their validity despite resistance. Here, too, the position of the particular scientist and the way he presents his theory are of crucial importance.

It makes a difference who presents the deviant scientific claim and to whom. Däniken's ancient astronaut theory was not written for the scientific community, whereas Crick's directed panspermia was first (1973) presented to scientists, although its later version (1981) was certainly directed to a larger audience. The type of motivational accounts used in each case, as well as the levels of scholarship, sophistication, and persuasiveness differ greatly. Schievella wrote in *Ancient Skies* (the official newsletter of the Ancient Astronaut Society) that scientists' reactions to Däniken's hypothesis are "irrational" and that the "scientific community has attacked both the hypothesis and von Däniken with outrage and abuse. His evidence has been dismissed with ridicule. The hypothesis is assailed with fallacious reasoning" (Nov.–Dec. 1983, p. 1).

In the early 1950s, nearly a decade before the Morrison-Cocconi paper was published in *Nature* (1959) suggesting preliminary ideas for SETI, Cocconi wrote a letter to Sir Bernard Lovell, then director of the Jodrell Bank radio telescope in England, suggesting a search for "beams of electromagnetic radiation, modulated in a rational way, e.g., in trains corresponding to the prime numbers." Edelson notes that the tone of Cocconi's letter was "half apologetic for proposing a project that at first . . . looks like science fiction" (1979, p. 126). Lovell was apparently very polite in his rejection of the request, saying that the Jodrell Bank radio telescope was too busy with other projects. Today any request for the use of a radio telescope for SETI research would not be automatically dismissed, even politely. SETI research provides us with another example for a motivational accounting system. The Dover edition (1979) of the now famous Morrison, Billingham, and Wolfe report from the NASA-sponsored 1977 conference reflects SETI thinking in the middle and late 1970s. In the introduction and first conclusion, the editors state "Great discoveries are often the result more of courage and determination than of the ultimate in equipment. The Niña, the Pinta, and the Santa Maria were not jet airliners, but they did the job" (p. 9).

In many cases, those who present or support deviant science tend to romanticize the proponents of deviant theories as underdogs, ostracized by the scientific community. They often present themselves as modern Galileos, the victims of jealous, cruel, and obtuse scientists who do not, and cannot, comprehend their ideas. In this way, the proponents of deviant theories provide motivational accounting systems both for themselves and for society at large. Many of those who make deviant knowledge claims enjoy describing themselves as the "true carriers of the light," or as the only real truth seekers. The history of science provides these people with ample precedents. We can therefore see how the generalized, macro-level motivational accounts are reflected in the micro-level motivational accounts. However, we also see that this process works in reverse. That is, we have many cases in which adherents of deviant sciences were successful in introducing change into science and in which the generalized, motivational accounts gradually changed to reflect the previously rejected motivational accounts of the deviant science.

In Conclusion

Deviance plays a crucial role in societies, and a better understanding of the nondeviant can be achieved by understanding the deviant. Deviance and the societal reaction to it must be seen as boundary maintenance phenomena within the context of change and stability as outlined in the classic Durkheimian approach. However, we must also be aware of the integration of the micro and macrosociological levels of analysis. C. Wright Mills' concept of the "motivational accounting system" anticipates this future task.

BIBLIOGRAPHY

Abell, G. O., and Barry Singer, eds. 1981. *Science and the Paranormal*. New York: Charles Scribner's Sons.

Abulafia, David. 1981. "Southern Italy and the Florentine Economy 1265–1370." *Economic History Review*, second series, 34 (3): 377–88.

Adler, Margot. 1979. *Drawing Down the Moon: Witches, Druids, Goddess Worshippers, and Other Pagans in America Today*. New York: Viking Press.

Agassi, Joseph. 1975. *Science in Flux*. Dordrecht. D. Reidel.

Alexander, J. C. 1979. "Paradigm Revision and 'Parsonianism.'" *Canadian Journal of Sociology*, 4 (4): 1343–58.

Alfred, R. H. 1976. "The Church of Satan." In *The New Religious Consciousness*, ed. C. Y. Glock and R. N. Bellah, pp. 180–202. Berkeley: University of California Press.

Anderson, Alan, and Raymond Gordon. 1978. "Witchcraft and the Status of Women—The Case of England." *British Journal of Sociology*, 29 (2): 171–82.

Anderson, Robert D. 1970. "The History of Witchcraft: A Review with Some Psychiatric Comments." *American Journal of Psychiatry* 126 (12): 1727–35.

Andreski, Stanislav. 1982. "The Syphilitic Shock." *Encounter* 58 (5): 7–26.

Arens, William. 1979. *The Man-Eating Myth: Anthropology and Anthropophagy*. Oxford: Oxford University Press.

Aries, Philippe. 1962. *Centuries of Childhood: A Social History of Family Life*. New York: Alfred A. Knopf.

Armstrong, J. Scott. 1982. "Research on Scientific Journals: Implications for Editors and Authors." *Journal of Forecasting* 1: 83–104.

Aronson, L. R. 1975. "The Case of the Midwife Toad." *Behavior Genetics* 5: 115–25.

Ashley, Michael, ed. 1975. *The History of the Science Fiction Magazines*. Chicago: Henry Regnery Company.

Ashtor, Eliyahu. 1975. "The Volume of Levantine Trade in the Later Middle Ages (1370–1498)." *Journal of European Economic History* 4 (3), 573–612.

———. 1976. "Observations on Venetian Trade in the Levant in the Fourteenth Century." *Journal of European Economic History* 5 (3): 533–86.

Ashworth, C. E. 1980. "Flying Saucers, Spoon Bending, and Atlantis: A Structural Analysis of New Mythologies." *Sociological Review* 28 (2): 353–76.

Asimov, Isaac. 1979. "Alas, All Human." *Magazine of Fantasy and Science Fiction* 56 (6): 131–49.

Babbage, C. 1975. *Reflections on the Decline of Science in England and on Some of Its Causes.* N.Y. Scholarly (reprint of 1930 edition).

Bainbridge, William S. 1976. "The Science Fiction Subculture." *The Spaceflight Revolution,* pp. 198–280. In New York: Wiley-Interscience.

———. 1978. *Satan's Power: A Deviant Psychotherapy Cult.* Berkeley: University of California Press.

Bainton, Ronald H. 1971. *Women of the Reformation in Germany and Italy.* Boston: Beacon Press.

———. 1973. *Women of the Reformation in France and England.* Boston: Beacon Press.

Balch, A. W., and D. Taylor. 1977. "Seekers and Saucers: The Role of Cultic Milieu in Joining a UFO Cult." *American Behavioral Scientist* 20 (6): 839–60.

Barber, Bernard. 1961. "Resistance by Scientists to Scientific Discovery." *Science* 134: 596-602.

Barnes, B. 1977. "On the Reception of Scientific Beliefs." In *The Sociology of Science,* ed. B. Barnes, pp. 269-291 Middlesex: Penguin Books.

———. 1982. *T.S. Kuhn and Social Science.* New York: Columbia University Press.

Baroja, J. C. 1965. *The World of the Witches.* Chicago: University of Chicago Press.

Bateson, Gregory, et al. 1956. "Toward a Theory of Schizophrenia." *Behavioral Science* 1: 251–264.

Becker, G. 1984. "Pietism and Science: A Critique of Robert K. Merton's Hypothesis." *American Journal of Sociology* 89 (5): 1065–90.

Becker, H. S. 1953. "Becoming a Marijuana User." *American Journal of Sociology* 59: 235–42.

———. 1963. *Outsiders.* New York: Free Press.

———. 1967. "Whose Side Are We On?" *Social Problems* 14 (3): 239–247.

———. 1978. "Arts and Crafts." *American Journal of Sociology* 83 (4): 862–89.

———. 1982. *Art Worlds.* Berkeley: University of California Press.

Bell, Daniel. 1977. "The Return of the Sacred? The Argument on the Future of Religion." *British Journal of Sociology* 28 (4), 419–49.

Bellah, R. N. 1965. "Epilogue: Religion and Progress in Modern Asia." In *Religion and Progress in Modern Asia,* pp. 168–226. Glencoe, Ill.: Free Press.

Ben-David, Joseph. 1960. "Roles and Innovations in Medicine." *American Journal of Sociology* 65: 557–86.

———. 1964. "Scientific Growth: A Sociological View." *Minerva* 2: 455–76.

———. 1971. *The Scientist's Role in Society,* Englewood Heights, N.J.: Prentice-Hall.

————. 1977. "Organization, Social Control, and Cognitive Change in Science." In *Culture and Its Creators: Essays in Honor of Edward Shils,* ed. J. Ben-David and T. Clark, pp. 244–65. Chicago: University of Chicago Press.

Ben-Yehuda, Nachman. 1980. "The European Witchcraze of the Fifteenth–Seventeenth Centuries: A Sociologist's Perspective." *American Journal of Sociology* 86 (1): 1–31.

————. 1981. "Problems Inherent in Socio-Historical Approaches to the European Witchcraze." *Journal for the Scientific Study of Religion* 20 (4): 326–38.

Berger, A. I. 1977. "Science Fiction Fans in Socio-Economic Perspective: Factors in the Social Consciousness of a Genre." *Science Fiction Studies* 4: 232–46.

Berger, Peter. 1979. *The Heretical Imperative: Contemporary Possibilities of Religious Affirmation.* Garden City, N.Y.: Anchor Press.

Berger, Peter, and Thomas Luchmann. 1966. *The Social Construction of Reality.* Middlesex, England: Penguin Books.

————. 1967. "Sociology of Religion and Sociology of Knowledge." In *Sociology of Religion,* ed. R. Robertson, pp. 61–73. Middlesex: Penguin Books.

Berger, P., et al. 1973. *The Homeless Mind.* Middlesex: Penguin Books.

Bergesen, A. J. 1977. "Political Witch Hunts: The Sacred and the Subversive in Cross National Perspective." *American Sociological Review* 42: 220–33.

Berkowitz, L. 1971. "Reporting an Experiment. A Case Study in Levelling, Sharpening, and Assimilation." *Journal of Experimental Social Psychology* 7: 237–43.

Berlitz, Charles, and William Moore. 1980. *The Roswell Incident.* London: Grenada.

Bernard, J. 1972. "Trade and Finance in the Middle Ages, 900–1500." In *The Middle Ages* Vol. 1 of *The Fontana Economic History of Europe,* ed. C. M. Cipolla, pp. 274–329. New York: Fontana Books.

Billingham, John, ed. 1981. *Life in the Universe.* Cambridge, Massachusetts: MIT Press.

Bird, F., and B. Reimer. 1982. "Participation Rates in New Religious and Para-Religious Movements." *Journal for the Scientific Study of Religion* 21 (1): 1–14.

Blake, J. A. 1979. "Ufology: The Intellectual Development and Social Context of the Study of Unidentified Flying Objects." In *On the Margins of Science: The Social Construction of Rejected Knowledge,* ed. Roy Wallis, pp. 315–37. University of Keele Press.

Bliss, Michael. 1982. *The Discovery of Insulin.* Chicago: University of Chicago Press.

Blum, Alan F. 1970. "The Sociology of Mental Illness." In *Deviance and Respectability,* ed. J. Douglas, pp. 31–60. New York: Basic Books.

Blumberg, Paul. 1962. "Magic in the Modern World." *Sociology and Social Research.* 47: 147–60.

Blumrich, J. F. 1974. *The Spaceships of Ezekiel.* New York: Bantam Books.

Bogucka, Maria. 1980. "The Role of Baltic Trade in European Development from the Sixteenth to the Eighteenth Centuries." *Journal of European Economic History* 9 (1), 5–20.

Bohm, David. 1980. *Wholeness and the Implicate Order.* London: Routledge and Kegan Paul.

Bonn, R. L. 1984. *Criminology.* New York: McGraw Hill.

Borrie, W. D. 1970. "The Population of the Ancient and Medieval World." In *The Growth and Control of World Population,* pp. 40–57. London: Weidenfeld and Nicolson.

Bova, Ben. 1978. "Trust the Force." *Analog* 48 (6): 5–10.

Bowyer, S., et al. 1983. "The Berkeley Parasitic SETI Program." *Icarus.* 53 (1): 147–55.

Bracewell, R. N. 1976. *The Galactic Club: Intelligent Life in Outer Space.* San Francisco: San Francisco Book Company.

Brannigan, Augustine. 1981. *The Social Basis of Scientific Discoveries.* New York: Cambridge University Press.

Bridbury, A. R. 1973. "The Black Death." *Economic History Review,* 2nd ser. 26 (4): 577–92.

———. 1977. "Before the Black Death." *Economic History Review,* 2nd series, *30* (no. 3): 393–410.

Bridenthal, R., and C. Koontz, eds. 1977: *Becoming Visible: Women in European History.* Boston: Houghton Mifflin.

Broad, W. J. 1979. "Paul Feyerabend: Science and the Anarchist." *Science* 206: 534–37.

———. 1980a. "Would Be Academician Pirates Papers." *Science* 208: 1438–40.

———. 1980b. "Imbroglio at Yale (1): Emergence of a Fraud." *Science* 210: 38–41.

———. 1980c. "Imbroglio at Yale (2): A Top Job Lost." *Science* 210: 171–173.

———. 1981. "Fraud and the Structure of Science." *Science* 212: 137–41.

———. 1982. "Harvard Delays in Reporting Fraud." *Science* 215: 478–82.

Broad, W. J., and N. Wade. 1982. *Betrayers of Truth,* N.Y., Simon and Schuster.

Bromberg, Walter. 1959. *The Mind of Man.* New York: Harper and Row.

Bromley, D. G., and A. D. Shupe. 1980. "Financing the New Religions: A Resource Mobilization Approach." *Journal for the Scientific Study of Religion* 19 (3): 227–39.

———. 1981. *Strange Gods.* Boston: Beacon Press.

Brown, Peter. 1969. "Society and the Supernatural: A Medieval Change." *Daedalus* 104: 133–51.

Bruce, Steven, and Roy Wallis. 1983. "Rescuing Motives." *British Journal of Sociology* 34 (1): 61–71.

Brush, S. G. 1974. "Should the History of Science Be Rated X?" *Science* 183: 1164–72.

———. 1980. "The Chimeral Cat: Philosophy of Quantum Mechanics in Historical Perspective." *Social Studies of Science* 10: 393–48.

Bullough, Vern L. 1964. *The History of Prostitution.* New York: University.

Bullough, Vern L., with Bonnie L. Bullough. 1974. *The Subordinate Sex.* New York: Penguin Books.

Capra, Fritjof. 1975. *The Tao of Physics,* New York: Bantam Books.

Carroll, Michael. 1977. "Of Atlantis and Ancient Astronauts: A Structural Study of Two Modern Myths." *Journal of Popular Culture* 11 (3): 541–50.

Carus, Paul. 1974. *The History of the Devil and the Idea of Evil.* La Salle, Ill.: Open Court.

Carus-Wilson, E. M. 1941. "An Industrial Revolution in the Thirteenth Century." *Economic History Review* 11: 39–60.

Cheney, Margaret. 1981. *Tesla: Man out of Time.* New York: Dell Publishing Co.

Chojnacki, Stanley. 1974. "Patrician Women in Renaissance Venice." *Studies in the Renaissance* 21: 176–203.

Christian, J. L., ed. 1976. *Extraterrestrial Intelligence: The First Encounter.* New York: Prometheus Books.

Cipolla, Carlo M. 1974. "The Plague and the Pre-Malthus Malthusians." *Journal of European History* 3 (2): 277–84.

———. 1976. *Before the Industrial Revolution.* London: Methuen.

———. 1978. *Economic History of World Population.* Baltimore: Penguin Books.

Clark, A. J. 1921. "Flying Ointments." In *The Witch Cult in Western Europe,* ed. M. A. Murray. London: Oxford University Press.

Clark, Stuart. 1980. "Inversion, Misrule, and the Meaning of Witchcraft." *Past and Present* 87: 98–127.

Claus, P. J. 1976. "A Structuralist Appreciation of 'Star Trek,'" In *The American Dimension. Cultural Myths and Social Realities,* ed. W. Arens and S. P. Montague, pp. 15–32. California, Alfred Publishing Co.

Clinard, M. B. 1974. *Sociology of Deviant Behaviour.* 3rd edition. New York: Holt, Rinehart and Winston.

Cohen, Albert. 1966. *Deviance and Control.* Englewood Cliffs, N.J.: Prentice-Hall.

Cohen, Stanley. 1972. *Folk Devils and Moral Panics.* London: MacGibbon and Kee.

Cohn, Norman. 1961. *The Pursuit of Millenium.* New York: Harper Torchbooks.

———. 1975. *Europe's Inner Demons: An Inquiry Inspired by the Great Witch Hunt* New York: Basic Books.

Cole, Steven. 1970. "Professional Standing and the Reception of Scientific Discoveries." *American Journal of Sociology.* 76: 286–306.

———. 1983. "The Hierarchy of the Sciences." *American Journal of Sociology* 81: 111–39.

Cole, Steven, J. R. Cole, and G. A. Simon. 1981. "Chance and Consensus in Peer Review." *Science* 214: 881–86.

Coleman, Emily. 1971. "Medieval Marriage Characteristics: A Neglected Factor in the History of Medieval Serfdom." In *The Family in History,* ed. T. K. Rab and R. I. Rothberg, pp. 1–15. New York: Harper and Row.

Colin, Morris. 1972. *The Discovery of the Individual.* London.
Colin, Norman. 1984a. "Stanford Investigates Plagiarism Charge." *Science* 224: 35–36.
———. (1984b): "No Fraud Found in Swiss Study. *Science*" 223: 913.
Colin, Wilson. 1971. *The Occult.* New York: Random House.
Colligan, D. 1981. "Global Cryptozoology." *Omni* 4, no. 2 (Nov.): 112.
Collins, H. M. 1981. "Son of Seven Sexes: The Social Destruction of a Physical Phenomenon." *Social Studies of Science.* 11: 33–62.
Collins, H. M. 1983. The Sociology of Scientific Knowledge: Studies of Contemporary Science. pp. 265–85 in Turner, R. H., and Short, J. F., eds.: *Annual Review of Sociology.* California: Annual Reviews Inc.
Collins, Randall. 1977. "Towards a Modern Science of the Occult." *Consciousness and Culture* 1 (1): 43–58.
Conklin, J. E. 1977. *Illegal but Not Criminal.* Englewood Cliffs, N.J.: Prentice-Hall.
Connor, John. 1975: "The Social and Psychological Reality of European Witchcraft Beliefs." *Psychiatry* 38: 366–80.
Connor, W. D. 1972. "The Manufacture of Deviance: The Case of the Soviet Purge, 1936–1938." *American Sociological Review* 37: 403–13.
Coon, Carleton S. 1969. *The Story of Man*, 3rd ed., New York: Knopf.
Craig, J. R., and S. C. Reese. 1973. "Retention of Raw Data: A Problem Revisited." *American Psychologist* 28: 723.
Crane, Diana. 1972. *Invisible Colleges.* Chicago: University of Chicago Press.
Cressy, D. R. 1962. "Role Theory, Differential Association, and Compulsive Crimes." In *Human Behavior and Social Processes,* ed. A. M. Rose. Boston: Houghton Mifflin.
Crick, F. H. C. 1981. *Life Itself: Its Origin and Nature.* New York: Simon and Schuster.
Crick, F. H. C., and L. E. Orgel. 1973. "Directed Panspermia." *Icarus,* 341; reprinted in Goldsmith 1980, pp. 34–37.
Culliton, B. J. 1974. "The Sloan-Kettering Affair (2): An Uneasy Resolution." *Science* 184: 1154–57.
———. 1983. "Coping with Fraud: The Darsee Case." *Science* 220 31–35.
Cumming, Elaine, and John Cumming. 1957. *Closed Ranks: An Experiment in Mental Health Education.* Cambridge: Harvard University Press.
Currie, E. P. 1968. "Crimes without Victims: Witchcraft and Its Control in Renaissance Europe." *Law and Society Review* 3: 7–32.
Davies, K., and J. Blake. 1956. "Social Structure and Fertility." *Economic Development and Cultural Change.* 4(3): 211–35.
Davies, Paul. 1980. *Other Worlds.* New York: Simon and Schuster.
———. 1981. *The Edge of Infinity.* New York: Simon and Schuster.
———. 1982a. *The Accidental Universe.* Cambridge: Cambridge University Press.
———. 1982b. "Looking Glass Universes." *Science Digest* 90 (2): 37.

Davis, F. J., and R. Stivers, eds. 1975. *The Collective Definition of Deviance.* New York: Free Press.

Davis, M. 1981. Review of *Ice* by Fred Hoyle. *Discover* 2 (11): 92–93.

Davis, Nanette. J. 1975. *Sociological Constructions of Deviance: Perspectives and Issues in the Field.* Dubuque, Iowa: William C. Brown Company.

Debus, Allen. 1970. *Science and Education in the Seventeenth Century.* New York: Elsevier.

Deevey, Edward S. 1960. "The Human Population." *Scientific American* 203(3): 194–206.

De Mause, L. ed. 1974. *The History of Childhood.* New York: Harper and Row.

De Mille, Richard. 1980. *The Don Juan Papers: Further Castaneda Controversies.* Santa Barbara: Ross-Erikson Publishers.

Demos, J. P. 1982. *Entertaining Satan: Witchcraft and the Culture of Early New England.* New York: Oxford University Press.

Dick, S. J. 1982. *Plurality of Worlds.* Cambridge: Cambridge University Press.

Diethelm, Oska. 1970. "The Medical Teachings of Demonology in the Seventeenth and Eighteenth Centuries." *Journal of the History of the Behavioral Sciences* 6: 3–15.

Ditton, J. 1977. "Alibis and Aliases: Some Notes on the 'Motives' of Fiddling Bread Salesmen." *Sociology* 11: 233–55.

Dolby, R. G. A. 1979. "Reflections on Deviant Science." In *On the Margins of Science: The Social Construction of Rejected Knowledge,* ed. R. Wallis, pp. 9–48. University of Keele Press.

Dorfman, D. D. 1978. "The Cyril Burt Question: New Findings." *Science* 201 (no. 4362): 1177–86.

Douglas, Jack. 1967. *The Social Meaning of Suicide.* Princeton: Princeton University Press.

———. 1970. "Deviance and Order in a Pluralistic Society." In *Theoretical Sociology: Perspectives and Developments.* ed. J. C. McKinney and E. A. Tiryakian, pp. 367–401. New York: Appleton-Century-Crofts.

———. 1977. "Shame and Deceit in Creative Deviance." *Deviance and Social Change,* In ed. E. Sagarin, pp. 59–86. Beverly Hills: Sage.

Douglas, Jack, and Frances Waksler. 1982. *The Sociology of Deviance: An Introduction.* Boston: Little Brown and Company.

Douglas, Mary. 1966. *Purity and Danger.* London: Routledge and Kegan Paul.

———. 1967. "Witch Beliefs in Central Africa." *Africa* 38 (1): 72–80.

Downes, David, and Paul Rock. 1982. *Understanding Deviance.* Oxford: Clarendon Press.

Drake, Frank. 1961. "Project Ozma." *Physics Today* 14 (4), 40–46.

Duncan, R., and M. Weston-Smith, eds. 1977. *The Encyclopedia of Ignorance. Everything You Ever Wanted to Know About the Unknown* New York: Pergamon Press.

Dunn, L. 1965. "Mendel, His Work and His Place in History." *Proceedings of the American Philosophical Society* 109: 189–98.

Durkheim, Emile. [1933] 1964. *The Division of Labor in Society*. New York: Free Press.

———. 1938. *The Rules of Sociological Method*. New York: Free Press.

———. 1973. *On Morality and Society*. Chicago: University of Chicago Press.

Dyson, Freeman J. 1960. "Search for Artificial Stellar Sources of Infrared Radiation." *Science* 131: 1667.

———. 1979. *Disturbing the Universe*. New York: Harper and Row.

Earle, Peter. 1969. "The Commercial Development of Ancona." *Economic History Review* 22 (1): 28–44.

Ebel, Henry. 1978. "The New Theology: Star Trek, Star Wars, Close Encounters, and the Crisis in Pseudo-rationality." *Journal of Psychohistory* 5 (4): 487–98.

Eckenstein, Lina (1896): *Women under Monasticism: Saint Lore and Convent Life between A.D. 500 and A.D. 1500*. Cambridge: Cambridge University Press.

Edelhertz, Herbert. 1970. *The Nature, Impact, and Prosecution of White Collar Crime*. U.S. Department of Justice, Law Enforcement Assistance Administration.

Edelson, E. 1979. *Who Goes There? The Search for Intelligent Life in the Universe*. New York: Doubleday and Company.

Edge, P. O., and M. J. Mulkay. 1976. *Astronomy Transformed: The Emergence of Radio Astronomy in Britain*. New York: John Wiley and Sons.

Ehrenreich, Barbara, and Deirdre English. 1972. *Witches, Midwives, and Curses: A History of Women Healers*. New York: Feminist Press.

Eisen, B. 1980. "Continental Drift: Intuition, Facts, or Temporary Truth?" *Machshavot* 49: 3–11 (Hebrew).

Eisenstadt, S. N. 1968. "The Development of Sociological Thought." In *International Encyclopedia of the Social Sciences,* ed. D. L. Sills, 15: 23–36. Macmillan Company and Free Press.

———. 1971. "Innovation and Tension between Different Types of Rationality." Paper presented before the International Seminar on the Social and Political Implications of Scientific and Technological Innovation in the Field of Information, the Adriane Olivetti Foundation, Courmayeur, 7–12 Sept.

Eisenstadt, S. N., with M. Curelaru. 1976. *The Forms of Sociology: Paradigms and Crises*. New York: John Wiley and Sons.

Eister, Allan W. 1978. "Religion and Science in A.D. 1977: Conflict? Accommodation? Mutual Indifference? or What?" *Journal for the Scientific Study of Religion* 17 (4): 347–58.

Eliade, Mircea. 1976. "The Occult and the Modern World." In *Occultism, Witchcraft, and Cultural Fashions,* pp. 47–68. Chicago: University of Chicago Press.

Ellwood, Robert S. 1973. *Religious and Spiritual Groups in Modern America*. Englewood Cliffs, N.J.: Prentice-Hall.

———. 1979. *Alternative Altars*. Chicago: The University of Chicago Press.

Elton, G. R. 1963. *Renaissance and Reformation, 1300–1648.* New York: Macmillan.

Erikson, Kai T. [1964] 1973. "Notes on the Sociology of Deviance." pp. 26-39 In *Deviance: The Interactionist Perspective,* ed. E. Rubington and M. S. Weinberg, pp. 26–39. New York: Macmillan Company.

———. 1966. *Wayward Puritans:* New York: John Wiley and Sons.

Etzioni, Amitai. 1978. "Seeking Solace from the Stars." *Current* 203: 47–48.

Evans, C. 1973. *Cults of Unreason.* New York: Dell Publishing.

Evans-Pritchard, E. E. 1937. *Witchcraft, Oracles, and Magic among the Azande.* London: Oxford University Press.

Eysenck, H., and D. K. B. Nias. 1982. *Astrology: Science or Superstition.* London: Maurice Temple Smith.

Farrell, R.A., and V. L. Swigert. 1982: *Deviance and Social Control.* Glenview, Ill.: Scott Foresman and Co.

Fawcett, Lawrence, and Barry L. Greenwood. 1984. *Clear Intent.* Englewood Cliffs, New Jersey: Prentice Hall.

Feinberg, Gerald. 1978. *What is the World Made Of?* Garden City, New York: Anchor Press, Doubleday.

Ferris, Timothy. 1977. *The Red Limit.* Bantam Books.

Feyerabend, Paul. 1975. *Against Method.* London: Verso.

Finer, S. E. 1954. "A Profile of Science Fiction." *The Sociological Review* 2: 239–55.

Fletcher, H. 1982. My Work with Millikan on the Oil-Drop Experiment. *Physics Today* 35: 43–47.

Forbes, T. R. 1966. *The Midwife and the Witch.* New Haven: Yale University Press.

Foucault, Michel. 1967. *Madness and Civilization.* London: Tavistock Publications.

Frankel, E. 1976. "Corpuscular Optics and the Wave Theory of Light: The Science and Politics of a Revolution in Physics." *Social Studies of Science* 6: 141–84.

Frazer, George J. 1963. *The Golden Bough,* abridged edition. New York: Macmillan Company.

Frazier, Charles E. 1976. *Theoretical Approaches to Deviance.* Columbus, Ohio: Charles E. Merrill Publishing co.

Frazier, Kendrick. 1978. "The Paranormal Reexamined." *Current* 203: 39–46.

———. ed. 1981. *Paranormal Borderlands of Science.* New York: Prometheus Books.

Frenkel, Henry. 1979. "The Reception and Acceptance of Continental Drift Theory as a Rational Episode in the History of Science." In *The Reception of Unconventional Science,* ed. Seymour H. Mauskopf, pp. 51–89. AAAS Selected Symposium 25, published by Westview Press.

Friedman, S. 1973. "Ufology and the Search for ET Intelligent Life." In *Proceedings of the 1973 Symposium of the Mutual UFO Network,* pp. 40–61. MUFON.

Galbreath, Robert. 1971a. "The Occult Today." *Journal of Popular Culture* 5: 629–36.

———. 1971b. "The History of Modern Occultism: A Bibliographical Survey." *Journal of Popular Culture* 5: 726–54.

Gardner, Martin. 1957. *Fads and Fallacies in the Name of Science,* New York: Dover.

———. 1981. *Science: Good, Bad, and Bogus.* New York: Prometheus Books.

———. 1982. "Eysenck's Folly." *Discover* 3, no. 10 (Oct.): 12.

Garfinkel, Harold. 1950. "Conditions of Successful Degradation Ceremonies." *American Journal of Sociology* 61: 420–24.

———. 1967. *Studies in Ethnomethodology,* Englewood Cliffs, N.J.: Prentice-Hall.

Garraty, J. A. 1978. *Unemployment in History,* New York: Harper and Row.

Garrett, Clarke. 1977. "Women and Witches: Patterns of Analysis." *Signs: Journal of Women in Culture and Society* 3 (2): 461–79.

Garvin, Richard. 1974. *The Crystal Skull,* New York: Pocket Books.

Geertz, Clifford. 1964. "Ideology as a Cultural System." In *Ideology and Discontent,* ed. David Apter, pp. 47–76. New York: Free Press.

Geis, Gilbert. 1978. "Lord Hale, Witches, and Rape." *British Journal of Law and Society,* 5(1), 26–44.

Geis, G. and R. Meier, eds. 1977. *White Collar Crime. Offenses in Business, Politics, and the Professions.* New York: Free Press.

Gieryn, T. F. 1983. "Boundary-work and the Demarcation of Science from Non-science: Strains and Interests in Professional Ideologies of Scientists." *American Sociological Review* 48 (6): 781–95.

Gies, Frances, and Joseph Gies. 1978. *Women in the Middle Ages.* New York: Thomas Y. Crowell Company.

Gilbert, Nigel G., and Peter Abell, eds. 1983. *Accounts and Action.* Hampshire, England: Gower.

Gliedman, J. 1982. "Scientists in Search of the Soul." *Science Digest* 90 (7): 77–79, 105.

Glock, C. Y., and R. N. Bellah, eds. 1976. *The New Religious Consciousness.* Berkeley: University of California Press.

Gmelch, G. 1978. "Baseball Magic." *Human Nature* 1: 32–39.

Goldsmith, Donald, ed. 1980. *The Quest for Extraterrestrial Life.* California: University Science Books.

Good, Irving John. 1962. *The Scientist Speculates.* New York: Basic Books.

Goode, Erich. 1978. *Deviant Behaviour: The Interactionist Approach.* Englewood Cliffs, N.J.: Prentice-Hall.

Goodsell, M. 1915. *History of the Family as a Social and Educational Institution.* New York: Macmillan Company.

Goran, Morris. 1979. *Fact, Fraud, and Fantasy.* New York: Barnes and Company.

Gordon, M. D. 1982. "How Socially Distinctive Is Cognitive Deviance in an

Emergent Science? The Case of Parapsychology." *Social Studies of Science* 12: 151–65.

Gottfried, Robert. 1978. *Epidemic Disease in Fifteenth-Century England: The Medical Response and the Demographic Consequences*. Leicester: Leicester University Press.

Gould, Stephen J. 1977. *Ever Since Darwin*. New York: W. W. Norton.

———. 1981. *The Mismeasure of Man*. New York: W. W. Norton.

Gouldner, Alvin. 1968. The Sociologist as Partisan: Sociology and the Welfare State. *The American Sociologist*, 3: 103–16.

Graus, F. 1967. "Social Utopias in the Middle Ages." *Past and Present*, no. 38, pp. 3–19.

Greco, Michael. 1978. "A Close Encounter with the Millennium." *Journal of Psychohistory* 5 (4): 499–508.

Greeley, Andrew M. 1970a. "Implication for the Sociology of Religion of Occult Behaviour in the Youth Culture." *Youth and Society* 2: 131–40.

———. 1970b. "Superstition, Ecstasy, and Tribal Consciousness." *Social Research* 37: 203–11.

———. 1981. "Religious Musical Chairs." In *In Gods We Trust,* ed. T. Robbins and D. Anthony, (eds.) pp. 127–40. London: Transaction Books.

Greenwell, J. R. (1979): "University of Colorado UFO Project." In *The Encyclopedia of UFOs,* ed. R. Story, pp. 77–79. Garden City, N.Y.: Doubleday.

———. 1979b. "Theories of Extraterrestrial Origin of Man." Pp. 118–20 in R. Story, ed.: *The Encyclopedia of UFO's*. New York: Doubleday.

———. 1979c. "A Review of UFO Witnesses' Reliability." *Zetetic Scholar* 5: 54–64.

Gribbin, J. R. and S. H. Plagemann. 1974. *The Jupiter Effect*. New York: Random House.

Griggs, D. B. 1980. *Population Growth and Agrarian Change*. New York: Cambridge University Press.

Grim, Patrick, ed. 1982. *Philosophy of Science and the Occult*. New York: SUNY Press.

Guerin, Pierre. 1979. Thirty Years after Kenneth Arnold: The Situation regarding UFOs. *Zetetic Scholar* 5: 35–49.

Gusfield, J. R. 1963. *Symbolic Crusade: Status Politics and the American Temperance Movement*. Chicago: University of Illinois Press.

———. 1981. *The Culture of Public Problems:, Drinking Driving and the Symbolic Order*. Chicago: The University of Chicago Press.

Gutting, G., ed. 1980. *Paradigms and Revolutions: Applications and Appraisals of Thomas Kuhn's Philosophy of Science*. Notre Dame: University of Notre Dame Press.

Hajnal, J. 1965. "European Marriage Patterns in Perspective." In *Populations in History*, ed. D. V. Glass and D. E. C. Eversley, pp. 101–43. London, Edward Arnold.

Hanen, M. P., M. J. Osler, and R. G. Weyant, eds. 1980. *Science, Pseudo-Science, and Society.* Canada: Wilfrid Laurier University Press.

Hansen, B. 1975. "Science and Magic." In *Science in the Middle Ages,* ed. D. C. Lindberg, pp. 483–500. Chicago: University of Chicago Press.

Hansen, Chadwick. 1969. *Witchcraft at Salem.* New York: Mentor Books.

Harner, M. J. 1972. "The Role of Hallucinogenic Plants in European Witchcraft." In *Hallucinogens and Shamanism,* pp. 127–50. New York: Oxford University Press.

Harper, Clive. 1977. "The Witches' Flying Ointment." *Folklore* 88: 105–106.

Harris, A. R. 1977. "Sex and Theories of Deviance: Toward a Functional Theory of Deviant Type Scripts." *American Sociological Review* 42: 3–16.

Harris, Marvin. 1974. *Cows, Pigs, Wars, and Witches: The Riddle of Culture.* New York: Vintage Books.

Harrison, E. R. 1980. "The Paradox of the Dark Night Sky." *Mercury* 9 (4): 83–101.

Harrison, Michael. 1973. *The Roots of Witchcraft.* London: Tandem Books.

Hart, M. H., and L. Zuckerman, eds. 1982. *Extraterrestrials: Where Are They?* New York: Pergamon Press.

Hartman, Patricia. 1976. "Social Dimension of Occult Participation: The Gnostica Study." *British Journal of Sociology,* 27 (2): 164–83.

Harvey, Bill. 1981. "Plausibility and the Evaluation of Knowledge: A Case Study of Experimental Quantum Mechanics." *Social Studies of Science* 11: 95–130.

Harvey, L. 1982. "The Use and Abuse of Kuhnian Paradigms in the Sociology of Knowledge." *Sociology* 16 (1): 85–101.

Hays, H. R. 1964. *The Dangerous Sex: The Myth of the Feminine Evil.* New York: Putnam's Sons.

Hearnshaw, L. S. 1979. *Cyril Burt: Psychologist.* New York: Vintage Books.

Heenan, Edward F. 1973. *Mystery, Magic, and Miracle: Religion in a Post Aquarian Age.* New York: Spectrum Books.

Heinsohn, Gunnar, and Otto Steiger. 1982. "The Elimination of Medieval Birth Control and the Witch Trials of Modern Times." *International Journal of Women's Studies* 5 (3): 193–214.

Heirich, Max. 1976. "Cultural Breakthroughs." *American Behavioral Scientist* 19 (6): 685–702.

Helleiner, K. F. 1957. "The Vital Revolution Reconsidered." *Canadian Journal of Economic and Political Science* 23 (1): 1–9.

———. 1967. "The Population of Europe from the Black Death to the Eve of the Vital Revolution." In *The Cambridge Economic History of Europe.* Vol. 4: *The Economy of Expanding Europe in the Sixteenth and Seventeenth Centuries,* ed. E. E. Rich and C. H. Wilson, pp. 1–96. Cambridge: Cambridge University Press.

Helmholtz, R. H. 1975. "Infanticide in the Province of Canterbury during the Fifteenth Century." *History of Childhood Quarterly* 2(3): 379–90.

Hendry, Allan. 1979. *The UFO Handbook. A Guide to Investigating, Evaluating, and Reporting UFO Sightings.* Garden City, N.Y.: Doubleday.

Henningsen, Gustav. 1980a. *The Witches' Advocate.* Reno: University of Nevada Press.

———. 1980b. "The Greatest Witch Trial of All: Navarre, 1609–1614." *History Today* 30: 36–39.

Henriques, F. 1963. *The Immoral Tradition.* London: Panther.

Henslin, James A. 1967. "Crops and Magic." *American Journal of Sociology* 73 (3): 316–30.

Herlihy, David. 1971. *Women in Medieval Society,* Smith History Lecture. Houston, Texas: University of Saint Thomas.

Hey, J. S. 1973. *The Evolution of Radio Astronomy.* New York: Science History Publications.

Hicks, John. 1969. *A Theory of Economic History.* New York: Oxford University Press.

Higgins, A. C. 1983. "The Games of Science: Science Watching." In *The Dark Side of Science,* ed. B. K. Kilbourne and M. T. Kilbourne, vol. 1, part 2, pp. 9–25. San Francisco: Pacific Division, AAAS.

Hills, S. L. 1980. *Demystifying Social Deviance.* New York: McGraw Hill Book Company.

Himes, Norman E. 1936. *A Medical History of Contraception.* New York: Schocken.

Hinnebusch, W. A. 1966. *The History of the Dominican Order.* New York: Alba.

Holmes, George. 1975. *Europe, Hierarchy, and Revolt, 1320–1450,* New York: Fontana.

Holton, G., and R.S. Morison, eds. 1979. *Limits of Scientific Inquiry.* New York: W. W. Norton.

Hood, Roger, and Richard Sparks. 1970. *Key Issues in Criminology.* New York: McGraw Hill Book Company.

Hooper, Dick. 1978. "Castaneda: Trickster-Teacher. A Conversation with Richard De Mille." *Zetetic Scholar* 1 (1): 27–30.

Horowitz, I. L., ed. 1974. *The Rise and Fall of Project Camelot.* London: MIT Press.

Horowitz, I. L., and M. Leibovitz. 1968. "Social Deviance and Political Marginality: Towards a Redefinition of the Relation between Sociology and Politics." *Social Problems* 15 (3): 280–97.

Hoyle, Fred. 1957. *The Black Cloud.* New York: Harper and Row.

———. 1981. *Ice.* New York: Continuum.

Hoyle, F., and N. C. Wickramasinghe. 1978. *Lifecloud.* London: J. M. Dent and Sons.

———. 1981. *Diseases from Space.* London: Sphere Books.

Hsu, F. L. 1960. "A Neglected Aspect of Witchcraft Studies." *Journal of American Folklore* 73: 35–38.

Hughes, Pennethorne. 1952. *Witchcraft.* Baltimore: Penguin Books.

Huyghe, P. 1983. "The Glowing Birds and 2,000 Other Mysteries That Stump Science." *Science Digest* 70–75: 109.

Hyman, Ray. 1980. "Pathological Science: Towards a Proper Diagnosis and Remedy." *Zetetic Scholar* 6: 31–39.

Hynek, J. A. 1972. *The UFO Experience.* New York: Ballantine Books.

———. 1977. *The Hynek UFO Report.* New York: Dell Books.

Ichheiser, Gustav. 1970. *Appearances and Realities.* San Francisco: Jossey-Bass.

Inverarity, J. 1980. "Theories of the Political Creation of Deviance: Legacies of Conflict Theory, Marx, and Durkheim." In *A Political Analysis of Deviance,* ed. P. Lauderdale, pp. 175–217. Minneapolis: University of Minnesota Press.

Irsigler, Frantz. 1977. "Industrial Production, International Trade, and Public Finances in Cologne." *Journal of European Economic History* 6 (2): 269–306.

Jacobs, D. M. 1975. *UFO Controversy in America.* New York: New American Library.

———. 1980. "The Debunkers." In *Proceedings of the First International UFO Congress,* ed. C. G. Fuller, pp. 123–138. New York: Warner Books.

Jarrett, Bede. 1926. *Social Theories of the Middle Ages, 1200–1500,* New York: Frederick Ungar Publishing Co. (reprinted 1966).

Jerome, L. E. 1977. *Astrology Disproved.* Buffalo, N.Y.: Prometheus Books.

Jones, T. A. 1981. "Durkheim, Deviance, and Development: Opportunities Lost and Regained." *Social Forces* 59 (4): 1009–24.

Jorgensen, D. L., and L. Jorgensen. 1982. "Social Meaning of the Occult." *Sociological Quarterly* 23: 373–89.

Judson, H. F. 1979. *The Eighth Day of Creation.* New York: Simon and Schuster.

Jung, C. G. 1960. *Synchronicity.* Princeton: Bellengen Press.

Kane, V. 1982. "Scientists Dispute Theory on Cretaceous Collision." *Astronomy* 10 (4): 78–79.

Kavolis, V. 1970. "Post Modern Man." *Social Problems* 17 (4): 435–48.

Kearney, H. F. 1971. *Science and Change, 1500–1700.* London: Weidenfeld and Nicholson.

Keller, E. F. 1983. *A Feeling for the Organism.* New York: W. H. Freeman and Company.

Kelso, Ruth. 1956. *Doctrine for the Lady in the Renaissance.* Urbana: University of Illinois Press.

Kendig, Frank. 1981. "Interview with Morris Kline." *Omni* 3 (9): 93–126.

Keniston, Kenneth. 1969. *The Uncommitted: Alienated Youth in American Society.* New York: Delta Books.

Kieckhefer, Richard. 1976. *European Witch Trials.* Berkeley: University of California Press.

Kilbourne, B. M., and M. T. Kilbourne, eds. 1983. *The Dark Side of Science.* San Francisco: AAAS/Pacific Division, California Academy of Science.

Kirsch, I. 1978. "Demonology and the Rise of Science: An Example of the Misperception of Historical Data." *Journal of the History of the Behavioral Sciences* 14: 149–57.

Klapp, O. E. 1969. *Collective Search for Identity.* New York: Holt, Rinehart and Winston.

Kline, Morris. 1980. *Mathematics: The Loss of Certainty*. New York: Oxford University Press.

Kluckhohn, Clyde. 1967. *Navaho Witchcraft*. Reprint of the 1944 ed. Boston: Beacon Press.

Knight, Damon. ed. 1975. *Science Fiction of the Thirties*. New York: Avon Books.

Koestler, Arthur. 1972a. *The Case of the Midwife Toad*. New York: Random House.

———. 1972b. *The Roots of Coincidence*. London: Hutchinson and Company.

Kolata, G. B. 1981. Reevaluation of Cancer Data Eagerly Awaited. *Science*, 214: 316–18.

Kors, A. C., and E. Peters, eds. 1972. *Witchcraft in Europe, 1100–1700*. Philadelphia: University of Pennsylvania Press.

Kraus, John. 1966. *Radio Astronomy*. New York: McGraw Hill.

———. 1981. "The First Fifty Years of Radio Astronomy. Part 1: Karl Jansky and His Discovery of Radio Waves from Our Galaxy." *Cosmic Search* 3 (4): 8–13.

———. 1982. "The First Fifty Years of Radio Astronomy. Part 2: Grote Reber and the First Radio Maps of the Sky." *Cosmic Search* 4 (1): 14–18.

Krupp, E. C. ed., 1977. *In Search of Ancient Astronomies*. New York: Doubleday.

Kuhn, T. S. 1962. *The Structure of Scientific Revolutions*. Chicago: University of Chicago Press.

———. 1972. *The Essential Tension*. Chicago: University of Chicago Press.

La Croix, P. 1926. *History of Prostitution*. 2 vols.. Chicago; Pascal Covici.

Lamb, H. H. 1982. *Climate History and the Modern World*. London: Methuen.

Landsman, G. 1972. "Science Fiction: The Rebirth of Mythology." *Journal of Popular Culture* 5 (4): 989–96.

Lane, F. C. 1932. "The Rope Factory and Hemp Trade in the Fifteenth and Sixteenth Centuries." *Journal of Economic and Business History* 4: 824–40.

———. 1933. "Venetian Shipping during the Commercial Revolution." *American Historical Review* 38(2): 219–37.

Langer, William. 1964. "The Black Death." *Scientific American* 210 (2): 114–21.

———. 1974a. "Further Notes on the History of Infanticide." *History of Childhood Quarterly* 2 (1): 129–34.

———. 1974b. "Infanticide: A History Survey." *History of Childhood Quarterly* 1 (3): 353–65.

Langmuir, I. 1953. *"Pathological Science."* Paper given at the colloquium at the Knolls Research Laboratory, Dec. 18. Printed in General Electric Research and Development Center Report, ed. R. Holl (1968).

Lankford, J. 1981. "Amateurs and Astrophysics: A Neglected Aspect in the Development of a Scientific Specialty." *Social Studies of Science* 11: 275–303.

Larner, Christina. 1981. *Enemies of God. The Witch Hunt in Scotland*. Baltimore: Johns Hopkins University Press.

Larsen, Egan. 1971. *Strange Sects and Cults: A Study of Their Origins and Influence.* New York: White Publishers.

Lasch, Christopher. 1979. *The Culture of Narcissism.* New York: Warner Books.

Latour, Bruno, and Steve Woolgar. 1979. *Laboratory Life: The Social Construction of Scientific Fact.* Beverly Hills: Sage Publications.

Laudan, Larry. 1983. The Demise of the Demarcation Problem. In *The Demarcation between Science and Pseudo Science,* ed. R. Laudan, pp. 7–36 Blacksburg, Va.: The Center for the Study of Science in Society, Virginia Polytechnic Institute and State University.

Lauderdale, Pat. 1976. "Deviance and Moral Boundaries." *American Sociological Review* 41: 660–64.

Lea, Henry C. 1901. *The History of the Inquisition of the Middle Ages.* 4 vols. Franklin Square, N.Y.: Harper.

———. 1957. *Materials towards a History of Witchcraft.* Edited by Arthur C. Howland. New York: Lincoln Burr.

Le Goff, Jacques. 1972. "The Town as an Agent of Civilization, 1200–1500." *The Fontana Economic History of Europe.* Vol. 1: *The Middle Ages,* ed. C. M. Cipolla, pp. 71–107. New York: Fontana.

———. 1980. *Time, Work, and Culture in the Middle Ages.* Chicago: University of Chicago Press.

Leff, Gordon. 1967. *Heresy in the Later Middle Ages.* Manchester: Manchester University Press.

Lemay, Rodnite H. 1978. "Some Thirteenth and Fourteenth Century Lectures on Female Sexuality." *International Journal of Women's Studies* 1 (4): 391–400.

Lerner, Robert E. 1970. "Medieval Prophecy and Religious Dissent." *Past and Present,* no. 72, pp. 3–24.

Leroy Ladurie, Emmanuel. 1971. *Times of Feast, Times of Famine: A History of Climate since the Year 1000.* London: Allen and Unwin.

Levy-Bruhl, Lucien. 1923. *Primitive Mentality.* Boston: Beacon Press.

Lévi-Strauss, Claude. 1963. *Structural Anthropology.* New York: Basic Books.

Lewin, R. 1983. "A Naturalist of the Genome." *Science* 222: 402–5.

Lewis, I. M. 1971. *Ecstatic Religion: An Anthropological Study of Spirit Possession.* Middlesex: Penguin Books.

Liazos, Alexander. 1972. "The Poverty of the Sociology of Deviance: Nuts, Sluts and Perverts." *Social Problems* 20: 103–20.

Lidz, C. W., and A. L. Walker. 1980. *Heroin, Deviance, and Morality.* London: Sage Publications.

Litchfield, E. Burr. 1966. "Demographic Characteristics of Florentine Patrician Families, Sixteenth to Nineteenth Centuries." *Journal of Economic History* 29: 191–205.

Lofland, John. 1969. *Deviance and Identity.* Englewood Cliffs, N.J.: Prentice-Hall.

Loos, Milan. 1974. *Dualist Heresy in the Middle Ages.* The Hague: Nijhoff.

Lopez, R. S. 1976. *The Commercial Revolution of the Middle Ages, 950–1350.* Cambridge: Cambridge University Press.

Lyman, S. M., and M. B. Scott. 1970. *A Sociology of the Absurd.* New York: Appleton-Century Crofts.

Lynch, F. R. 1979. "'Occult Establishment' or 'Deviant Religion'? The Rise and Fall of a Modern Church of Magic." *Journal of the Scientific Study of Religion* 18 (13): 281–98.

MacAndrew, Craig. 1969. "On the Notion that Certain Persons Who are Given to Frequent Drunkenness Suffer from a Disease Called Alcoholism." In *Changing Perspectives in Mental Illness,* ed. S. C. Plog and R. B. Edgerton, pp. 483–501. New York: Holt, Rinehart and Winston.

MacDougall, C. D. 1940. *Hoaxes.* New York: Dover.

MacFarlane, Alan. 1970. *Witchcraft in Tudor and Stuart England.* London: Routledge and Kegan Paul.

MacIntyre, Alasdair. 1981. *After Virtue.* Notre Dame: University of Notre Dame Press.

Mackal, Roy R. 1980. *Searching for Hidden Animals: An Inquiry into Zoological Mysteries.* Garden City, N.Y.: Doubleday.

MacKay, Charles. [1841] 1932. *Memories of Extraordinary Popular Delusions.* New York: Fordham University Press.

Madaule, Jacques. 1967. *The Albigensian Crusade: A Historical Essay.* New York: Fordham University Press.

Maher, B. W. and B. Maher. 1982. "The Ships of Fools." *American Psychologist* 37 (no. 7): 756–61.

Malawist, Marion. 1974. "Problems of Growth of the National Economy of Central-Eastern Europe in the Late Middle Ages." *Journal of European Economic History* 3 (2): 319–57.

Malinowsky, Bronislaw. 1955. *Magic, Science, and Religion and Other Essays.* Garden City, N.Y.: Anchor Doubleday.

Mandonnet, P. 1944. *St. Dominic and His Work.* St. Louis: Herder.

Martin, Michael. 1982. "Defining UFO." *Zetetic Scholar* 9: 84–89.

Marty, Martin. 1970. "The Occult Establishment." *Social Research* 37: 212–30.

———. 1981. "The Many Faces of Religion in America." *Horizons* 38: 25–29.

Masson, J. M. 1984. *The Assault on Truth.* New York: Farrar, Straus and Giroux.

Masters, Robert E. L. 1962. *Eros and Evil: The Sexual Psychopathology of Witchcraft.* New York: AMA Press.

Matalene, Carolyn. 1978. "Women as Witches." *International Journal of Women's Studies* 1: 573–87.

Matza, David. 1964. *Delinquency and Drift.* New York: John Wiley and Sons.

———. 1969. *Becoming Deviant.* Englewood Cliffs, N.J.: Prentice-Hall.

Mauskopf, Seymour H., ed. 1979. *The Reception of Unconventional Science.* AAAS Selected Symposium 25, published by Westview Press.

Mauskopf, S. H., and M. R. McVaugh. 1979. "The Controversy over Statistics in Parapsychology, 1934–1938". Pp. 105–23 in Mauskopf, S. H., ed.: *The Reception of Unconventional Science,* AAAS Selected Symposium 25, published by Westview Press.

Mcaulay, Robert. 1978. "Velikovsky and the Infrastructure of Science: The Metaphysics of a Close Encounter." *Theory and Society* 6 (3): 313–42.

McCaghy, C. H. 1976. *Deviant Behavior.* New York: Macmillan Publishing Company.

McDonnell, E. W. 1954. *The Beguines and Beghards in Medieval Culture,* New Brunswick, N.J.: Rutgers University Press.

McKean, Kevin. 1981. "A Scandal in the Laboratory." *Discover* 2 (11): 18–23.

McNeill, W, William H. 1976. *Plagues and People,* Garden City, N.Y.: Doubleday, Anchor Books.

Mead, G. H. 1918. "The Psychology of Punitive Justice." *American Journal of Sociology* 23: 586–92.

Merton, Robert K. 1938. "Social Structure and Anomie." *American Sociological Review* 3 (October): 672–82.

Merton, R. K. (1968): "Science and Democratic Social Structure," pp. 604-615 in *Social Theory and Social Structure* N.Y., Free Press.

———. 1973. *The Sociology of Science: Theoretical and Empirical Investigations.* Chicago: University of Chicago Press.

———. 1984. "The Fallacy of the Latest Word: The Case of *Pietism and Science.*" *American Journal of Sociology* 89 (5): 1091–121.

Metz, William D. 1977. "Astrophysics: Discovery and the Ubiquity of Black Holes." *Science* 195: 276–77.

Michelet, Jules. 1965. *Satanism and Witchcraft.* London: Tandem Books.

Midelfort, Erik H. C. 1972. *Witch Hunting in Southwestern Germany, 1562–1684.* Stanford, California: Stanford University Press.

Midelfort, Erik H. C. 1981. "Heartland of the Witchcraze: Central and Northern Europe." *History Today,* February, 27–31.

Mills, C. Wright. 1940. "Situated Actions and Vocabularies of Motives." *American Sociological Review* 5: 904–13.

———. 1943. "The Professional Ideology of Social Pathologists." *American Journal of Sociology* 49: 165–80.

Molenda, Danuta. 1976. "Investments in Ore Mining in Poland from the Thirteenth to the Seventeenth Centuries." *Journal of European Economic History* 5(1): 151–69.

Monter, W. E. 1969. *European Witchcraft.* New York: Wiley.

———. 1976. *Witchcraft in France and Switzerland.* Ithaca: Cornell University Press.

———. 1980. "French and Italian Witchcraft." *History Today* 30: 31–35.

Moody, E. J. 1974. "Magical Therapy: An Anthropological Investigation of Contemporary Satanism." In *Religious Movements in Contemporary America,* ed. I. I. Zaretsky and M. P. Leone, pp. 355–82. Princeton: Princeton University Press.

Moorcock, Michael. 1962. *Elric of Melnibone.* New York: Daw Books.

Moore, Sally F., and B. G. Myerhoff, eds. 1977. *Secular Ritual.* Assen/Amsterdam: Van Garcum.

Morewedge, Rosemarie Thee, ed. 1975. *The Role of Women in the Middle Ages.* Albany: State University of New York Press.

Morrison, P., J. Billingham and J. Wolfe, eds. 1979. *The Search for Extraterrestrial Intelligence.* New York: Dover.

Mulkay, M. J. 1972a. "Conformity and Innovation in Science." In *The Sociology of Science,* ed. P. Halmos, pp. 5–23. University of Keele Press.

Mulkay, M. J. 1972b. *The Social Process of Innovation. A Study in the Sociology of Science.* London: Macmillan Co.

Mulkay, M. J., and G. N. Gilbert. 1982. "Accounting for Error: How Scientists Construct Their Social World When They Account for Correct and Incorrect Belief." *Sociology* 16 (2): 166–83.

Murray, B., S. Gulkis, and E. Edelson. 1978. "Extraterrestrial Intelligence: An Observational Approach." *Science* 199: 485–92.

Murray, Henry A. 1962. "The Personality and Career of Satan." *Journal of Social Issues* 18 (4): 36–54.

Murray, M. A. 1918. "Child Sacrificing among European Witches." *Man* 18: 60–62.

———. 1921. *The Witch Cult in Western Europe.* London: Clarendon Press.

Nate, Davis. 1978. "High Prices in Early Fourteenth Century England: Causes and Consequences." *Economic History Review,* 2d series 28 (1):

National Astronomy and Ionosphere Center. 1975. "The Arecibo Message of November 1974." *Icarus* 26(4): 462–66.

Neaman, J. 1975. *Suggestion of the Devil: The Origins of Madness.* New York, Doubleday, Anchor Books.

Nelson, Mary. 1971. "The Persecution of Witchcraft in Renaissance Europe: An Historical and Sociological Discussion." Photocopy.

———. 1975. "Why Witches Were Women." In *Women: A Feminist Perspective,* ed. J. Freeman, pp. 335–50 Palo Alto, Cal.: Mayfield Publishing Company.

Nettler, Gwynn. 1972. *Explaining Crime.* New York: McGraw Hill Book Company.

Nicholas, David. 1976. "Economic Reorientation and Social Change in Fourteenth Century Flanders." *Past and Present,* no. 70, pp. 3–29.

Nicholls, Peter, ed. 1979. *The Science Fiction Encyclopedia.* Garden City, N.Y.: Doubleday.

———. 1983. *The Science in Science Fiction.* New York: Alfred A. Knopf.

Niven, Larry. 1968. *Neutron Star,* New York: Ballantine Books.

———. 1970. *Ringworld.* New York: Ballantine Books.

———. 1975. *Tales of Known Space,* New York: Ballantine Books.

Noonan, J. T. 1965. *Contraception: A History of Its Treatment by the Catholic Theologians and Canonists.* Cambridge: Harvard University Press, Belknap.

———. 1968. "Intellectual and Demographic History." *Daedalus* 97: 463–85.

Norman, H. J. 1933. "Witch Ointments." Appendix to *The Werewolf,* ed. M. Summers. London: Kegan Paul and Trench and Trubner.

Nowotny, Helga, and Hillary Rose, eds. 1979. *Counter-Movements in the Sciences.* Boston: D. Reidel Publishing Company.

Nye, Mary Jo. 1980. "N-rays: An Episode in the History and Psychology of Science." *Historical Studies in the Physical Sciences* 11: 125–26.

Oberg, James. 1980. "Alone Again." *Omni* 2 (5): 32, 122.

———. 1982. *UFOs and Outer Space Mysteries.* New York: Donning.

O'Dea, Thomas. 1966. *The Sociology of Religion.* Englewood Cliffs, N.J.: Prentice-Hall.

O'Faolain, Julia, and Lauro Martines. 1973. *Not in God's Image.* New York: Harper and Row Torchbooks.

O'Keefe, D. L. 1982. *Stolen Lightning: The Social Theory of Magic.* New York: Continuum.

Oliver, B. M., and J. Billingham. 1971. *Project Cyclops Report.* NASA, CR 114445.

Orne, M. T. 1969. "Demand Characteristics and the Concept of Quasi-Controls." In *Artifacts in Behavioral Research,* ed. R. Rosenthal and R. L. Rosnow, pp. 143–79. N.Y., Academic Press.

Palmer, Jeremy N. Y. 1979. "The Damp Stones of Positivism: Eric von Däniken and Paranormality." *Philosophy of Social Sciences* 9: 129–47.

Panshin, Alexei, and Cory Panshin. 1981. "Science Fiction and the Dimension of Myth." *Extrapolation* 22 (2): 127–39.

Papagiannis, M. D., ed. 1980. *Strategies for the Search for Life in the Universe.* Holland: D. Reidel.

Parrinder, Geoffrey. 1958. *Witchcraft.* Harmondsworth: Penguin Books.

Parsons, Talcott. 1951. *The Social System.* Glencoe, Ill.: Free Press.

———. 1966. *Societies, Evolutionary and Comparative Perspectives.* Englewood Cliffs, N.J.: Prentice-Hall.

———. 1971. *The System of Modern Societies.* Englewood Cliffs, N.J.: Prentice-Hall.

Pattison, E. M., and R. M. Wintrob. 1981. "Possession and Exorcism in Contemporary America." *Journal of Operational Psychiatry* 12: 13–20.

Patton, Robert. 1982. "Ooparts." *Omni* 4 (12): 53–105.

Pauling, Linus. 1976. *Vitamin C, the Common Cold, and the Flu.* San Francisco: Freeman.

Payer, Pierre J. 1980. "Early Medieval Regulations Concerning Marital Sexual Relations." *Journal of Medieval History,* 6 (4): 353–76.

Penrose, Bois. 1962. *Travel and Discovery in the Renaissance, 1420–1620.* New York: Atheneum.

Pesch, Peter, and Roland Pesch 1977. "The Dogon and Sirius." *Observatory* 97 (1016): 26–28.

Peters, D. P., and S. J. Ceci. 1980. "A Manuscript Masquerade." *The Sciences* 35: 16–19.

Peters, Ted. 1980. "The Future of Religion in a Post-Industrial Society." *The Futurist,* October, pp. 21–25.

Pierce, J. J. 1977. "The Golden Age." *Galaxy* 38 (9): 157–58.

Piers, Maria W. 1978. *Infanticide.* New York: W. W. Norton and Company.

Pinch, Trevor J. 1979. "Normal Explanations of the Paranormal: The Demarcation Problem and Fraud in Parapsychology." *Social Studies of Science* 9: 229–48.

Pirenne, Henry. 1937. *Economic and Social History of Medieval Europe.* New York: Harcourt Brace.

Polanyi, Michael. 1967. "The Growth of Science in Society." *Minerva* 5 (4): 533–45.

———. 1969. "The Republic of Science: Its Political and Economic Theory." *Knowing and Being,* ed. Marjorie Grene, pp. 54–55. Chicago: University of Chicago Press.

Policelli, Eugene F. 1978. "Medieval Women: A Preacher's Point of View." *International Journal of Womens Studies* 1 (3): 281–96.

Ponnamperuma, Cyril, ed. 1981. *Comets and the Origin of Life.* New York: D. Reidel.

Pontell, H. J., P. D. Jesilow, and G. Geis. 1982. "Policing Physicians: Practitioner Fraud and Abuse in Government Medical Programs." *Social Problems* 30 (1): 117–25.

Postan, N. M. 1950. "Some Economic Evidence of Declining Population in the Later Middle Ages." *Economic History Review,* 2d ser. 2(3): 221–46.

Postan, N. M., and E. R. Rich, eds. 1952. *The Cambridge Economic History of Europe.* Vol. 2: *Trade and Industry in the Middle Ages.* Cambridge: Cambridge University Press.

Pounds, N. J. C. 1979. *A Historical Geography of Europe.* New York and London: Cambridge University Press.

Power, Eileen. 1926. "The Position of Women." Pp. 401–37 in C. G. Crump and E. F. Jacob, eds. *The Legacy of the Middle Ages.* Oxford: Clarendon.

———. 1975. *Medieval Women,* edited by M. M. Postan. Cambridge: Cambridge University Press.

Project Icarus. 1979. MIT student project. Cambridge: MIT Press.

Provine, W. B. 1973. "Genetics and the Biology of Race Crossing." *Science* 790–96.

Puech, Henry-Charles. 1974. "Manicheism." *Encyclopedia Britannica,* vol. 11. Chicago: Encyclopedia Britannica.

Quinney, Richard. 1964. The Study of White-Collar Crime: Toward a Reorientation in Theory and Research. *Journal of Criminal Law, Criminology, and Police Science* 55: 208–14.

Radbill, S. X. 1974. "A History of Child Abuse and Infanticide." In *Violence in the Family,* ed. S. L. Steinmets and L. A. Strauss, pp. 173–79. New York: Dodd, Mead.

Rattansi, P. M. 1972. "The Social Interpretation of Science in the Seventeenth Century." In *Science and Society, 1600–1900,* ed. P. Mathias, pp. 1–32. London: Cambridge University Press.

Reber, Grote. 1983. "Radio Astronomy between Jansky and Reber." Paper given at the Jansky Memorial Conference, National Radio Astronomy Observatory, Green Bank, West Virginia, May.

Reed, G. 1983. The Discovery of Pulsars. *Astronomy* 11 (12): 24–28.

Rensberger, B. 1977. "Fraud in Research Is a Rising Problem in Science." *New York Times,* Jan. 23, pp. 1, 44.

Rice, Edward. 1980. *Eastern Definitions.* Garden City, N.Y.: Doubleday Anchor Books.

Richardson, James T., ed. 1978. *Conversion Careers: In and Out of New Religions.* California: Sage Publications.

Ridpath, Ian. 1975. *Worlds Beyond: A Report on the Search for Life in Space.* New York: Harper and Row.

Robbins, Russell Hope. 1959. *The Encyclopedia of Witchcraft and Demonology.* New York: Crown Publishers.

———. 1978. *Witchcraft: An Introduction to the Literature of Witchcraft.* New York: Kta Press.

Robbins, Thomas. 1979. "The Sociology of Contemporary Religious Movements." *Annual Review of Sociology* 5: 75–89.

Robbins, Thomas and O. Anthony, eds. 1981. *In Gods We Trust.* London: Transaction Books.

Robock, Alan. 1979. "The 'Little Ice Age': Northern Hemisphere Average Observations and Model Calculations." *Science* 206: 1402–4.

Rock, Paul. 1973a. *Deviant Behavior.* London: Hutchinson University Library.

———. 1973b. "Phenomenalism and Essentialism in the Sociology of Deviance." *Sociology* 7: 17–29.

———. 1974. "The Sociology of Deviance and Conception of Moral Order." *British Journal of Criminology* 14 (2): 139–49.

Rondinone, P. 1982. "UFO Update." *Omni* 4 (7): 101.

Rood, Robert T., and James S. Trefil. 1981. *Are We Alone?.* New York: Charles Scribner's Sons.

Rorvik, D. 1982. "Sperm from Deep Space: Interview with Francis Crick." *Omni* 4 (6): 74–84.

Rose, Elliot E. 1962. *A Razor for a Goat:* Toronto: Toronto University Press.

Rose, Mark. 1981. *Alien Encounters.* Cambridge: Harvard University Press.

Rosen, George. 1969. *Madness in Society.* New York: Harper Torchbooks.

Rosenhan, D.C. 1973. "On Being Sane in Insane Places." *Science* 179: 250–58.

Rosenthal, R., et al. 1979. *Sensitivity to Nonverbal Communication: The PONS Test.* Baltimore: Johns Hopkins University Press.

Roshier, Bob. 1977. "The Function of Crime Myth." *Sociological Review* 25 (2): 309–23.

Roszak, Theodore. 1981. "In Search of the Miraculous." *Harper's,* January, pp. 54–62.

Roth, Cecil. 1971. "Inquisition." *Encyclopedia Judaica,* pp. 1379–1407.

Roth, J. A. 1966. "Hired Hand Research." *American Sociologist,* 10: 190–96.

Rubington, Earl, and M. S. Weinberg, eds. 1971. *The Study of Social Problems.* New York: Oxford University Press.

———. 1978. *Deviance: The Interactionist Perspective,* 3d edition. New York: Macmillan Publishing Company.

Runciman, Steven. 1955. *The Medieval Manichee.* London: Cambridge University Press.

Ruppelt, E. J. 1956. *The Report on Unidentified Flying Objects.* New York: Ace Books.

Russell, Jeffrey Burton. 1971. *Religious Dissent in the Middle Ages.* New York: John Wiley and Sons.

————. 1972. *Witchcraft in the Middle Ages.* Ithaca: Cornell University Press.

————. 1977. *The Devil:* Ithaca: Cornell University Press.

Rutledge, H. D. 1981. *Project Identification.* Englewood Cliffs, N.J.: Prentice-Hall.

Sachs, Margaret. 1980. *The UFO Encyclopedia,* New York: G. P. Putnam's Sons, A Perigee Book.

St. James–Roberts, Ian. 1976. "Cheating in Science." *New Scientist* 72, no. 1028 (Nov. 25): 466–69.

Sagan, Carl. 1973. *The Cosmic Connection.* New York: Dell Books.

————. ed. 1979. *Murmurs of Earth.* New York: Ballantine Books.

Sagan, Carl, and T. Page, eds. 1972. *UFOs: A Scientific Debate.* New York: W. W. Norton and Co.

Sagan, Carl, and I. S. Shklovkii. 1966. *Intelligent Life in the Universe.* New York: Delta Books.

Sagarin, Edward. 1977. *Deviance and Social Change.* Beverly Hills: Sage Publications.

Saler, Benson. 1977. "Supernatural as a Western Category." *Ethos* 5 (1): 31–53.

Sanderson, I. T. 1957. *Uninvited Visitors: A Biologist Looks at UFOs.* New York: Cowles Education Corporation.

Sanger, William W. 1937. *The History of Prostitution.* New York: Eugenics.

Sapir, Edward. 1960. *Culture, Language, and Personality.* Berkeley: University of California Press.

Sarbin, Theodore S. 1969. "The Scientific Status of the Mental Illness Metaphor." In *Changing Perspectives in Mental Illness,* ed. S. C. Plog and R. B. Edgerton, pp. 9–31. New York: Holt, Rinehart and Winston.

Sayre, Anne. 1975. *Rosalind Franklin and DNA.* New York: W. W. Norton and Company.

Schlussel, Y. R. 1983. *Structural Determinants of Resistance to Innovation: Peer Review, Disciplinary Paradigm, and Formal Organizations.* Paper read at the annual meeting of the New York State Sociological Association, Potsdam, N.Y.

Schmidt, Stanley. 1979. "Irreproducible." *Analog* 49 (9): 5–10.

————. 1981. "Portrait of You." *Analog* 101 (5): 5–14.

Schoeneman, T. J. 1977. "The Role of Mental Illness in the European Witch Hunts of the Sixteenth and Seventeenth Centuries: An Assessment." *Journal of the History of the Behavioral Sciences* 13: 337–51.

Scholes, Robert, and E. S. Rabkin. 1977. *Science Fiction: History, Science, Vision.* New York: Oxford University Press.

Schur, E. M. 1979. *Interpreting Deviance.* New York: Harper and Row.

———. 1980. *The Politics of Deviance*. Englewood Cliffs, N.J.: Prentice-Hall.

Scott, George Ryley. 1936. *A History of Prostitution*. London: Laurie.

Scull, Andrew. 1984. "Competing Perspectives on Deviance" *Deviant Behavior* 5:275–89.

Sebald, Hans. 1978. *Witchcraft: The Heritage of a Heresy*. New York: Elsevier.

Senter, Donovan. 1947. "Witches and Psychiatrists." *Psychiatry* 10: 49–56.

Shapin, Steven. 1982. The Sociology of Science. *History of Science* 20 (49): 157–211.

Sheaffer, Robert. 1981. *The UFO Verdict*. New York: Prometheus Books.

Shelley, L. I. 1981. *Crime and Modernization*. Carbondale: Southern Illinois University Press.

Shepherd, William C. 1972. "Religion and the Counter Culture—A New Religiosity?" *Sociological Inquiry* 42 (1): 3–9.

Shils, Edward. 1975. *Center and Periphery: Essays in Macrosociology*. Selected Papers of Edward Shils. Vol. 2. Chicago: University of Chicago Press.

Shumaker, Wayne. 1972. *The Occult Sciences in the Renaissance*. Berkeley: University of California Press.

Silberner, J. 1982. "Cheating in the Labs." *Science Digest* 90 (8): 38, 40, 41.

Silk, Joseph. 1980. *The Big Bang*. San Francisco: W. H. Freeman and Company.

Singer, B., and V. A. Benassi. 1981. "Occult Beliefs." *American Scientist* 69: 49–55.

Slater, Philip. 1975. *The Wayward Gate: Science and the Supernatural*. Boston: Beacon Press.

Smith, M. S. 1980. "Projects Sign and Grudge." Pp. 276–78 in Story, R., ed.: *The Encyclopedia of UFOs*. New York, Garden City: Doubleday.

Solzhenitsyn, A. I. 1975. *The Gulag Archipelago*. New York: Harper and Row.

Sontag, S. 1967. *Against Interpretation*. New York: Dell Books.

Sorokin, P. A. 1956. *Fads and Foibles in Modern Society and Related Sciences*. Chicago: Henry Regnery.

Spanos, N. P. 1978. "Witchcraft in Histories of Psychiatry: A Critical Analysis and an Alternative Conceptualization." *Psychological Bulletin* 85 (2): 417–39.

Spengler, J. J. 1968. "Demographic Factors and Early Modern Economic Development." *Daedalus* 97: 433–43.

Sprenger, J., and H. Kramer [1487–89] 1968. *Malleus maleficarum*, translated by Montague Summers. London Folio Society.

Stark, Rodney, and William Sims Bainbridge. 1980. "Networks of Faith: Interpersonal Bonds and Recruitment to Cults and Sects." *American Journal of Sociology* 85 (6): 1376–95.

Stark, Rodney, and Charles V. Glock. 1968. *American Piety: The Nature of Religious Commitment*. Berkeley: University of California Press.

Staude, John R. 1970. "Alienated Youth and the Cult of the Occult." In *Sociology for the Seventies*, ed. M. C. Medley and J. E. Conyers, pp. 86–95. New York: John Wiley and Sons.

Stent, Gunther. 1981. "A Close Encounter." *New York Times Review of Books* 28 (19): 34–36.

Stoneley, Jack., and A. T. Lawton. 1976. *CETI—Communication with Extra-Terrestrial Intelligence.* New York: Warner Books.

Stoner, Carol, and Jo Ann Park. 1977. *All God's Children: The Cult Experience—Salvation or Slavery.* Harmondsworth, England: Penguin Books.

Storer, Norman W. 1977. "The Sociological Context of the Velikovsky Controversy." In *Scientists Confront Velikovsky,* ed. D. Goldsmith, pp. 29–39. New York: W. W. Norton and Company.

Story, R. D. 1976. *The Space Gods Revealed: A Close Look at the Theory of Eric von Däniken,* New York: Harper and Row.

———. ed. 1980a. *The Encyclopedia of UFOs.* New York: Doubleday.

———. 1980b. *Guardians of the Universe.* New York: St. Martin's Press.

Story, R. D., and Richard Greenwell. 1981. *UFOs and the Limits of Science.* New York: William Morrow.

Stromer, Wolfgang von. 1970. "Nurnberg in the International Economics of the Middle Ages." *Business History Review* 44 (2): 210–21.

Struve, Otto. 1962. *The Universe.* Cambridge: MIT Press.

Stuard, Susan M., ed. 1976. *Women in Medieval Society.* Philadelphia: University of Philadelphia Press.

Suchar, Charles S. 1978. *Social Deviance: Perspectives and Prospects.* New York: Holt, Rinehart and Winston.

Sullivan, Walter. 1964. *We Are Not Alone.* New York: Signet Books.

———. 1979. *Black Holes,* New York: Warner Books.

Sullivan, Woodruf T. 1982. *Classics in Radio Astronomy.* Dordrecht: D. Reidel Company.

———. 1984. *Early Years of Radio Astronomy.* Cambridge Cambridge University Press.

Summers, Montague. 1956: *The History of Witchcraft and Demonology.* New York: University Books.

Sumption, Jonathan. 1978. *The Albigensian Crusade.* London: Faber and Faber.

Swift, P. W. 1981. "Parallel Universe: A Tale of Two SETIs." *Astronomy* 9 (10): 24–28.

Sykes, G. M., and D. Matza. 1957. "Techniques of Neutralization: A Theory of Delinquency." *American Sociological Review* 22: 664–70.

Szasz, Thomas. 1970. *The Manufacture of Madness.* New York: Harper and Row.

Tarter, J. 1982. Search for Them. *Astronomy* 10 (10): 6–22.

Taylor, Ian, Paul Walton, and Jack Young. 1973. *The New Criminology: For a Social Theory of Deviance.* London: Routledge and Kegan Paul.

Taylor, Laurie. 1972. "The Significance and Interpretation of Replies to Motivational Questions: The Case of Sex Offenders." *Sociology* 6: 23–40.

Temple, R. K. 1976. *The Sirius Mystery.* New York: St. Martin's Press.

———. 1981. "On the Sirius Mystery: An Open Letter to Carl Sagan." *Zetetic Scholar* 8: 29–37.

Teske, Richard. 1982. "Asteroid Collisions with Earth." *Astronomy* 10 (1): 18–22.

Thio, Alex. 1983. *Deviant Behavior*. 2nd ed. Boston: Houghton Mifflin Company.

Thomas, Keith. 1971. *Religion and the Decline of Magic*. New York: Charles Scribner's Sons.

Thompson, J. D. 1967. *Organizations in Action*. New York: McGraw Hill Book Company.

Thorndike, Lynn. 1941. *History of Magic and Experimental Science*. New York: Columbia University Press.

Thrupp, S. L. 1972. "Medieval Industry, 1000–1500." In *The Middle Ages*. Vol. 1 of *The Fontana Economic History of Europe*, ed. C. M. Cipolla, pp. 221–74. New York: Fontana.

Tipler, F. J. 1983a. "Extraterrestrial Intelligence: A Skeptical View of Radio Searches" *Science* (Jan. 14) 219 (4581): 110–11.

———. 1983b. "We are Alone." *Discover* 4 (3): 56–61.

Tiryakian, Edward A. 1972. "Toward the Sociology of Esoteric Culture." *American Journal of Sociology* 78: 401–12.

———. ed. 1981. "Durkheim Lives." *Social Force, Special Issue,* 59 (4).

Toch, Hans. 1981. "Cast the First Stone? Ethics as a Weapon." *Criminology* 19 (2): 185–94.

Tönnies, Ferdinand. 1957. *Community and Society*. New York: Harper Torchbooks.

Trevor-Roper, H. R. 1967. *The European Witch Craze of the Sixteenth and Seventeenth Centuries and Other Essays*. New York: Harper Torchbooks.

Trexler, Richard C. 1973. "Infanticide in Florence: New Sources and First Results." *History of Childhood Quarterly* 1 (1): 98–116.

Truzzi, Marcello. 1972. "The Occult Revival as Popular Culture: Some Random Observations on the Old and Nouveau Witch." *Sociological Quarterly* 13: 130–40.

———. 1974. "Toward a Sociology of the Occult: Notes on Modern Witchcraft." In *Religious Movements in Contemporary America,* ed. I. I. Zaretsky and M. P. Leone, pp. 628–45. Princeton: Princeton University Press.

———. 1979. "On the Reception of Unconventional Scientific Claims." In *The Reception of Unconventional Science*. ed. S. H. Mauskopf, pp. 125–37 AAAS Selected Symposium 25, published by Westview Press.

Tuck, Donald H., ed. 1978. *The Encyclopedia of Science Fiction and Fantasy*. Chicago, Ill.: Advent Publishers.

Tucker, E. 1980. "Antecedents of Contemporary Witchcraft in the Middle Ages." *Journal of Popular Culture* 14 (1): 70–78.

Turberville, A. S. 1964. *Medieval Heresy and the Inquisition*. London: Archon.

Turner, Victor. 1969. *The Ritual Process*. Ithaca: Cornell University Press.

———. 1977. "Variations on a Theme of Liminality." In *Secular Ritual,* ed. S. F. Moore and R. G. Myerhoff, pp. 36–52. Assen/Amsterdam: Van Gorcum.

Tymm, M. B., R. C. Schlobin, and L. W. Currey. 1977. *A Research Guide to Science Fiction Studies*. New York: Garland Publishing.

U. S. Congress. House. 1981. *Fraud in Biomedical Research*. Report prepared for the Subcommittee on Investigations and Oversight of the Committee on Science and Technology 97th Cong., 1st sess. No. 1.

Usher, A. D. 1956. "The History of Population and Settlement in Euro-Asia." In *Demographic Analysis,* ed. J. J. Spengler and D. D. Duncan. Glencoe, Ill.: Free Press.

Valdes, F., and R. A. Freitas. 1983. "A Search for Objects Near the Earth-Moon Lagrangian Points." *Icarus* 53: 453–57.

Vallee, J. 1965. *UFOs in Space.* New York: Ballantine Books.

Van der Wee, Herman. 1975. "Structural Changes and Specialization in the Industry of the Southern Netherlands." *Economic History Review,* 2d series 28(2): 203–21.

Wade, Nicholas. 1975. "Discovery of Pulsars: A Graduate Student's Story." *Science* 189: 358–64.

———. 1976. "IQ and Heredity: Suspicion of Fraud Beclouds Classic Experiment." *Science* 194: 916–19.

———. 1981. "A Diversion of the Quest for Truth." *Science* 211: 1022–25.

———. 1983. "Fraud and the State of Science." *SUNY Research* 2 (4): 3–6.

Wagner, M. W., and M. Monnet. 1979. "Attitudes of College Professors toward Extra-Sensory Perception." *Zetetic Scholar* 5: 7–17.

Wakefield, W., and A. Evans, eds. 1969. *Heresies of the High Middle Ages.* New York: Columbia University Press.

Waldorf, M. M. 1982. "Astronomy and Astrophysics for the 1980s." *Science* 216: 282.

Wallace, A. F. C. 1966. *Religion: An Anthropological View.* New York: Random House.

Wallis, C. 1983. "Fraud in a Harvard Lab." *Time* (International Edition), Feb. 28, p. 41.

Wallis, Roy. 1977. *The Road to Total Freedom: A Sociological Analysis of Scientology.* New York: Columbia University Press.

———. ed. 1979. *On the Margins of Science: The Social Construction of Rejected Knowledge.* University of Keele Press.

Wallis, R., and S. Bruce. 1983. "Accounting for Action: Defending the Common Sense Heresy." *Sociology* 17 (1): 97–111.

Wallwork, E. 1972. *Durkheim: Morality and Milieu.* Cambridge: Harvard University Press.

Warner, Marina. 1976. *Alone of All Her Sex: The Myth and Cult of the Virgin Mary.* New York: Alfred A. Knopf.

Waugh, C. G., E. F. Libby, and C. Waugh. 1975. "Demographic, Intellectual, and Personality Characteristics of Science Fiction Fans." A paper presented at the 1975 Science Fiction Research Association Annual Meeting.

Waugh, C. G., and D. J. Schroeder 1980. "Here's Looking at You Kids: A Profile of Science Fiction Fans." In *Science Fiction Reference Book,* ed. M. Tymm.

Webb, S. D. 1972. "Crime and the Division of Labour: Testing a Durkheimian Model." *American Journal of Sociology* 78 (3): 643–56.

Weber, Max. 1964. *The Sociology of Religion.* Boston: Beacon Press.

Webster, Charles, ed. 1979: *Health, Medicine, and Mortality in the Sixteenth Century*. Cambridge: Cambridge University Press.

Weinberg, Steven. 1977. *The First Three Minutes*. New York: Basic Books.

Weiner, S. J. 1980. *The Piltdown Forgery*. New York: Dover (Reprint of the 1955 edition).

Weinstein, Deena. 1978. *Fraud in Science*. A paper given at the Seventy-third Annual Meeting of the American Sociological Association, San Francisco.

———. 1979. "Fraud in Science." *Social Science Quarterly* 59 (4): 639–52.

Weisman, Richard. 1984. *Witchcraft Magic and Religion in 17th Century Massachusetts*. Amherst: The University of Massachusetts Press.

Wescott, R. W. 1982. "Anomalistics: A New Field of Interdisciplinary Study." *Fortean Times* (Winter):4–10.

Westfall, R. S. 1980. "The Influence of Alchemy on Newton." In *Science, Pseudo-Science, and Society*, ed. M. P. Hanen, M. J. Osler, and R. G. Weyant, pp. 145–70. Wilfrid Laurier University Press.

Westrum, Ron. 1977. "Social Intelligence about Anomalies: The Case of UFOs." *Social Studies of Science* 7: 271–302.

———. 1978. "Science and Social Intelligence about Anomalies: The Case of Meteorites." *Social Studies of Science* 8: 461–93.

———. 1982. "Crypto-Science and Social Intelligence about Anomalies." *Zetetic Scholar* 10: 89–136.

Westrum, R., and Marcello Truzzi. 1978. "Anomalies: A Bibliographic Introduction with Some Cautionary Remarks." *Zetetic Scholar* 1: 69–78.

Wheeler, S. 1960. "Sex Offenders: A Sociological Critique." *Law and Contemporary Problems* 25: 258–278.

Wheeler, S., D. Weisburg, and N. Bode. 1982. "Sentencing the White Collar Offender: Rhetoric and Reality." *American Journal of Sociology* 47 (5): 641–59.

White, Andrew Dickson. 1913. *A History of the Warfare of Science with Theology*. New York: D. Appleton and Company.

White, John, and Stanley Krippner, eds. 1977. *Future Science*. New York: Doubleday.

Williams, Charles. 1959. *Witchcraft*. New York: Meridian Books.

Williams, J. 1978. "The Next Century of Science Fiction." *Analog* 48 (2): 5–15.

Wilson, Clifford. 1978. *War of the Chariots*. San Diego: Master Books.

Wilson, Brian. 1979. "The Return of the Sacred." *Journal for the Scientific Study of Religion* 18 (3): 268–80.

Wilson, Monica. 1951. "Witch Beliefs and Social Structure." *American Journal of Sociology* 56 (4): 307–13.

Wilson, R. A. 1982. "Mere Coincidences?" *Science Digest*, 90 (1): 84–95.

Winslow, R. W. 1970. *Society in Transition: A Social Approach to Deviancy*. New York: Free Press.

"Witchcraft." 1975. *The New Encyclopedia Britannica*. Vol. 19, pp. 895–900. Chicago.

Wolfgang, M. E., L. Savitz, and N. Johnson, eds. 1970. *The Sociology of Crime and Delinquency.* New York: John Wiley and Sons.

Wolins, L. 1962. "Responsibility for Raw Data." *American Psychologist* 17: 657–58.

Woolf, Patricia. 1981. "Fraud in Science: How Much, How Serious?" *The Hastings Center Report* 11 (5): 9–14.

Wright, S. 1966. "Mendel's Ratios." Pp. 173–75 in Stern, C., and Sherwood, E. eds.: *The Origins of Genetics: A Model Sourcebook.* San Francisco: W. H. Freeman.

Wrigley, E. A. 1969. *Population and History.* London: Weidenfeld and Nicolson.

Wynne, Brian. 1979. "Between Orthodoxy and Oblivion: The Normalization of Deviance in Science." In *On the Margins of Science,* ed. R. Wallis, pp. 67–83. University of Keele.

Zablocki, Benjamin. 1971. *The Joyful Community.* Baltimore: Penguin Books.

Zaretsky, Irving I., and Mark P. Leone, eds. 1974. *Religious Movements in Contemporary America,* Princeton: Princeton University Press.

Zguta, Russell. 1977. "Witchcraft Trials in Seventeenth Century Russia." *American Historical Review* 82 (5): 1187–1207.

Ziegler, Philip. 1971. *The Black Death.* New York: Harper and Row.

Zilboorg, Gregory. 1935. *The Medical Man and the Witch during the Renaissance.* Baltimore: Johns Hopkins University Press.

Zilboorg, Gregory, with G. W. Henry. 1941. *A History of Medical Psychology.* New York: W. W. Norton and Company.

Zinder, N. D. 1983. "Fraud in Science." *Science 83* 4: 94–95.

Zuckerman, Harriet. 1968. "Patterns of Name-Ordering among Authors of Scientific Papers." *American Journal of Sociology* 74: 276–91.

———. 1977. "Deviant Behaviour and Social Control in Science." In *Deviance and Social Change,* ed. E. Sagarin, pp. 87–138. Beverly Hills: Sage Publications.

Zukav, Gary. 1979. *The Dancing of Wu Li Masters.* New York: William Morrow and Company.

INDEX

249